Walk With Me
To Everest and back for CMT

Kev Howlett

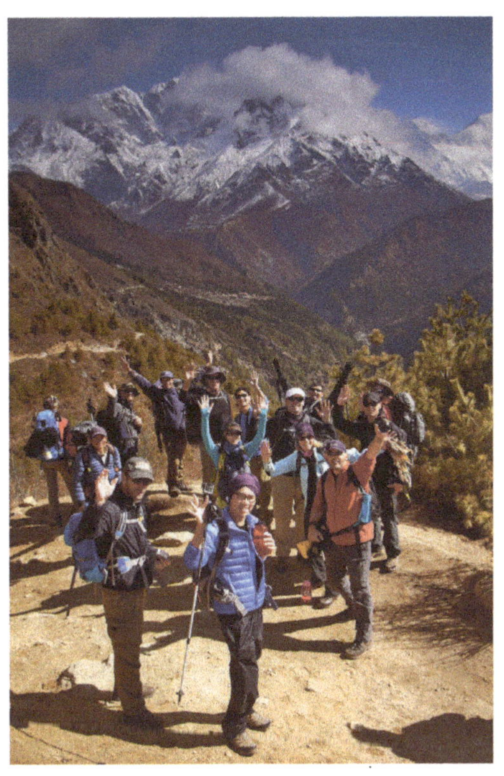

First published by Busybird Publishing 2014

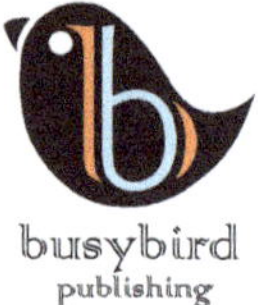

busybird
publishing

ISBN: 978-1-922691-95-8

Cover image by Kev Howlett
Cover and book design by Jason Farrugia
Layout and typesetting by Jason Farrugia
All photographs where Kev appears were taken by Norman Krueger

This book will raise funds and awareness for Charcot-Marie-Tooth Association Australia
Inc.
For more information about this condition please see the website www.cmt.org.au

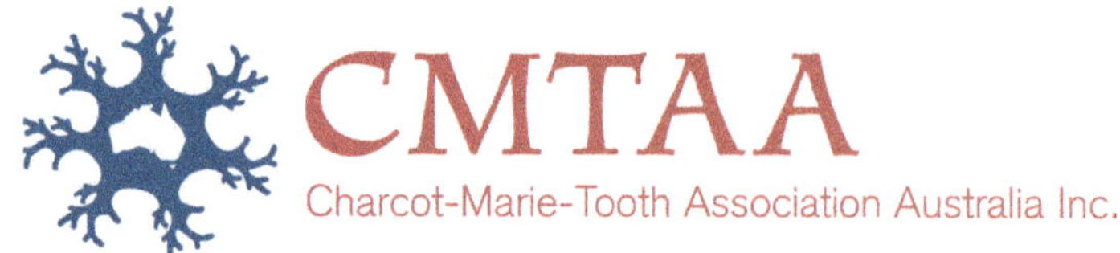

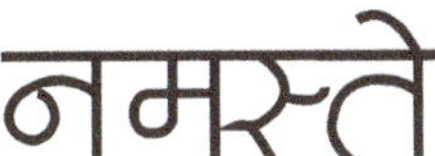

नमस्ते

Namaste – hello/welcome

The whole *Walk With Me* project – the trek, the book, the exhibition – is a dedication to all those suffering from CMT.

'What is CMT?' you ask.

CMT is a disease named after its founders – Charcot, Marie, Tooth – that is a degeneration of the nerve coatings, affecting first the feet, and then the hands.

It's also a disease that my oldest son, Dylan, has. Dylan was a champion footballer in his teens, but struggled with balance as his feet curled up from the nerve degeneration. He had to have both feet reconstructed (the Achilles cut, lengthened, and the toes wired straight), and now struggles with distance and exertion. Potentially, if there are no further advancements in the treatment of CMT, it's surgery he will have to face again in 10–15 years because even now, the CMT is fighting the reconstructions.

Doing this trek is partly a fundraiser for the CMTAA (Charcot-Marie-Tooth Association Australia Inc), who do an amazing job considering they are not funded and struggle to be heard over the more high profile – and, I guess – popular diseases. The other part of the trek is a symbolic gesture to highlight that this is an adventure, which involves a lot of hard walking and, most likely, can't be completed by those suffering with CMT.

Before I left I was talking to a few people who had completed the EBC (Everest Base Camp) trek with their sons, daughters, etc., and it made me realise that this is something I couldn't complete or ever share with Dylan and I felt a little sad about that.

This idea itself to trek up to EBC originally started simply with two mates, both photographers, thinking of photographing an amazing and unusual off-the-beaten track location, as well as a way of getting fitter as we approached the big five-oh. But as the ball got rolling it evolved into a massive project and fundraiser where 70+ amazing people and businesses pledged money through Pozible, excited to support and try and help those suffering with CMT like Dylan and also back my efforts to get to Mount Everest Base Camp.

Most importantly, they were keen to hear and learn more about CMT and our struggles with Dylan over the years. Nearly all the people I mentioned CMT to looked at me blankly. Well, apart from achieving a lifetime bucket list adventure with the eighteen-day trek to Mount Everest, the thing I am most proud of is that more people on this planet won't look blankly again if CMT is mentioned to them. I would hope they will spread the word about CMT a little wider into the community, making it more talked about than it was before I started all this. Hopefully, it will also encourage more funding. My goal is to see a cure for this disease sometime in Dylan's lifetime and I thank you for supporting me in any way to help this to one day become a reality.

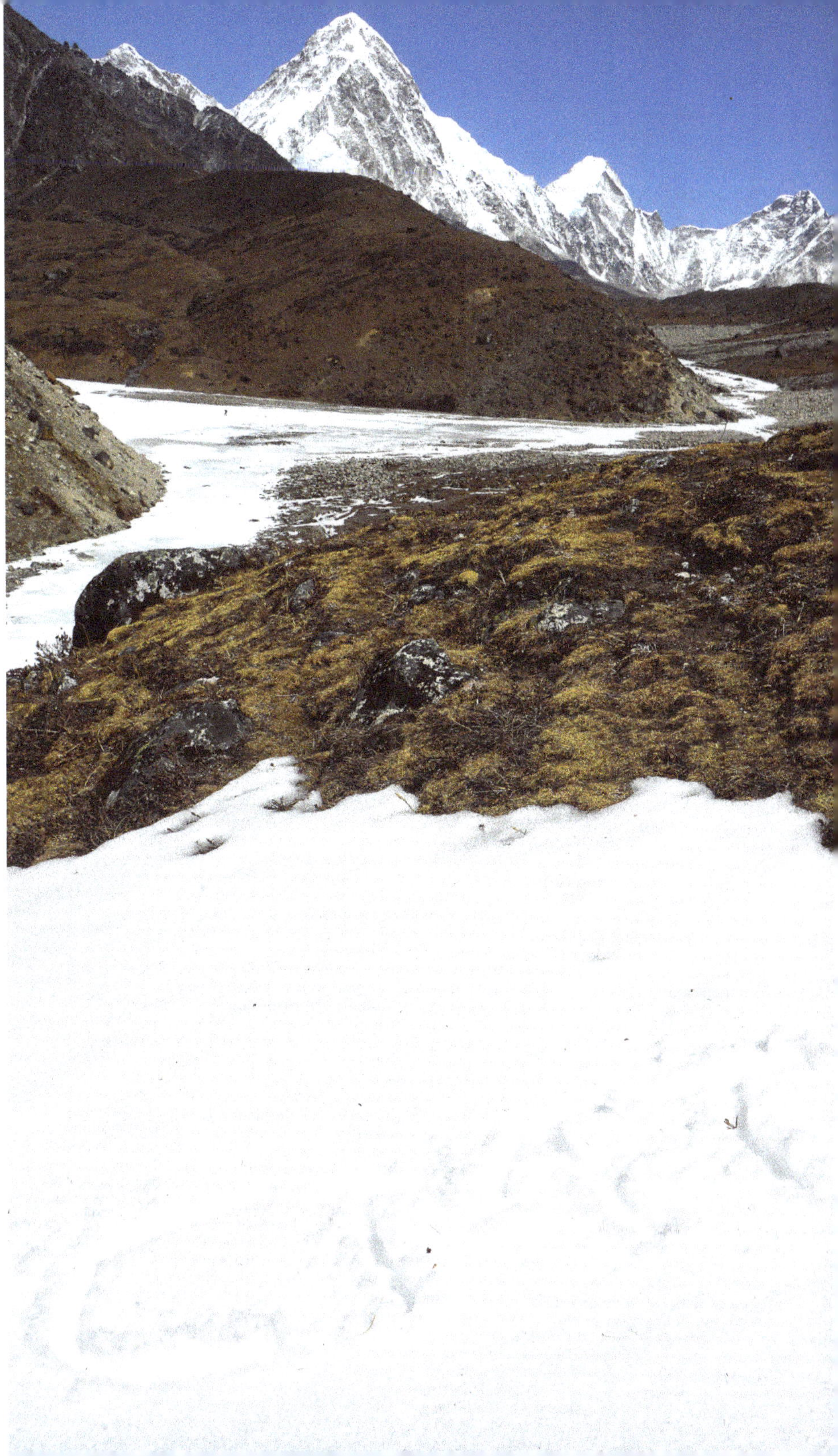

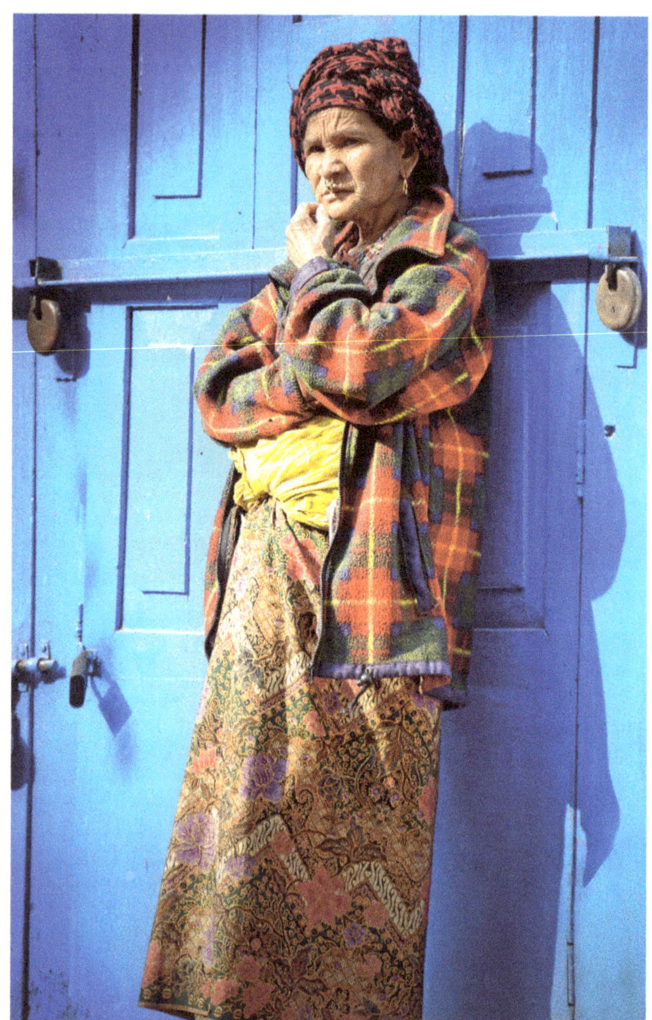

One of those places you quickly realise where chaos and disorder can actually work. The people are so kind and generous and the city just as inviting. I loved wandering around, stopping now and then to hide on a corner photographing and watching Nepalese life hustle by. It's a place I will go back to for sure. It has that crazy romance in a city you easily get addicted to.

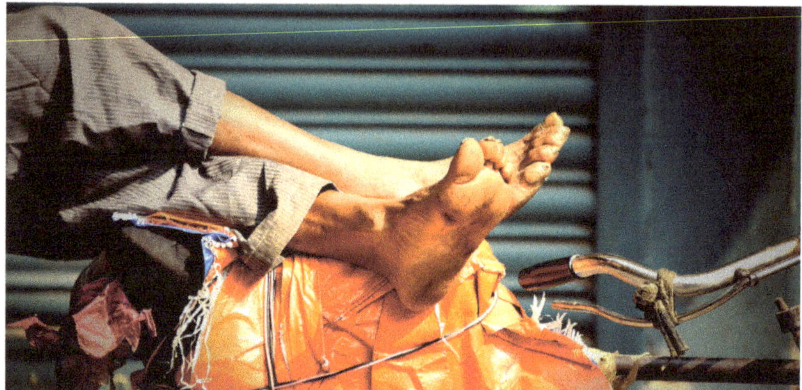

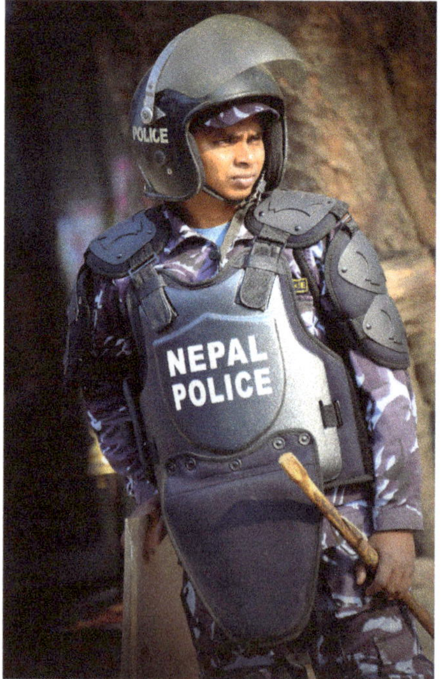

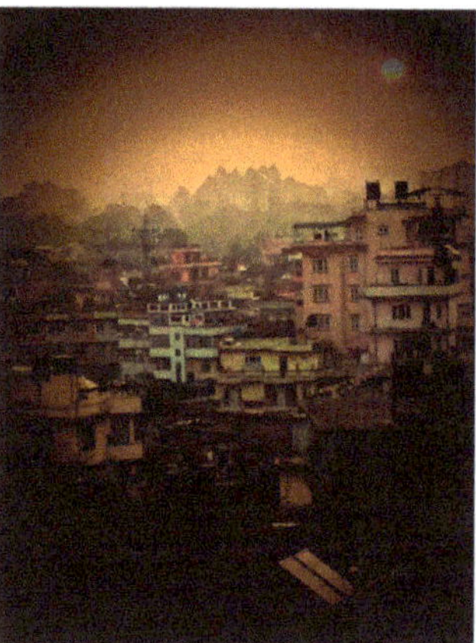

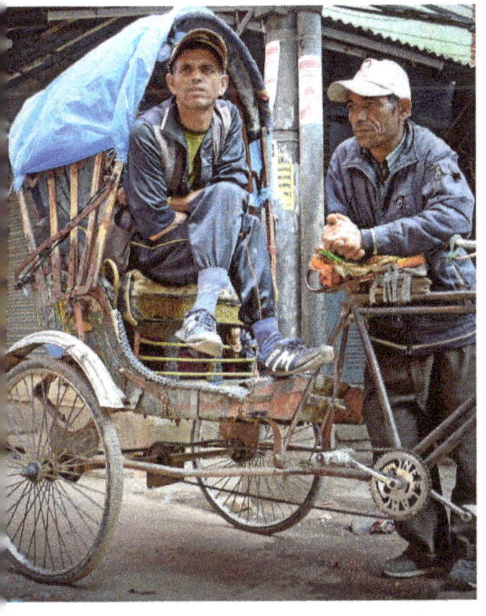

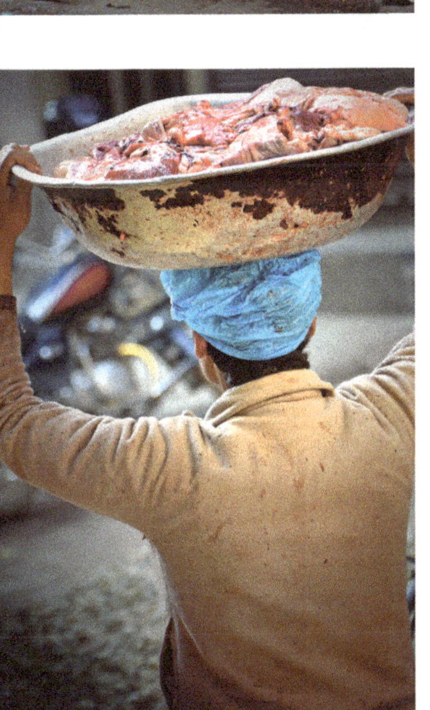

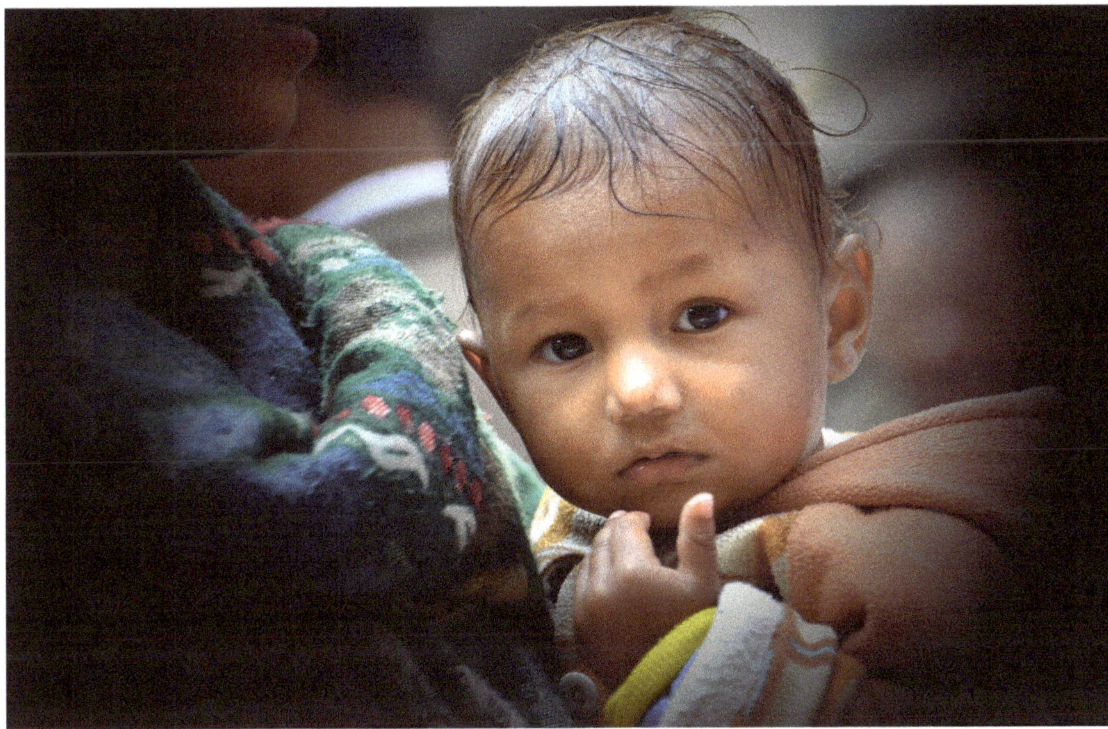

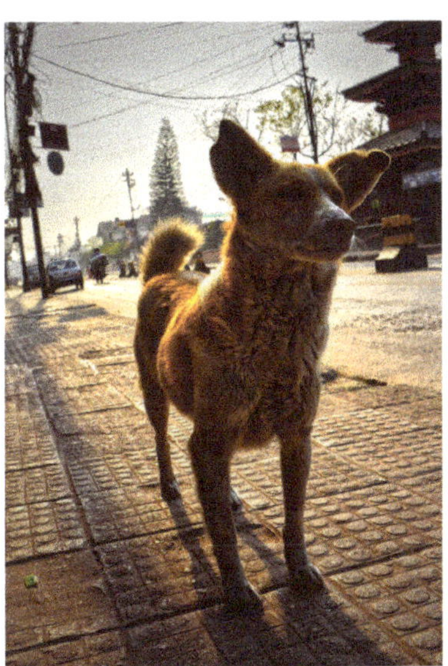

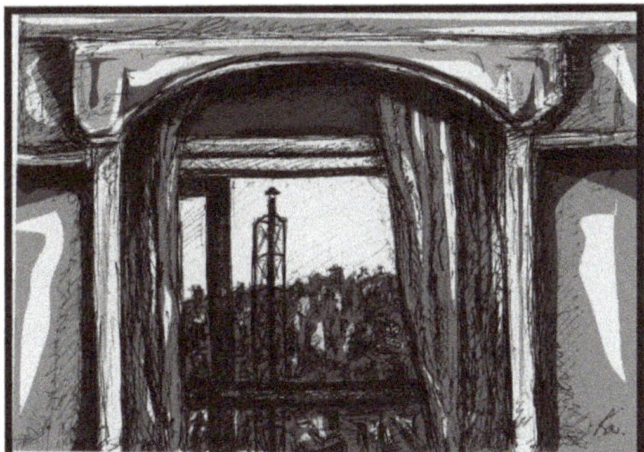

Radisson Hotel Room 302

Through the frame of the new

Is the old and the dusty

Standing tall and so grand

Is the chimney old and rusty

As the city hustles by in a rush and a haze

We look out on the streets on the baffiling maze.

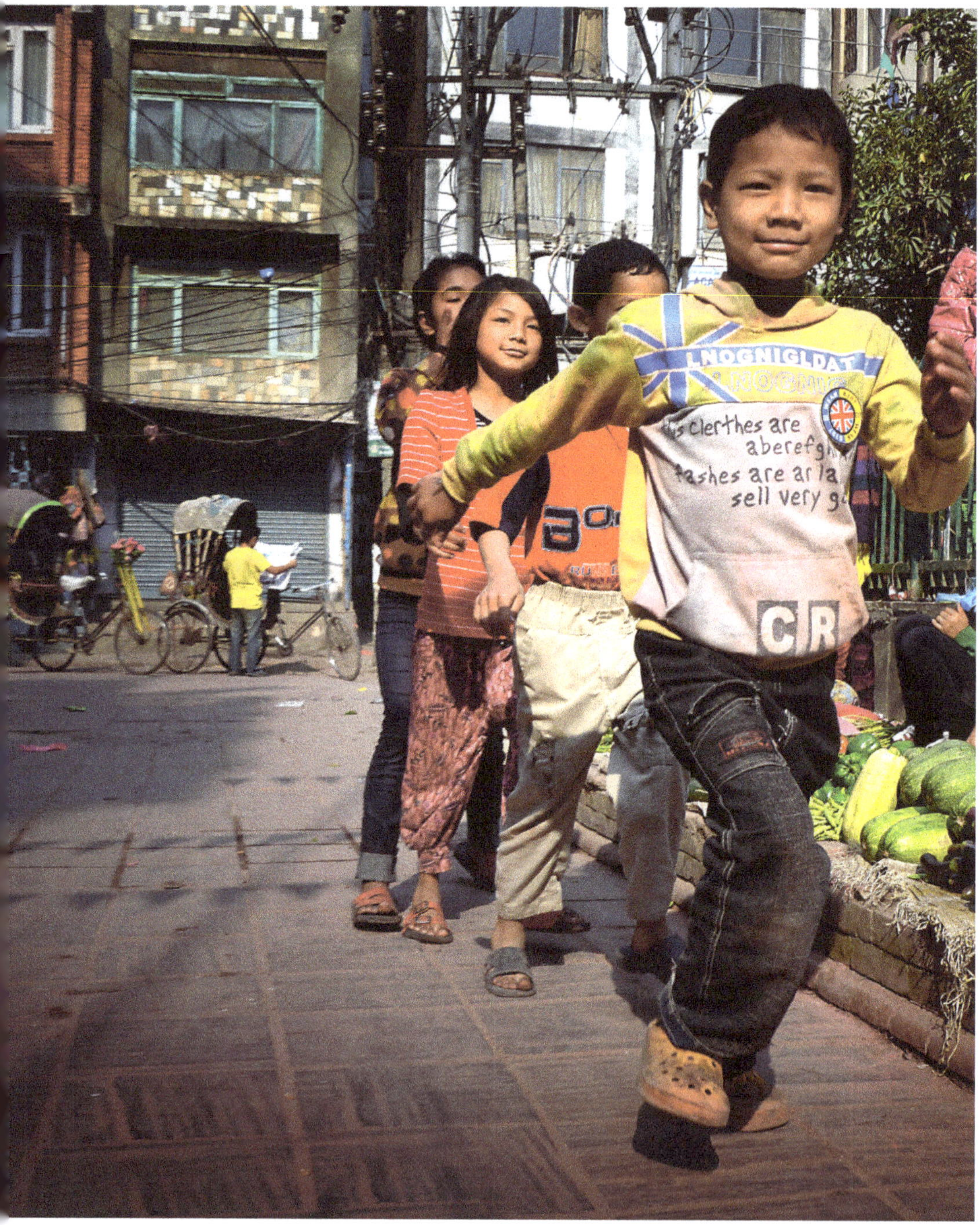

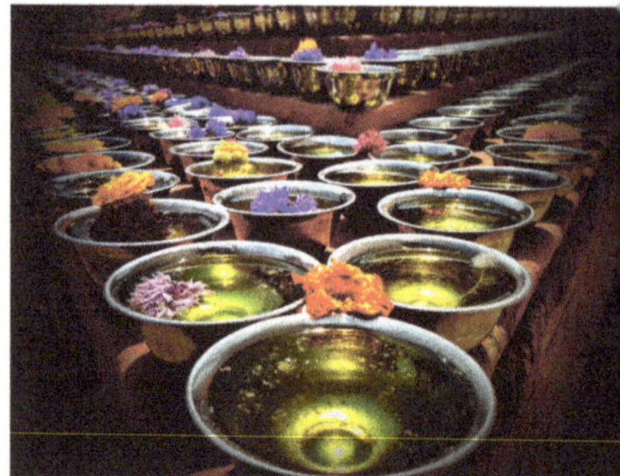

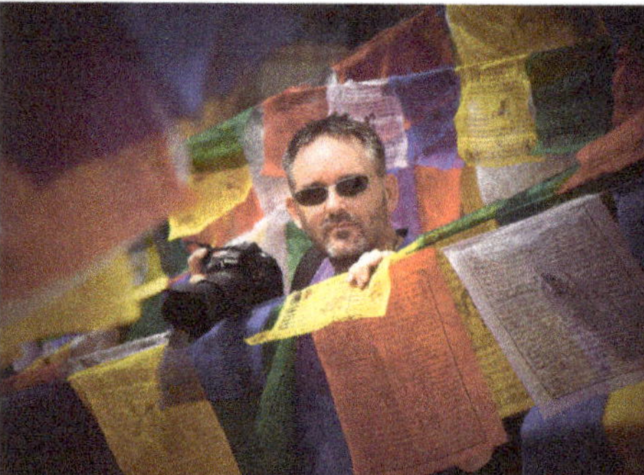

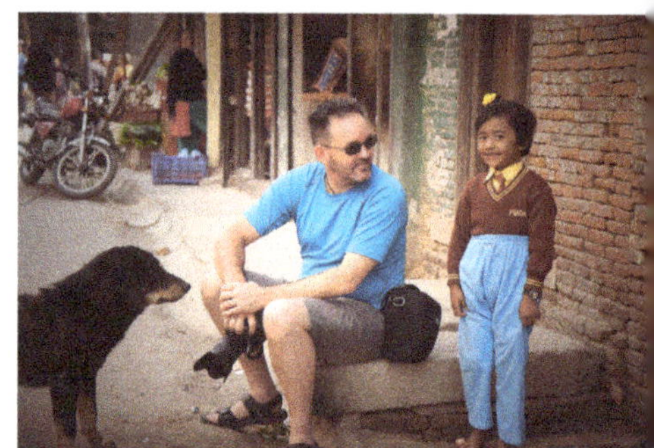

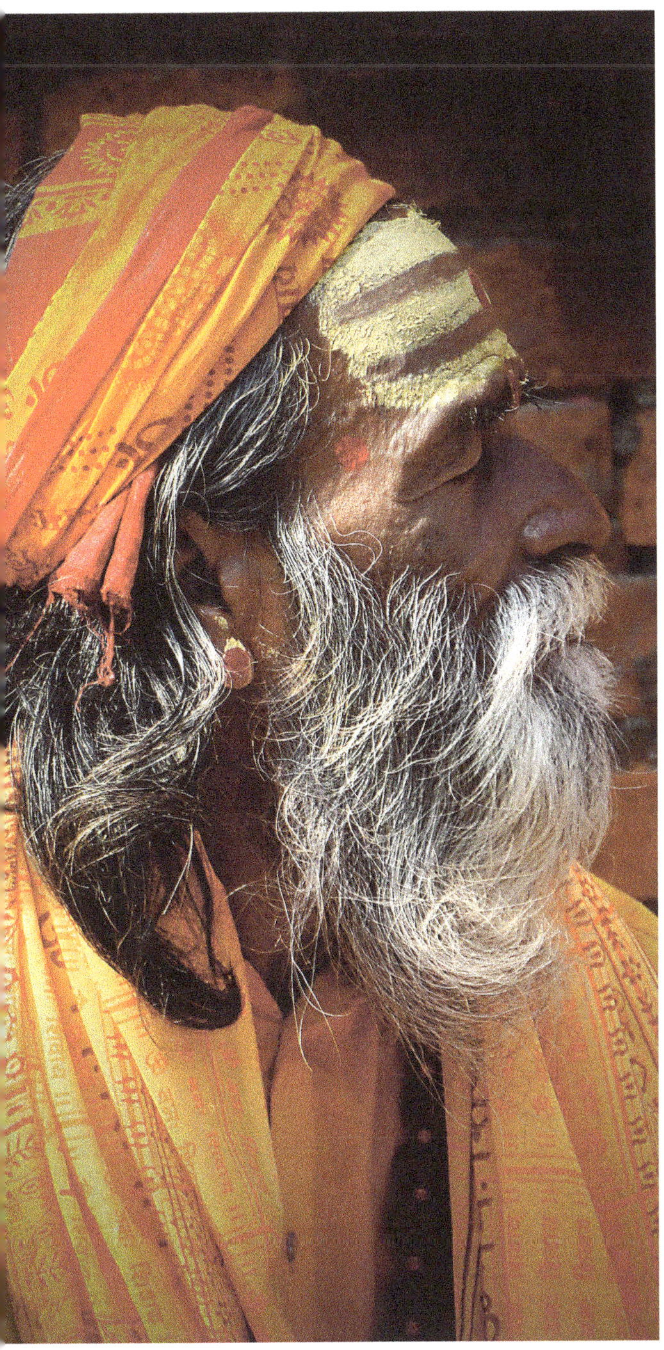

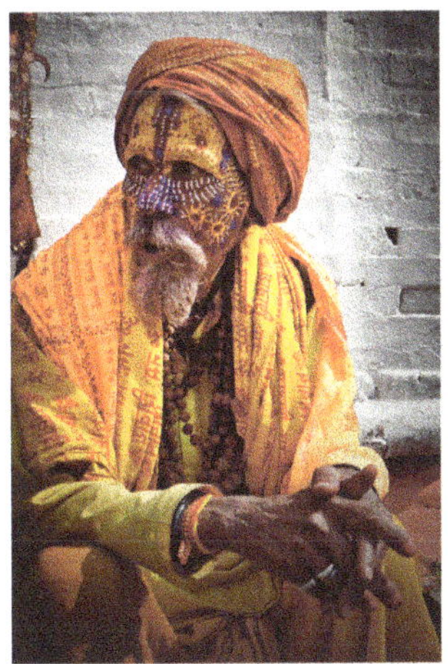

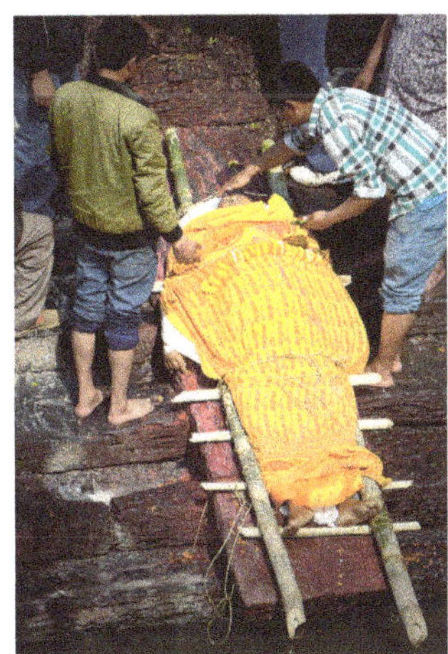

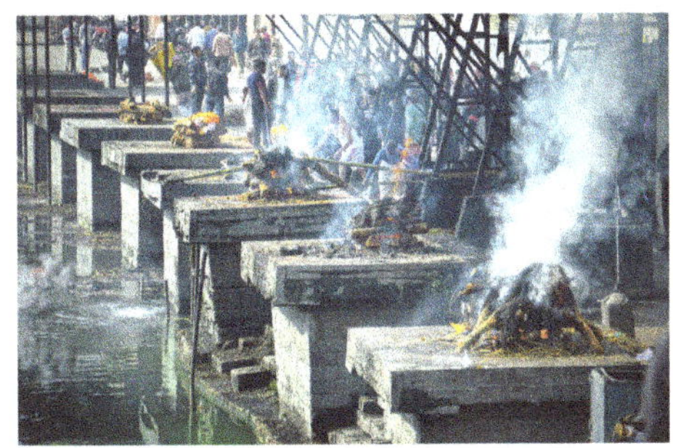

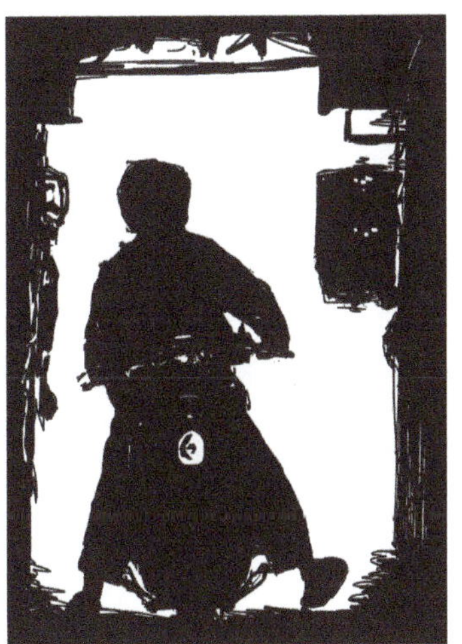

The bikes rush right by. tooting their horns like a song

As they zip right past me. in a frenzy, then they're gone

Its orderly chaos but it works like a charm

Strolling the streets , no one ever comes to harm

Through arches and lanes, through streets and the crowd

You suddenly get used to the chaos oh so loud

You stroll along shopping dodging the bikers and the cows

But it's the stimulation of the senses that this place allows.

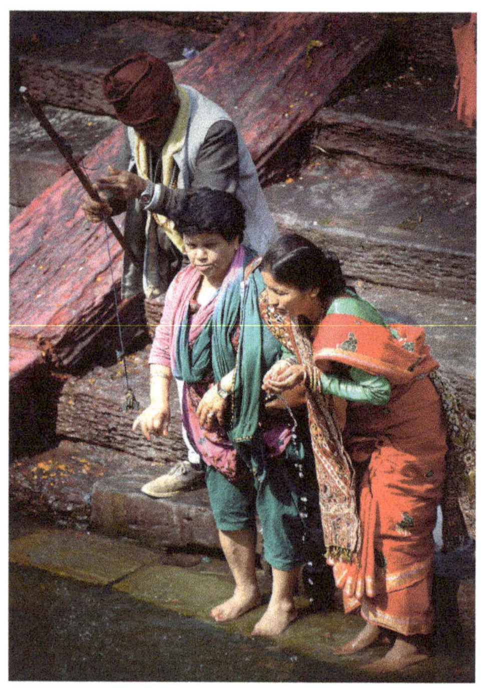
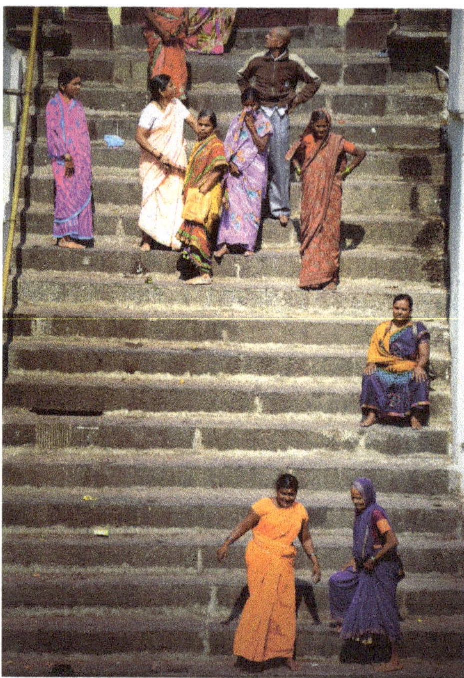
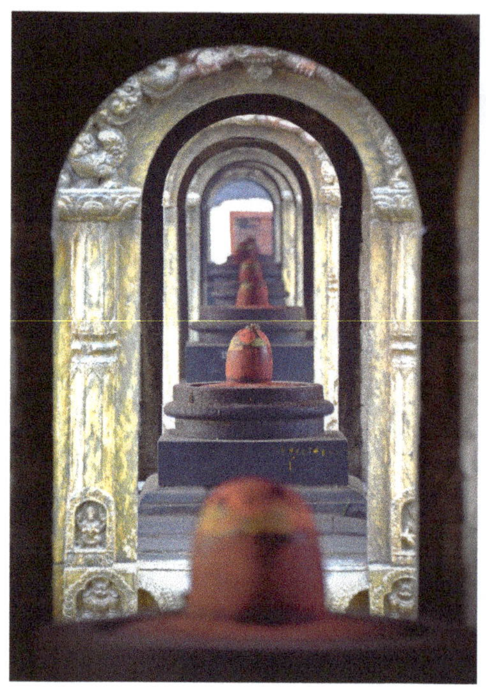
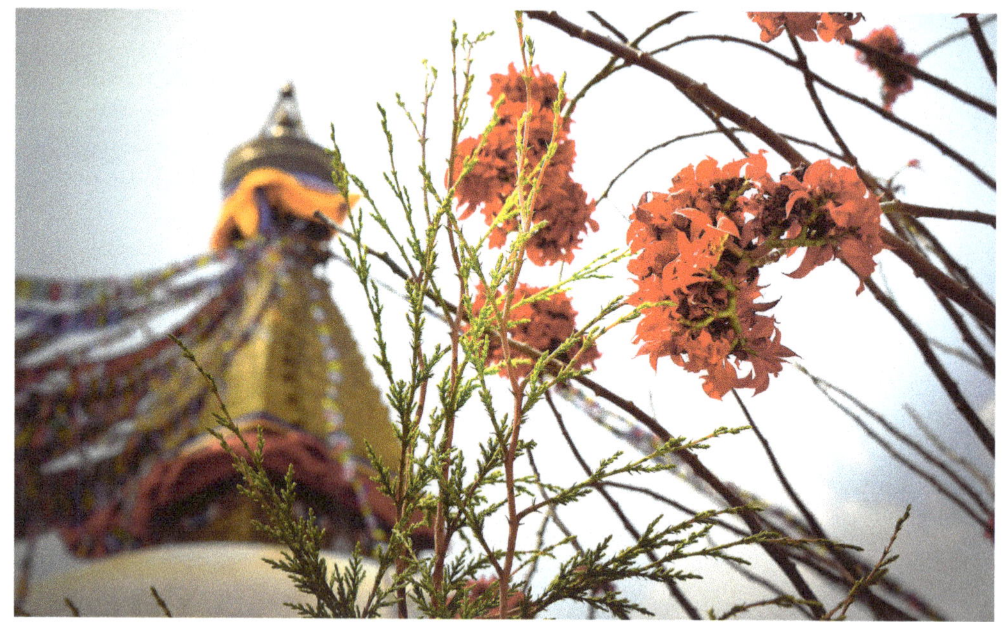

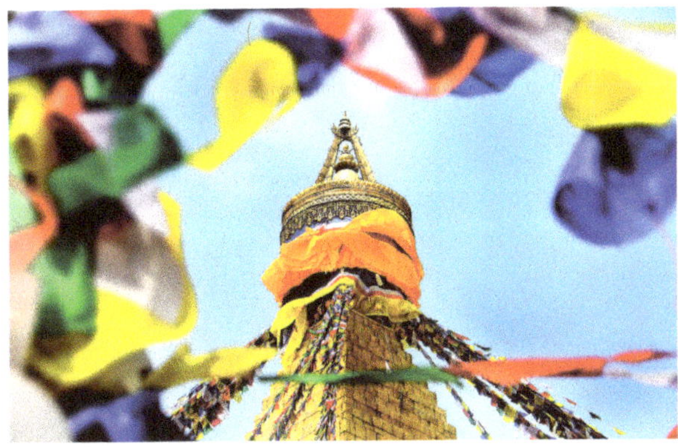

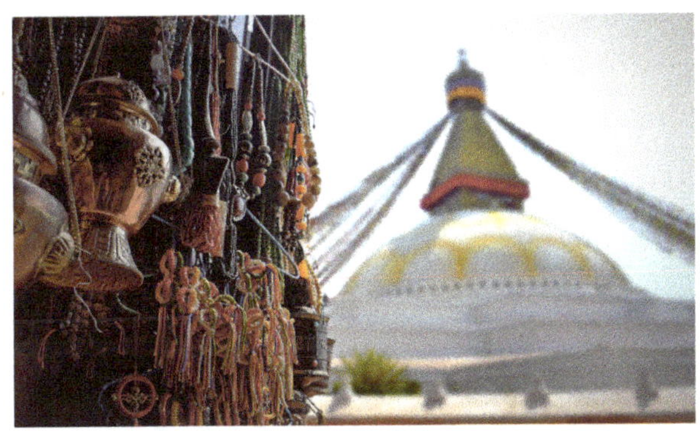

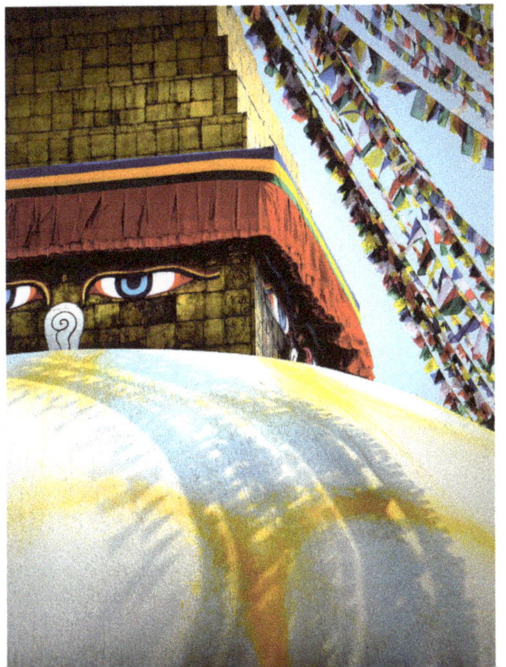

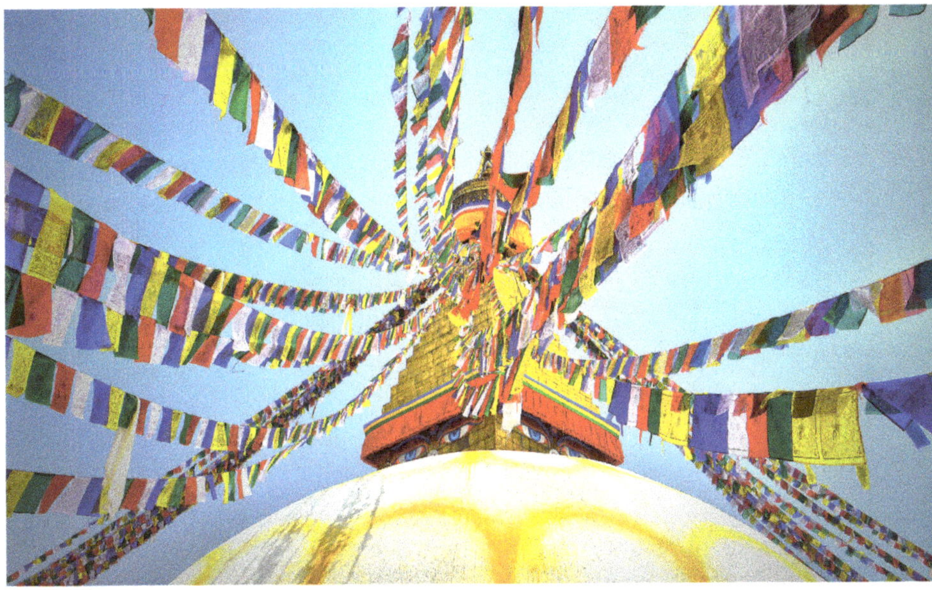

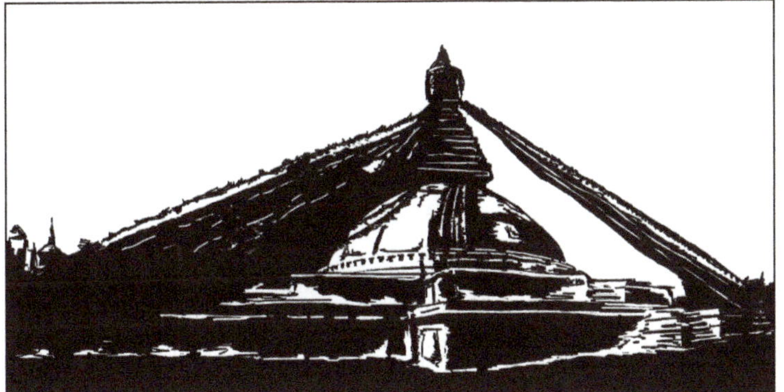

The second biggest stupa in the world they did say
On a hot and steamy but typical Kathmandu sightseeing day
With its tower and flags and huge religious pride
It shelters some parts of Bhudda locked away deep inside
as the locals wander by and the tourists snap away
it's great just to sit and watch the people stop and pray
as the shops and the noise seem to vanish in its grace
it's the glow and the grandeur of the stupa that rules this place.

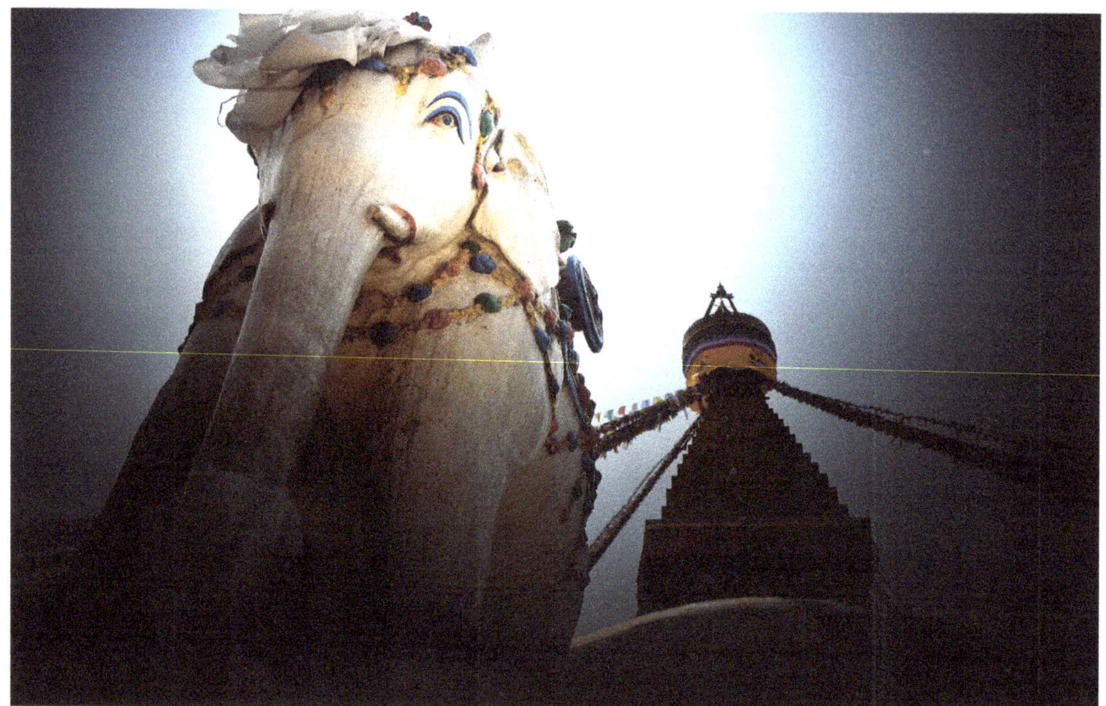

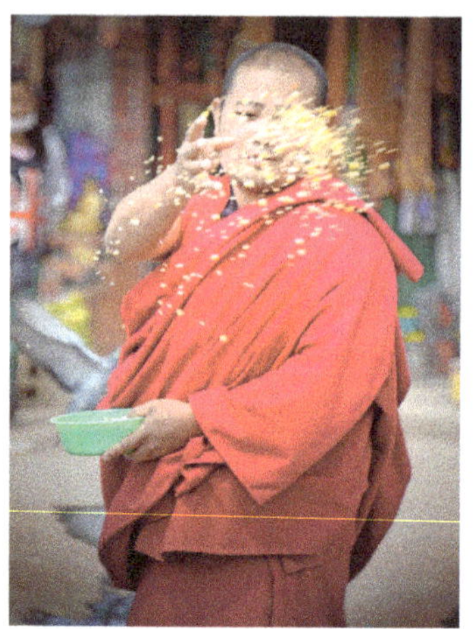

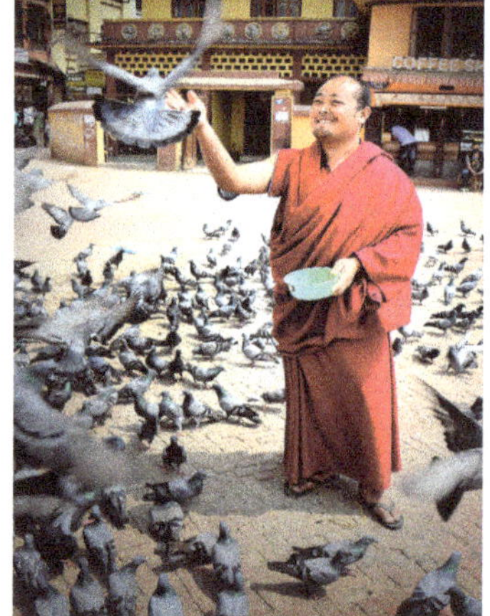

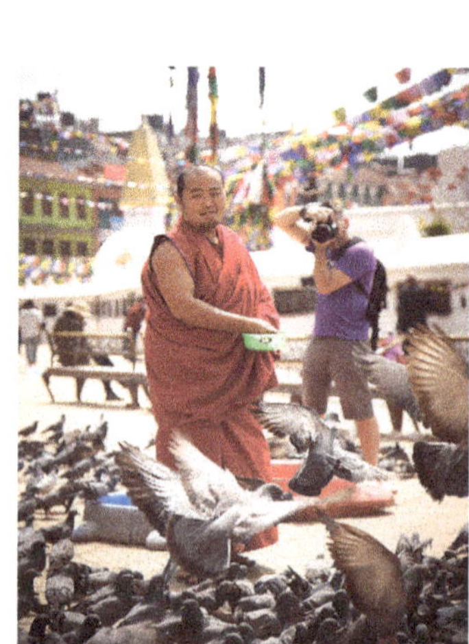

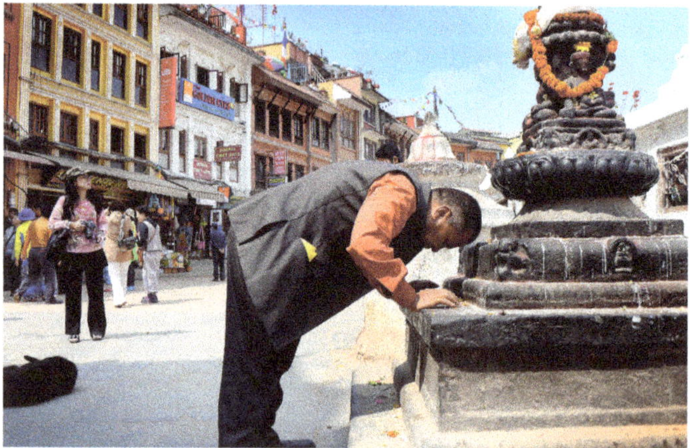

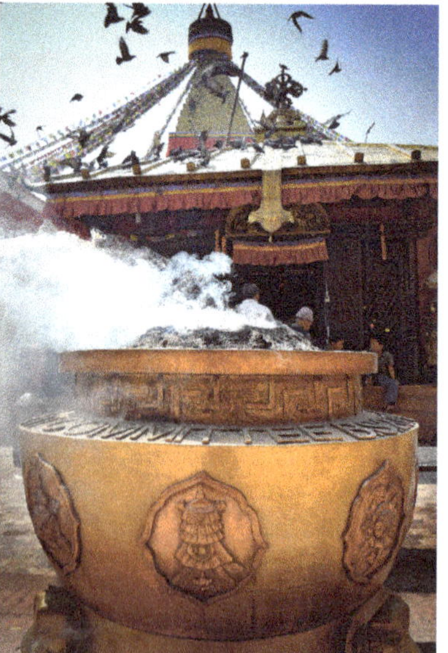

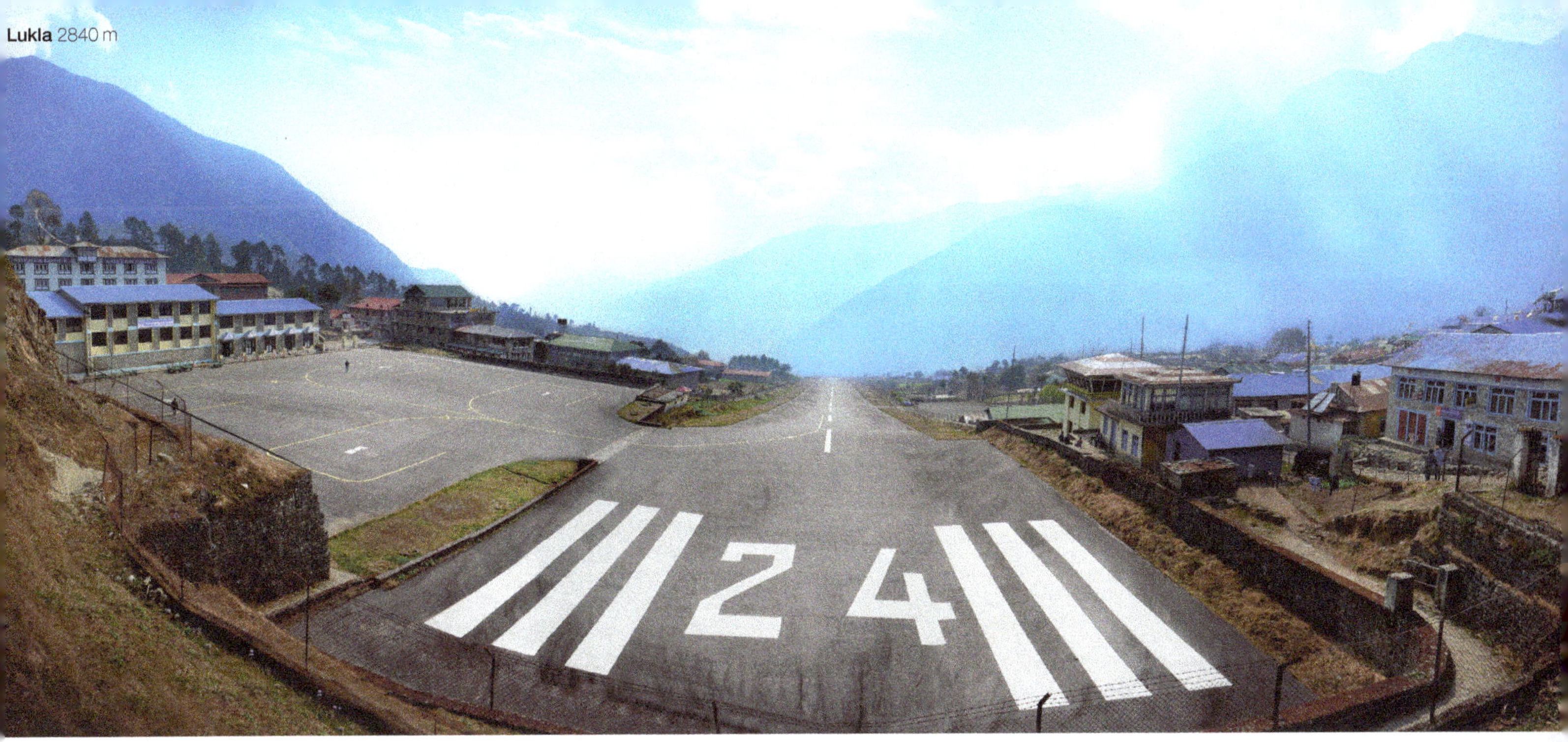

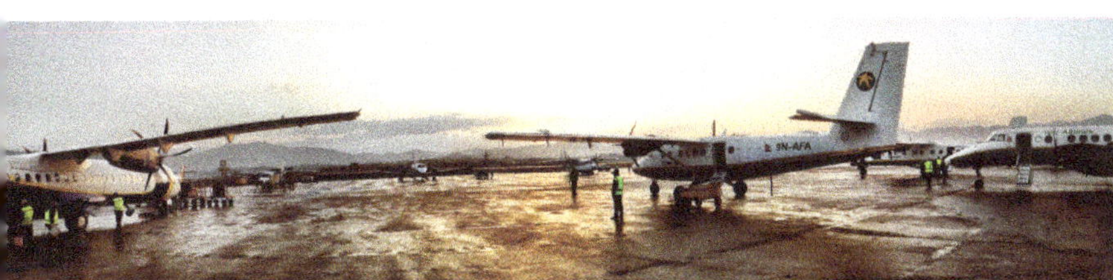

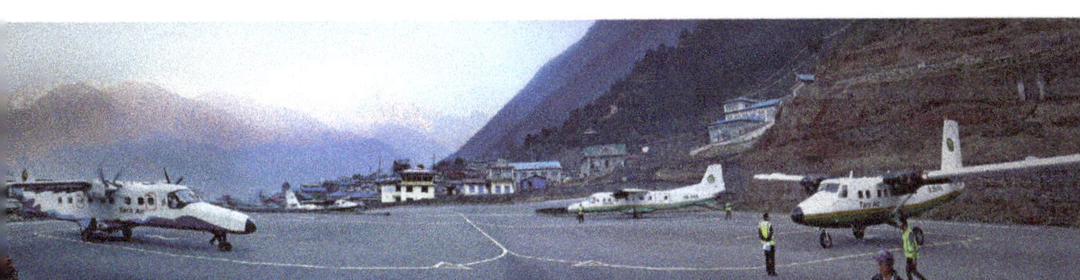

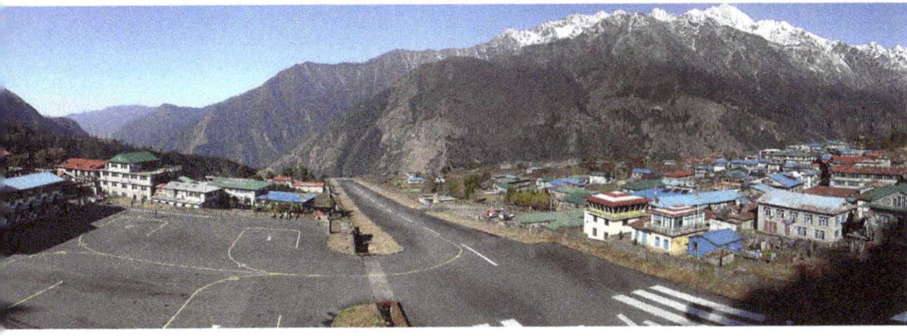

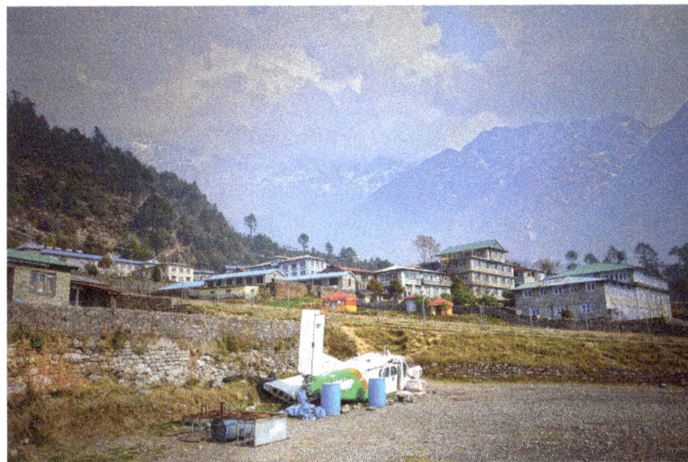

Ever since I became a plane nerd as a child, I knew about Lukla and its airport. For any aviation nut it's a bucket list item to land into and I finally got to do it. It's the only time I have landed into a place and everyone on board has cheered and clapped that we made it safely. Voted the most dangerous airport in the world due to the 2000 metre drop off at one end of the runway and the steep vertical cliff at the other, pilots have no room for second decisions. I have done it, I survived and I so want to do it again.

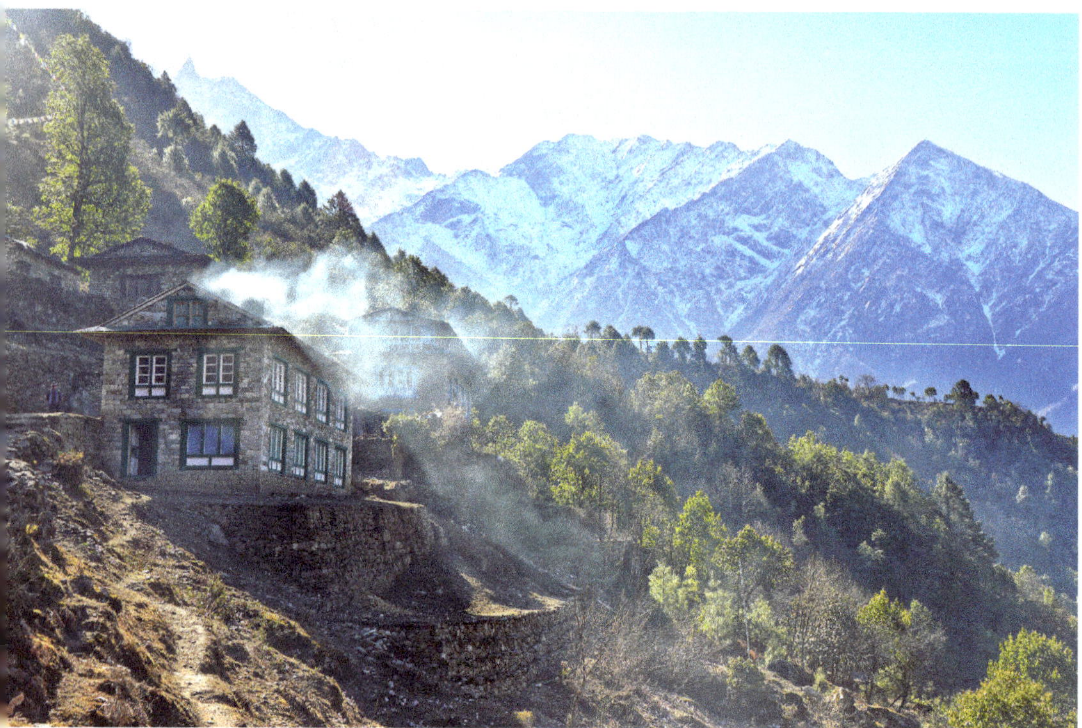

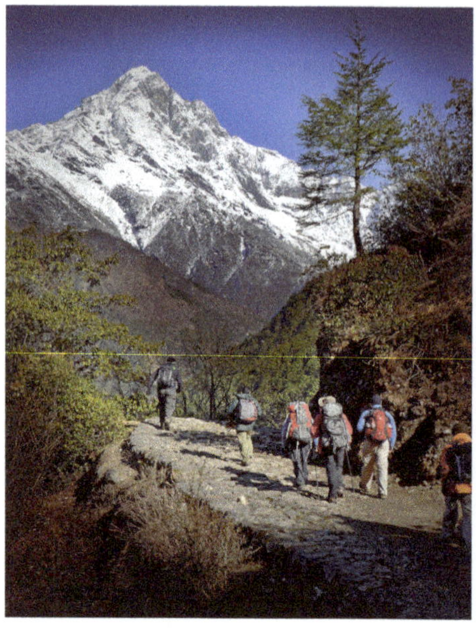

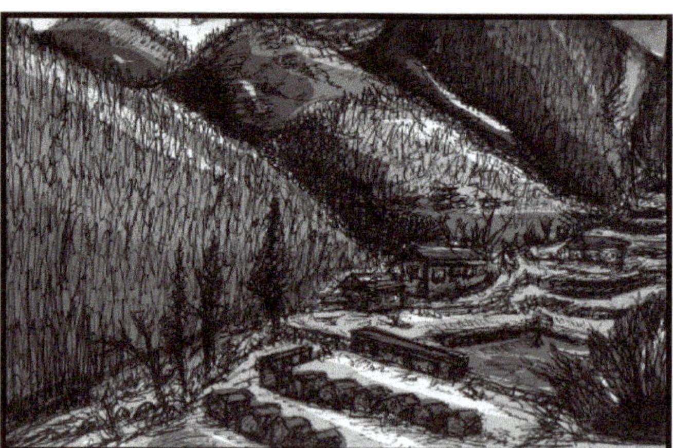

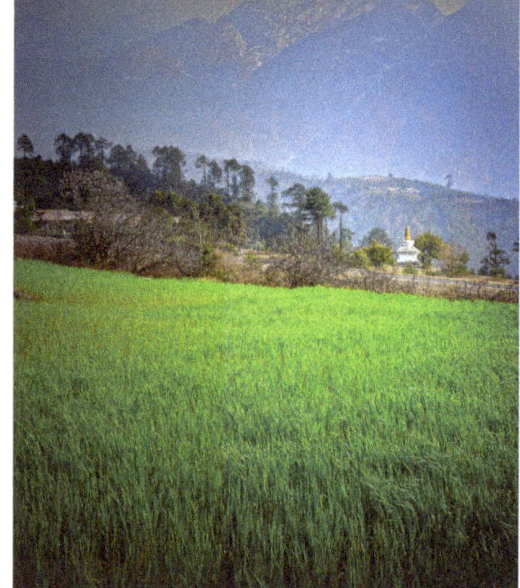

Looking down to the valley so deep

Lies the village with its cliffs so steep

See our tents so waterproof and untorn

Keeping us weary trekkers so snug and so warm.

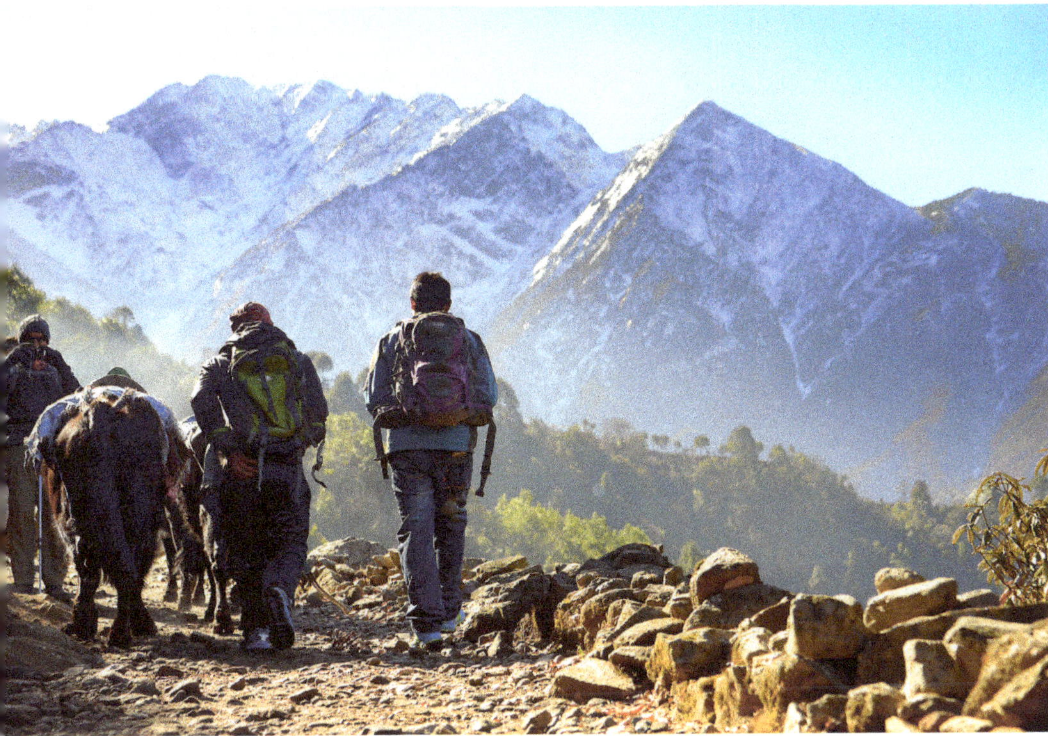

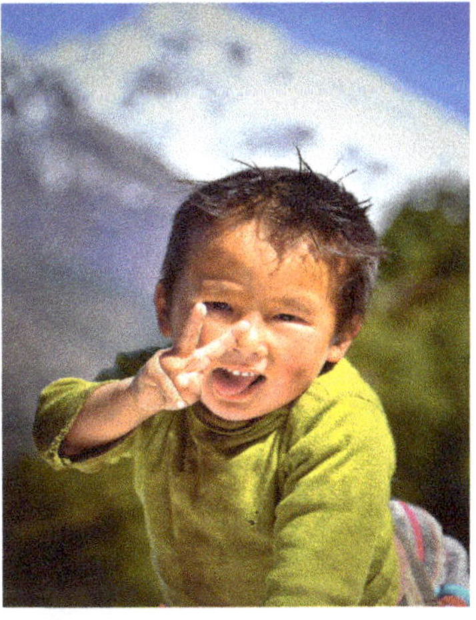

After surviving the flight into the most dangerous airport in the world, we set off into the mountains so naïve and extremely excited. The first part is unusually downhill, which was unexpected knowing we were on our way up the mountain. The sight of our red tents all in rows beside the river from Everest was a welcome surprise and a great place to stop and marvel at where we were in the world.

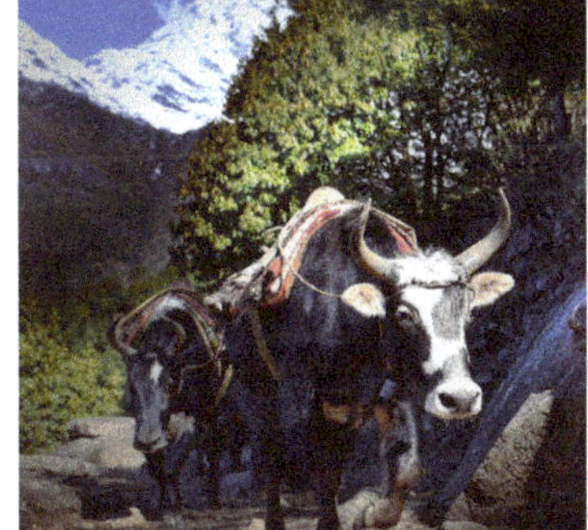

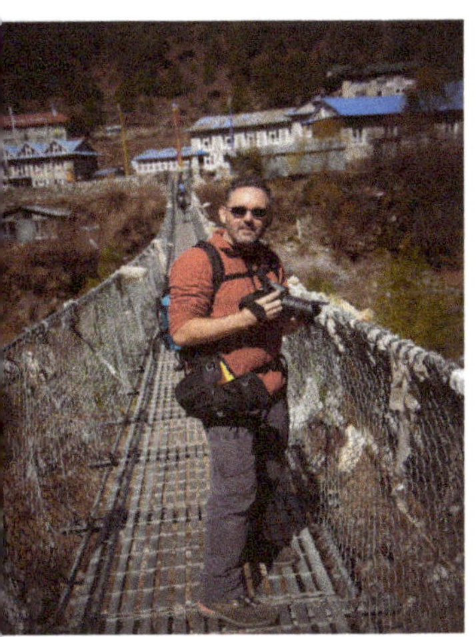

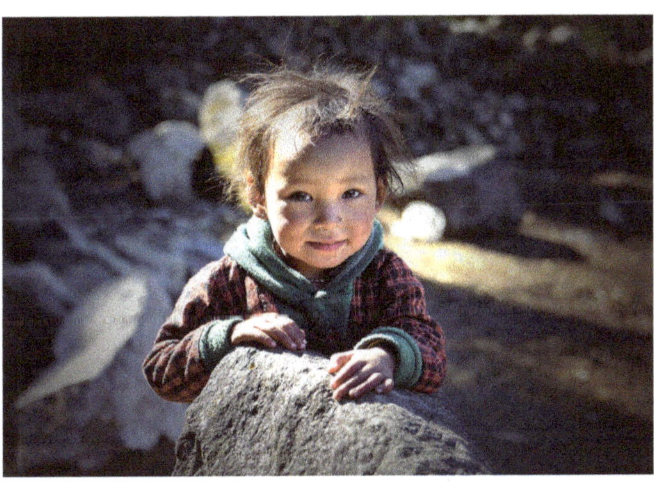

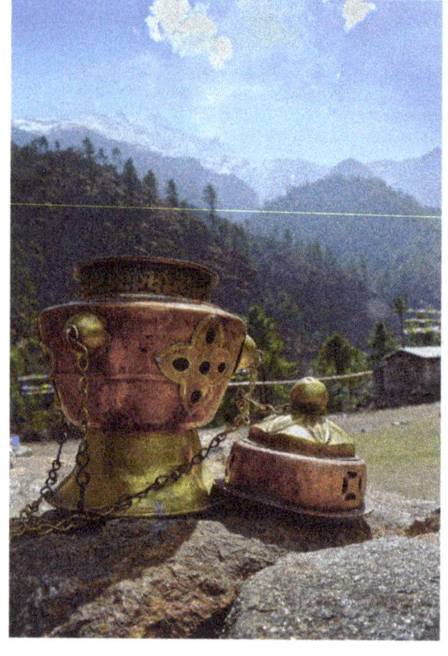

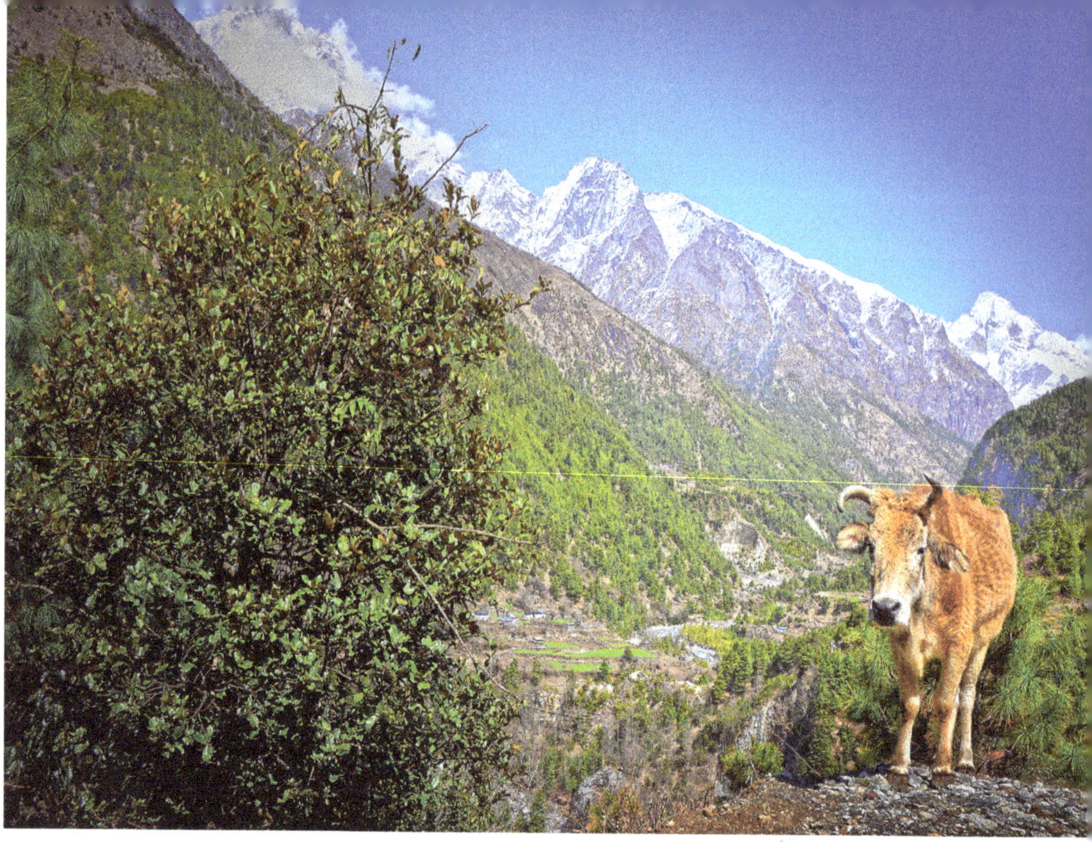

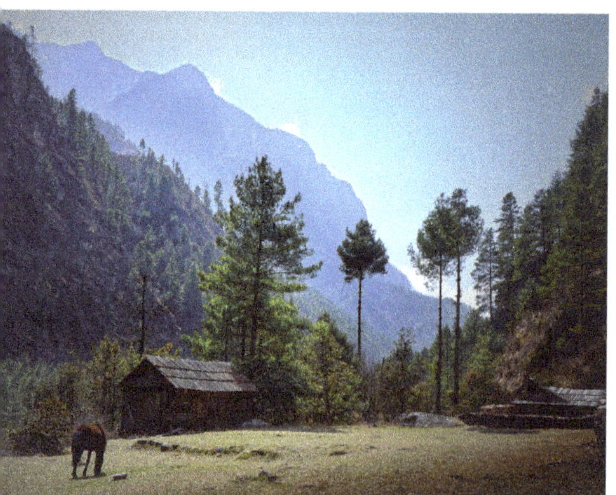

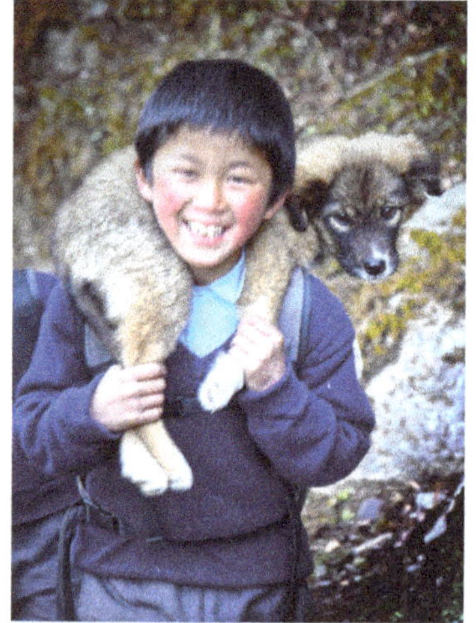

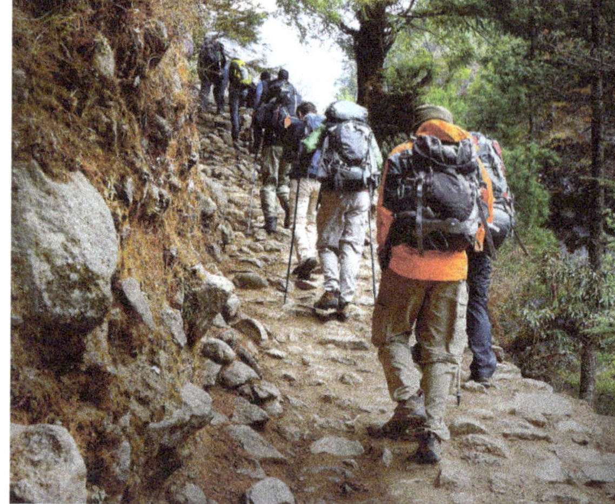

Sagarmatha National Park

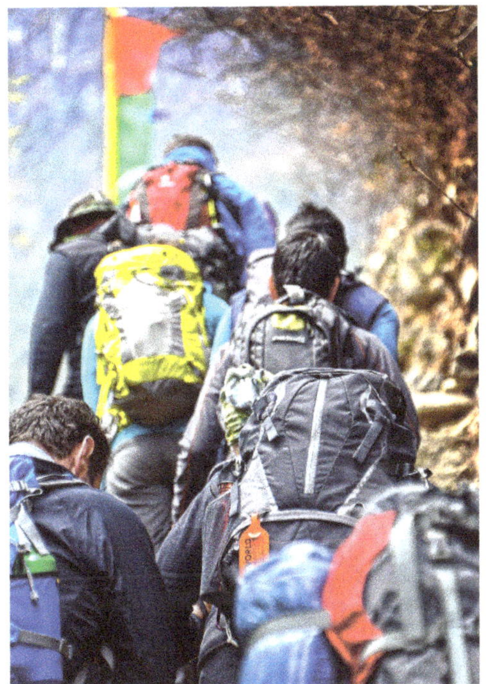

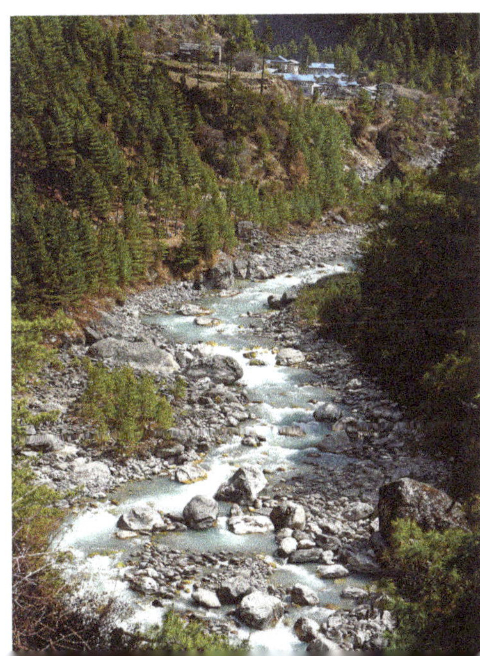

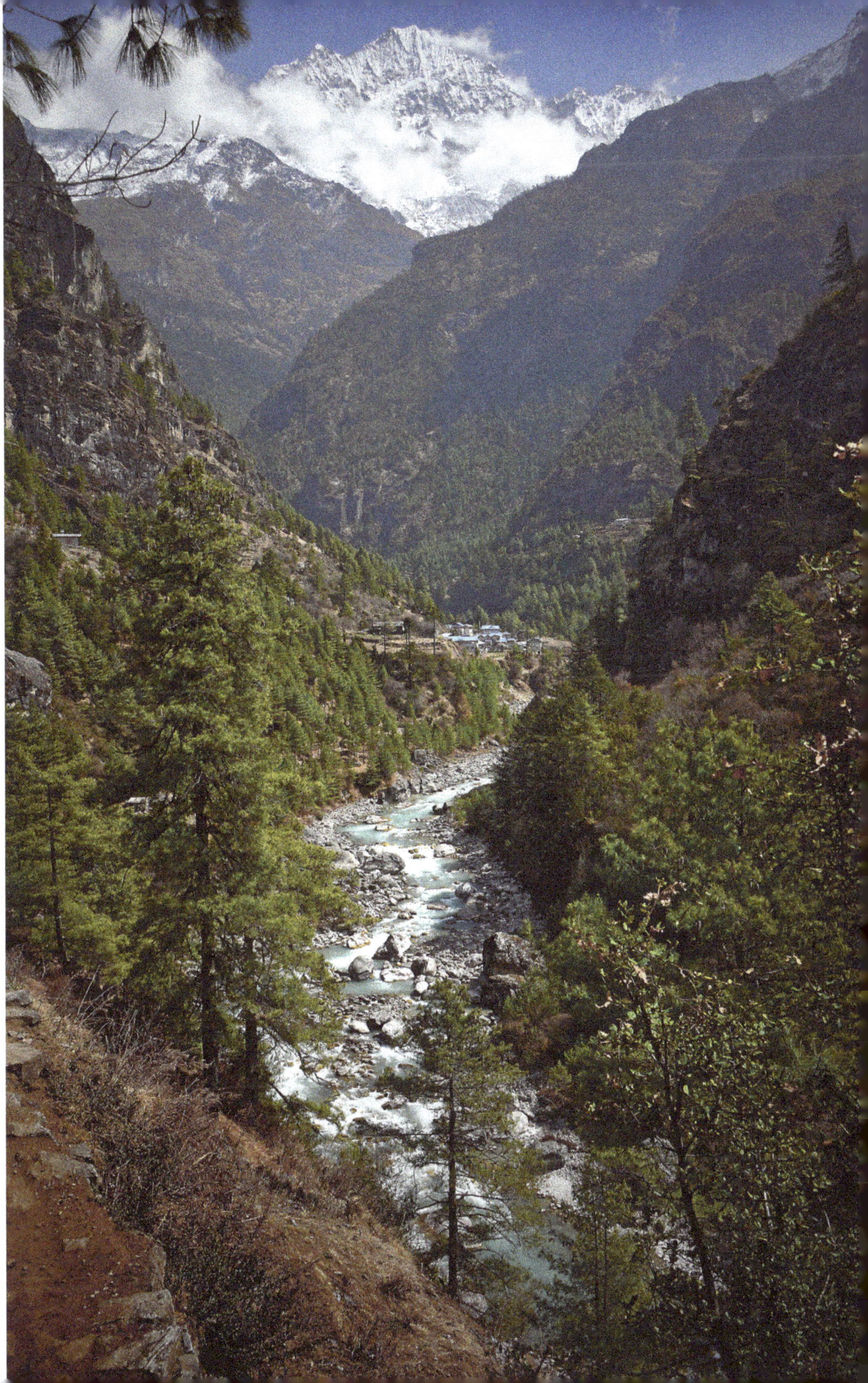

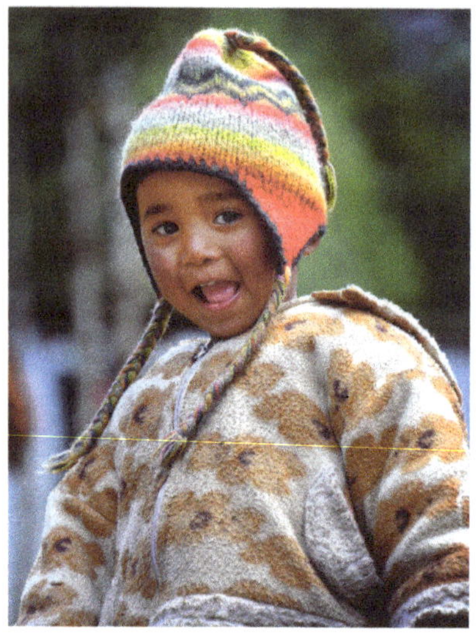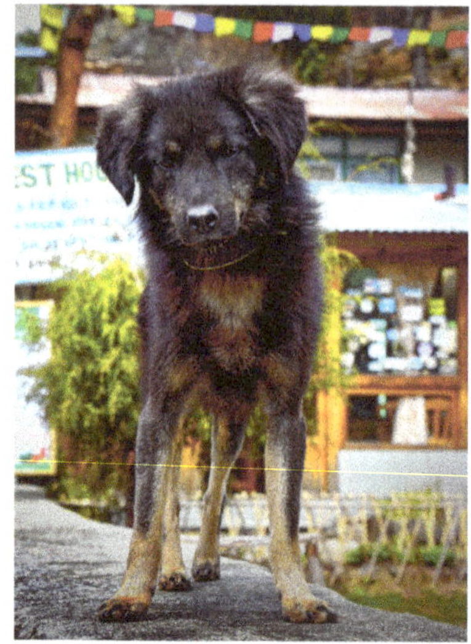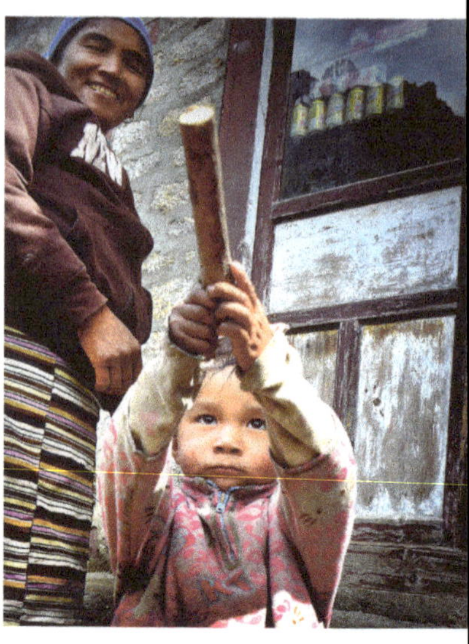

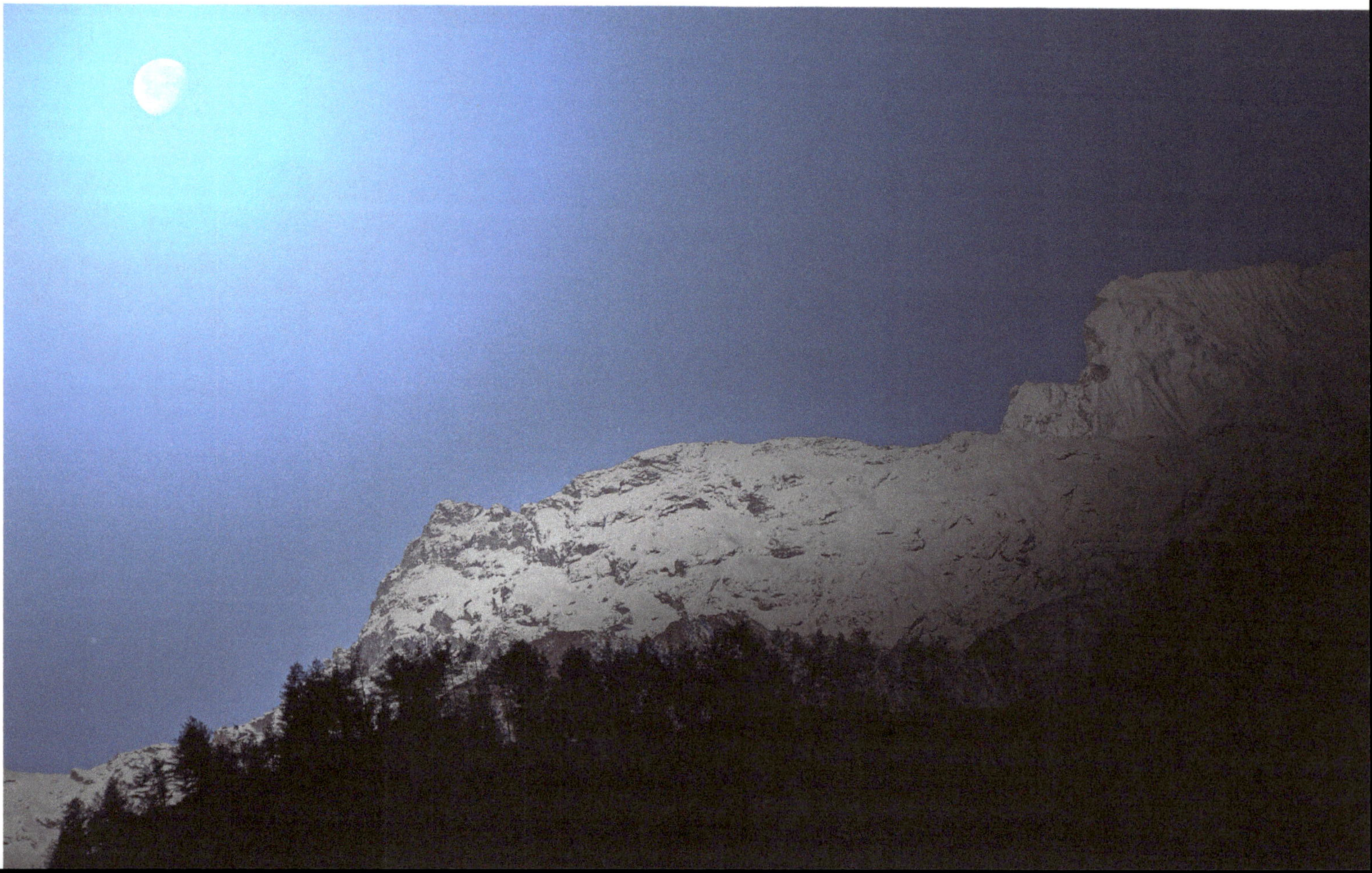

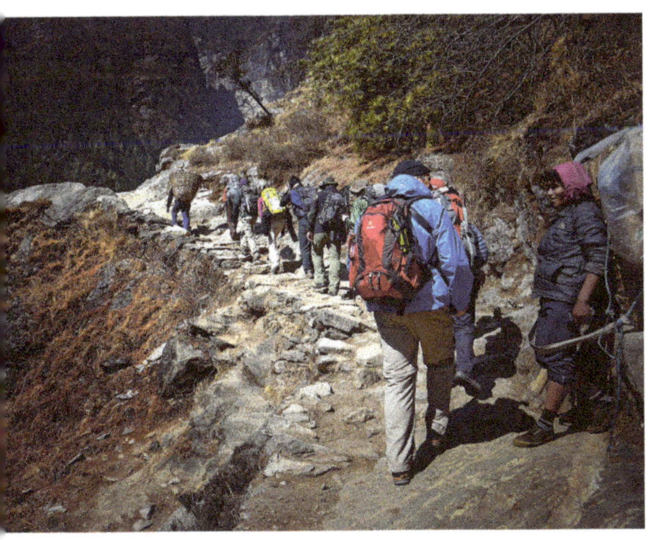
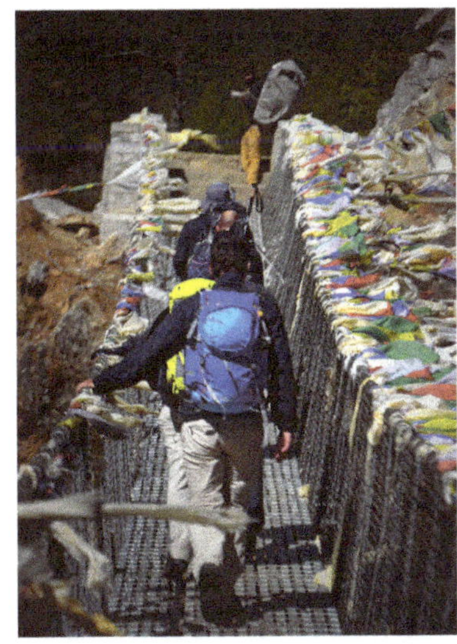
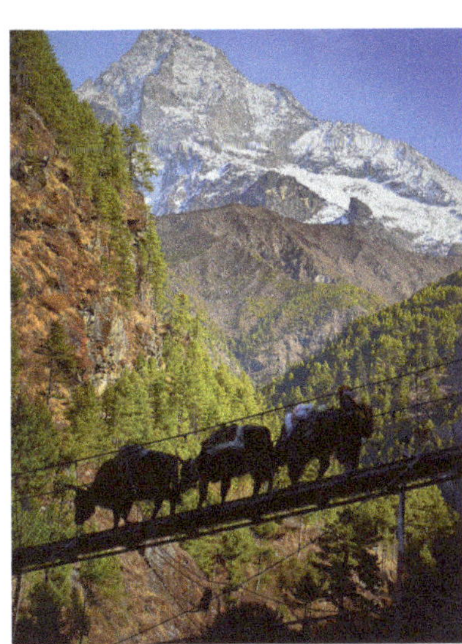
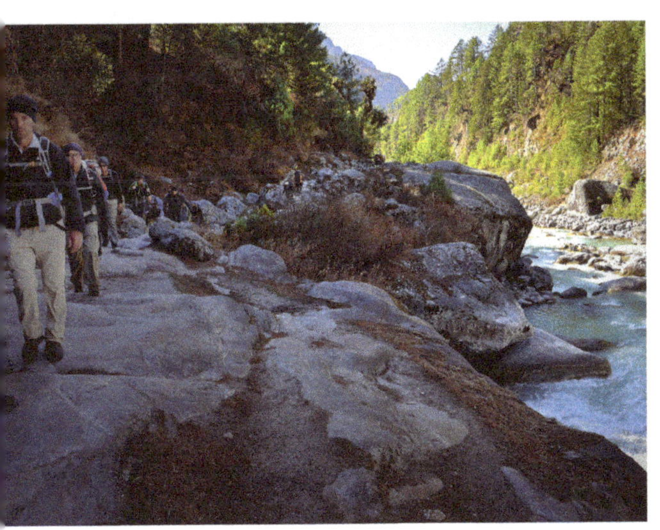
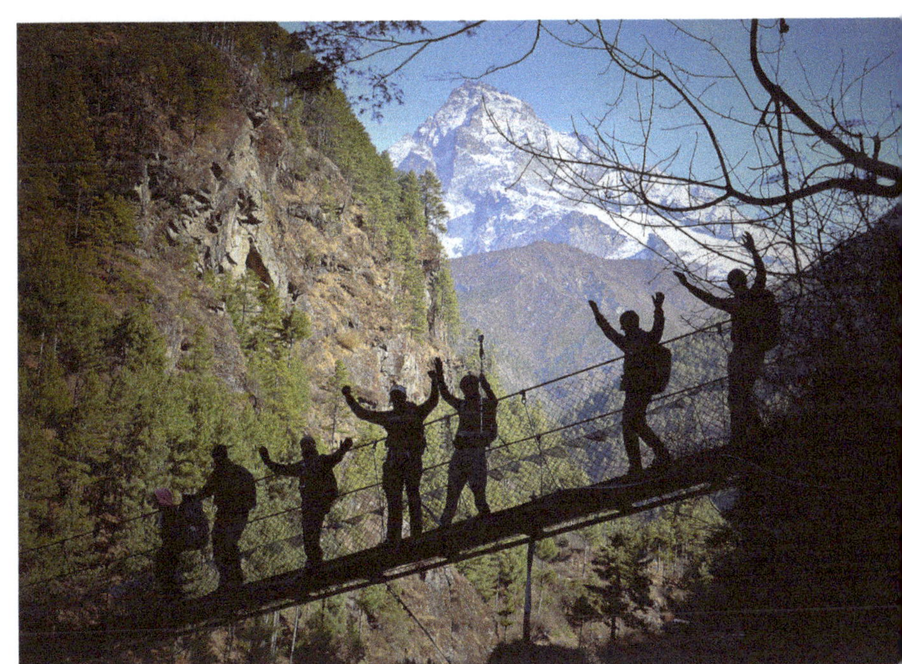

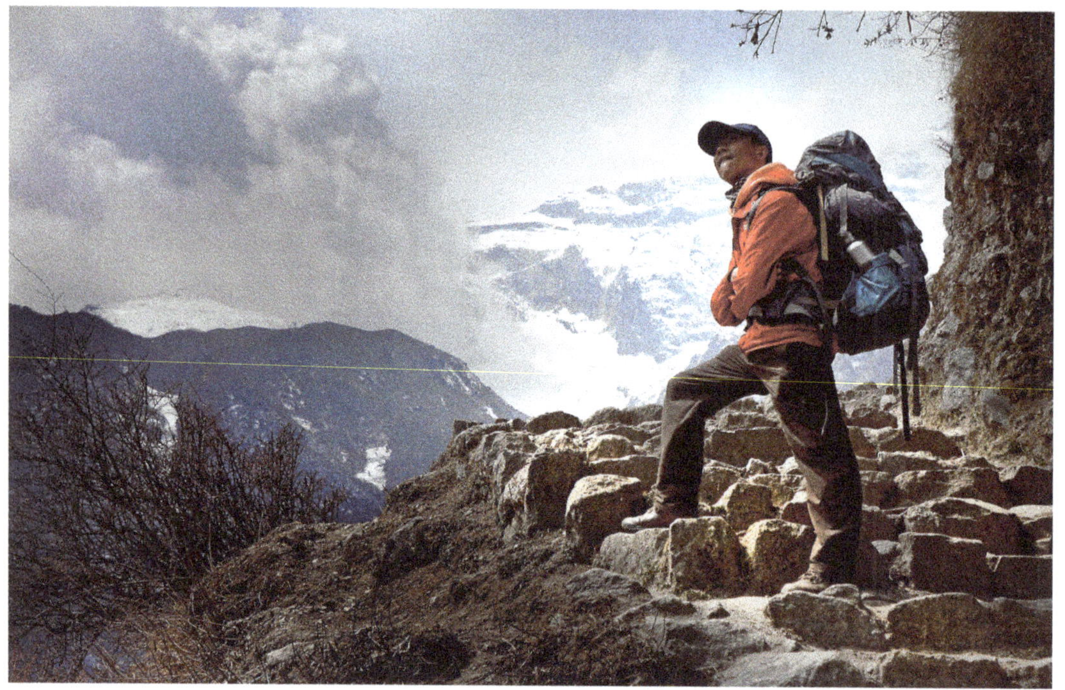

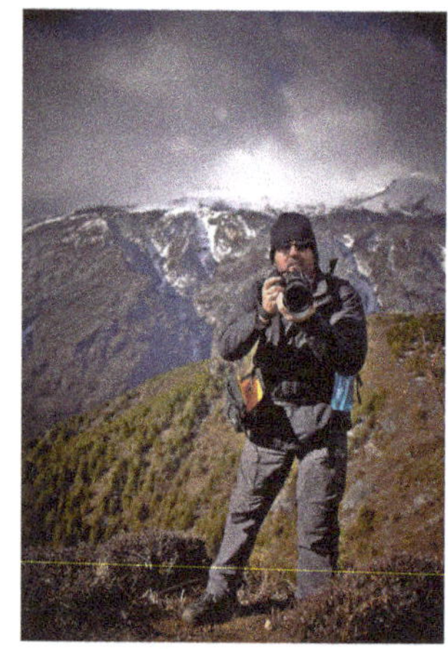

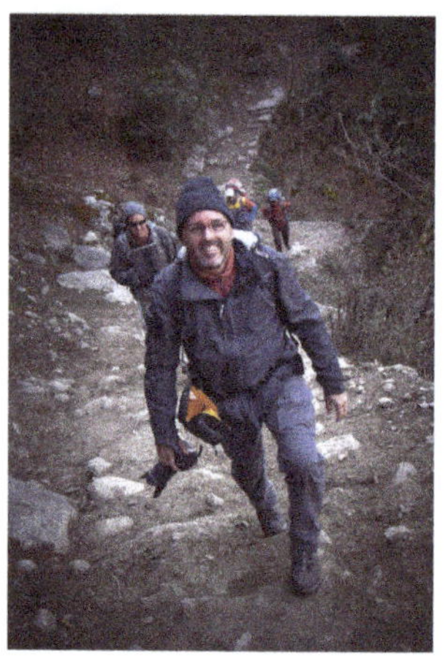

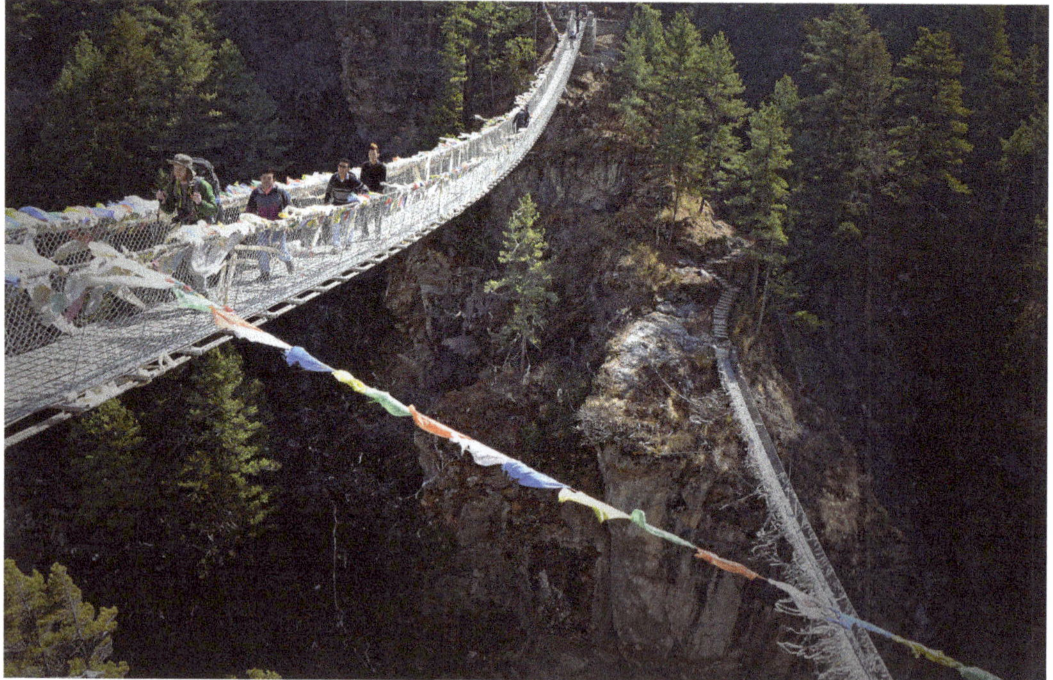

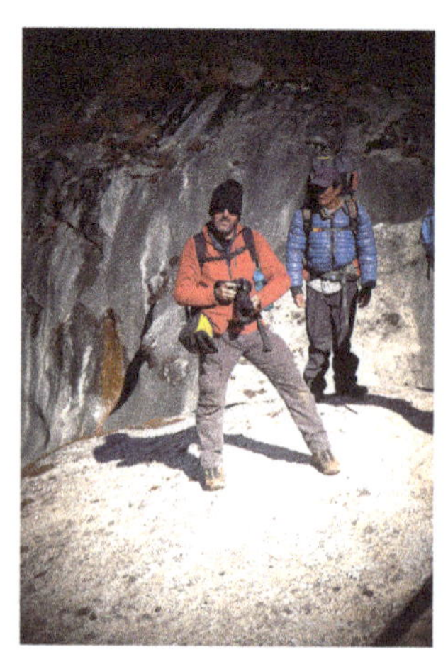

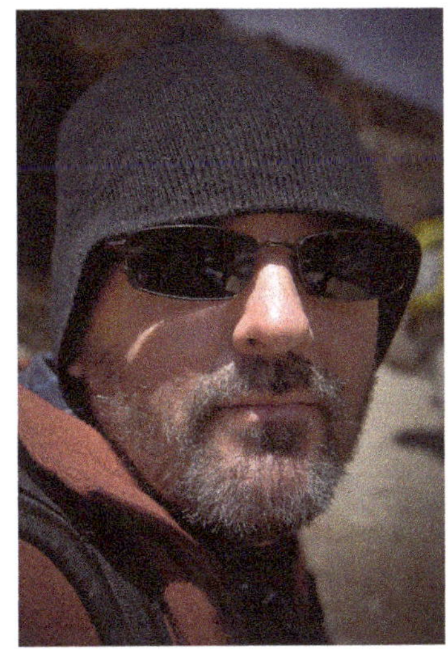
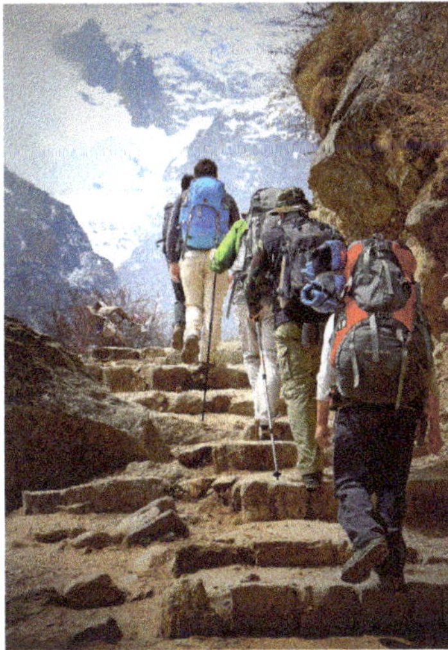
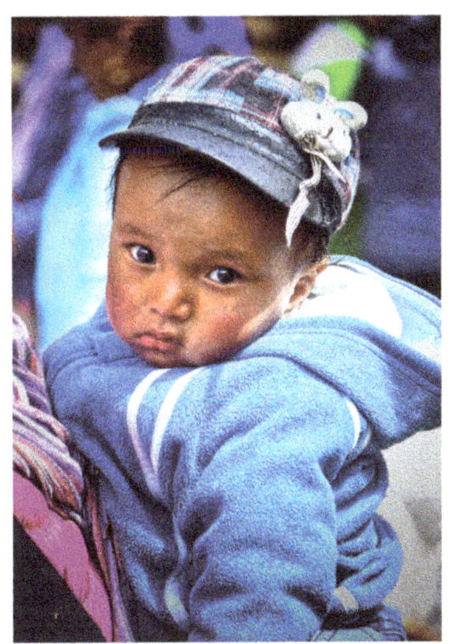

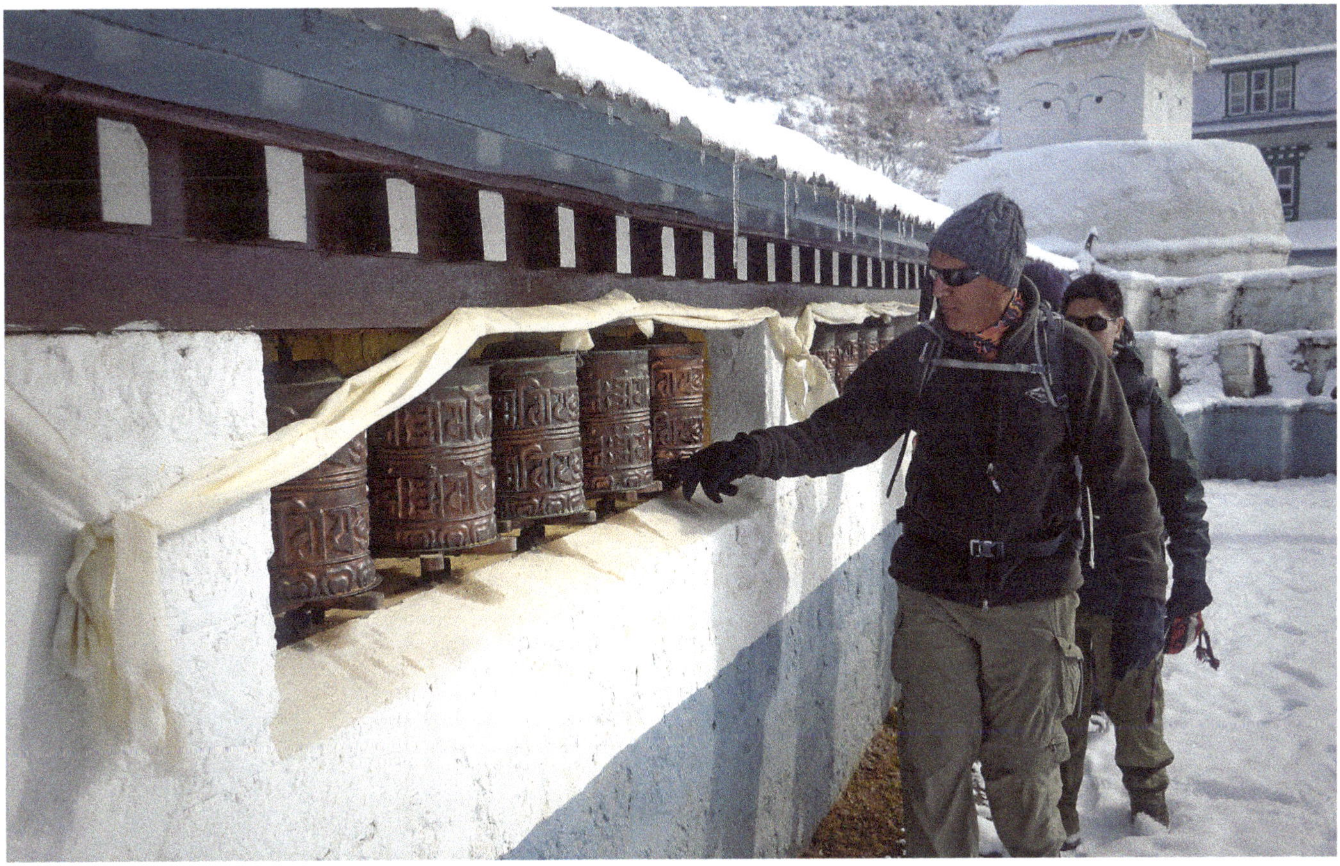

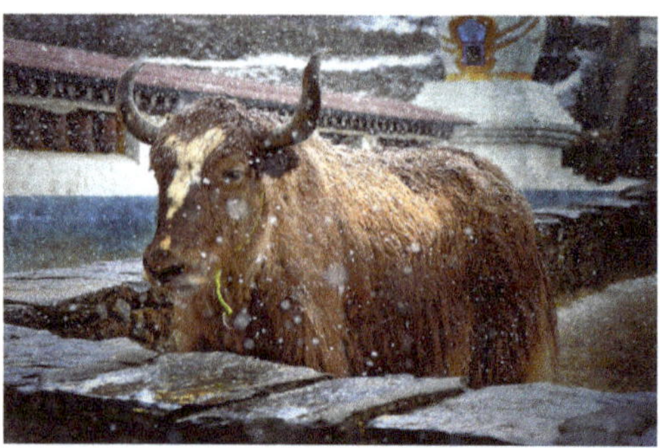

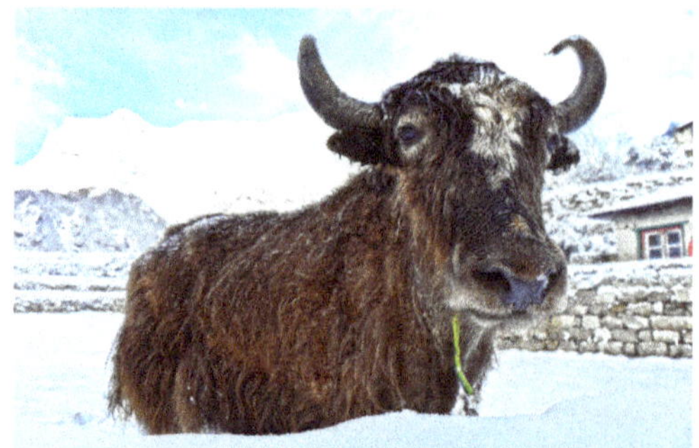

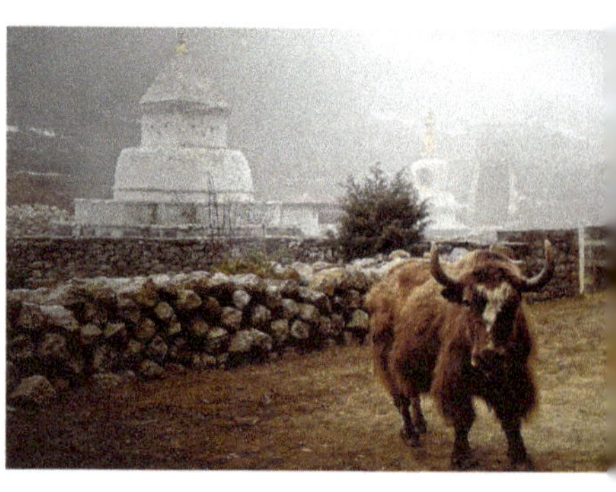

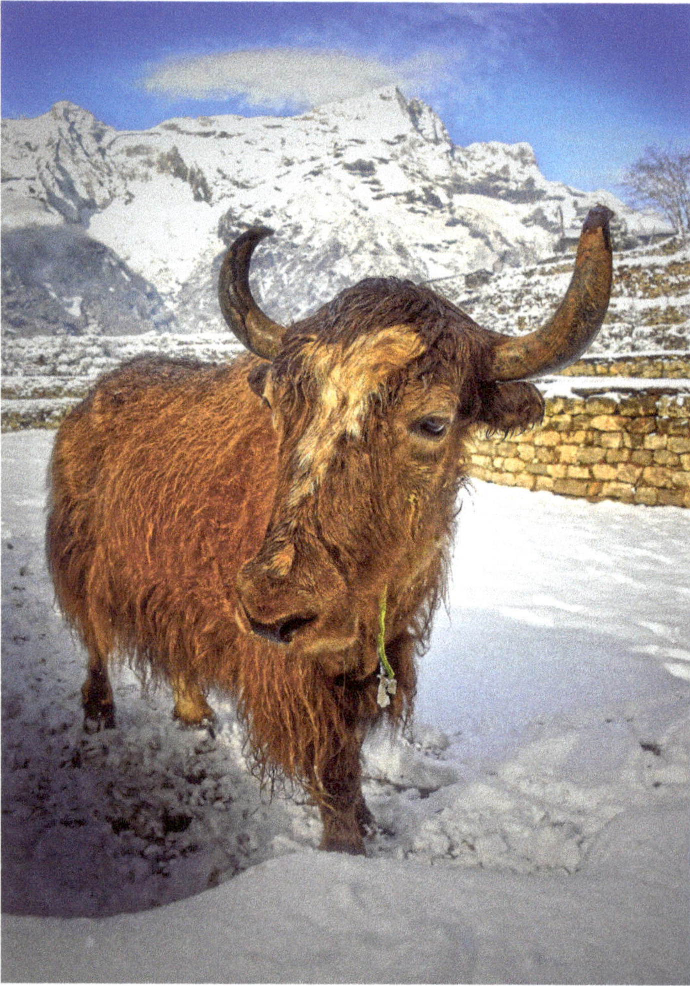

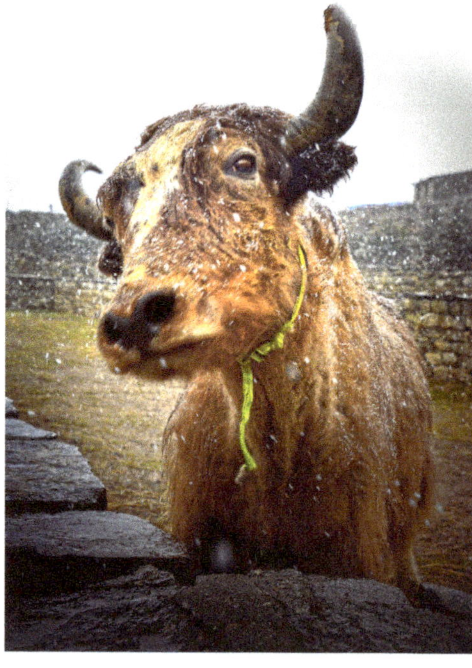

Yakky

At the lower altitudes you come across what you think are yaks but they are actually an animal called a 'dzo', which is a crossbreed between a yak and common cattle. You get all excited that you have seen a yak and then get told they are not. It's only later as you get into the real heights that dzos can't work and only purebred yaks are used. The initial excitement and novelty is quickly gone after your twentieth stop to let them pass on the trail as they have right of way.

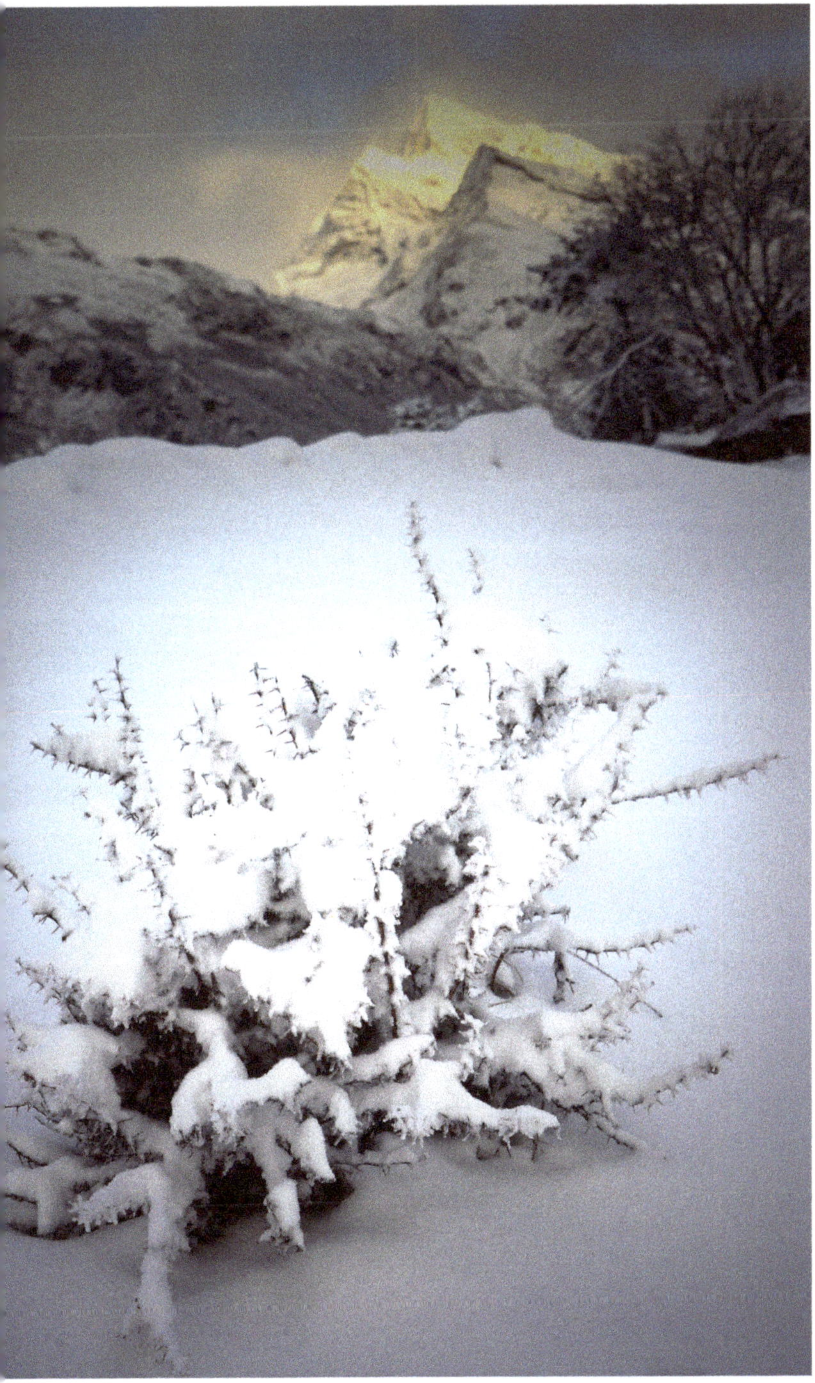

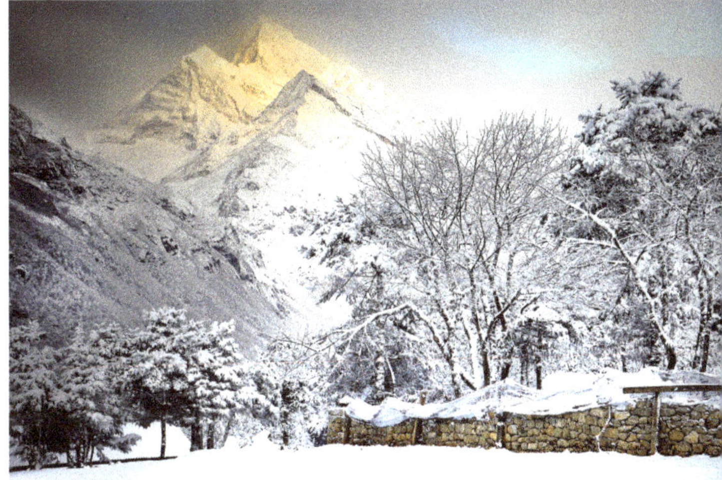

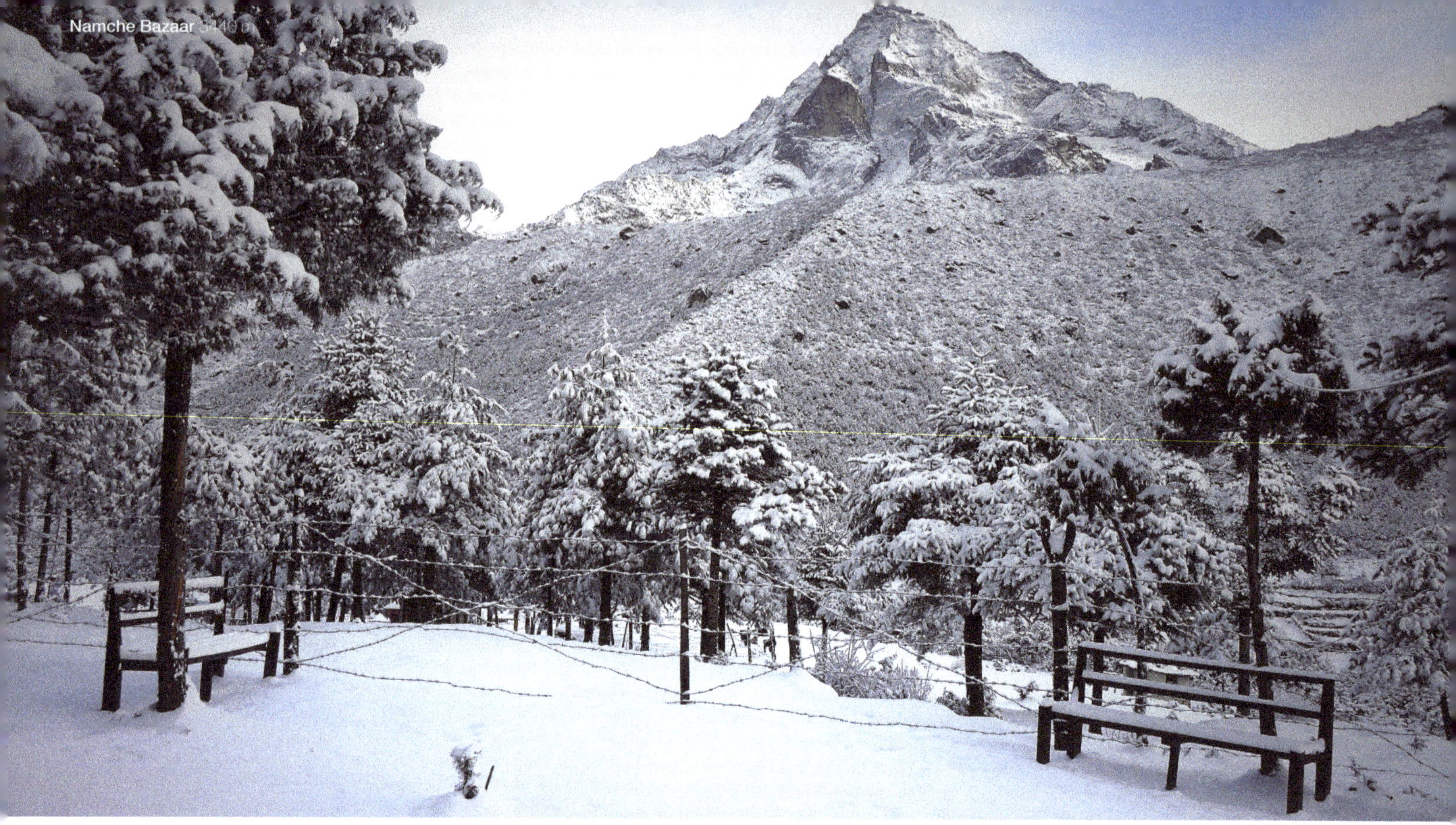

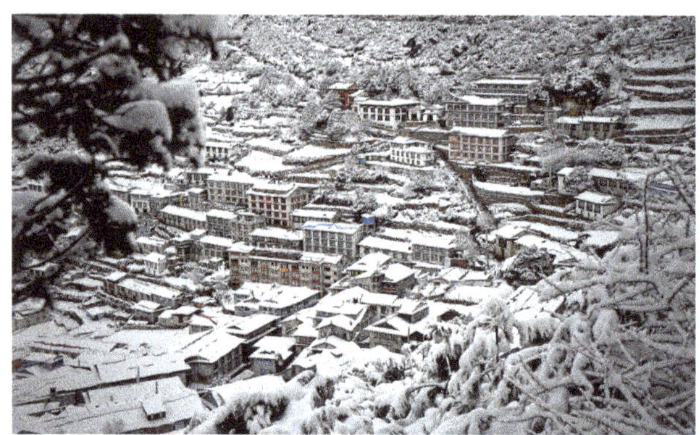

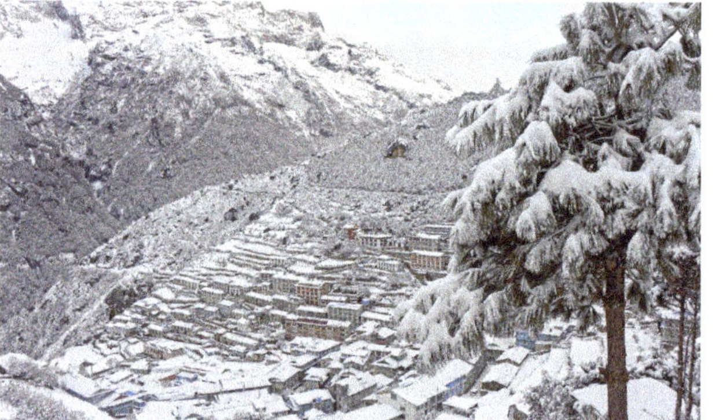

After the long and frustrating climb into Namche you are greeted with one of the special places on this Earth. Built into the curved hillside it is a feat of engineering to even exist. The town, its markets, shops and simplistic life are unique. Waking up to a snow-covered Namche on our first morning there was one of the special times on the entire trek. It's a day I will always remember.

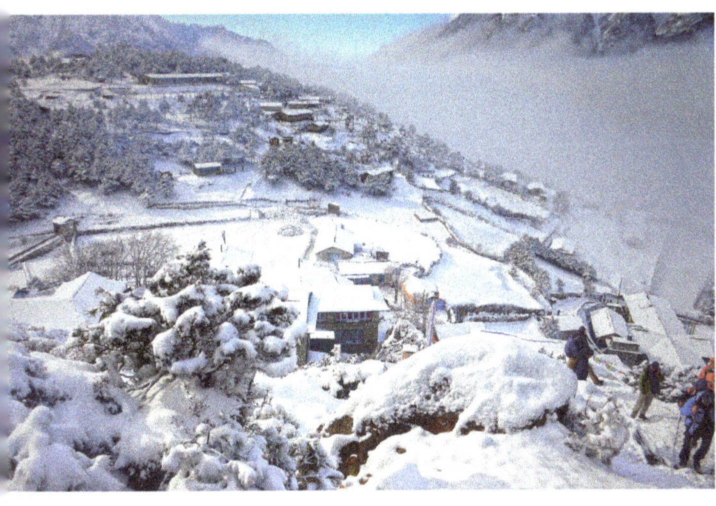

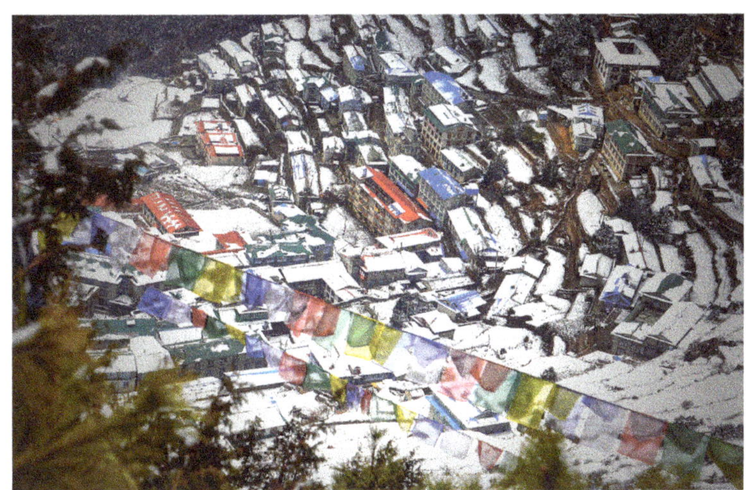

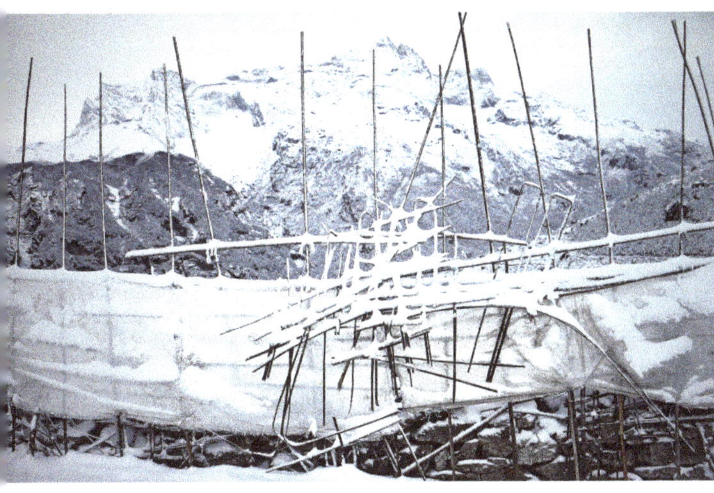

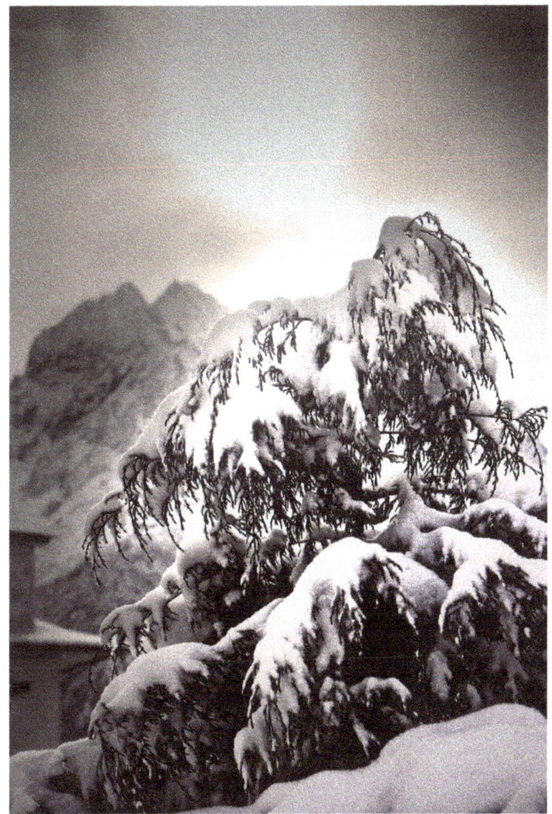

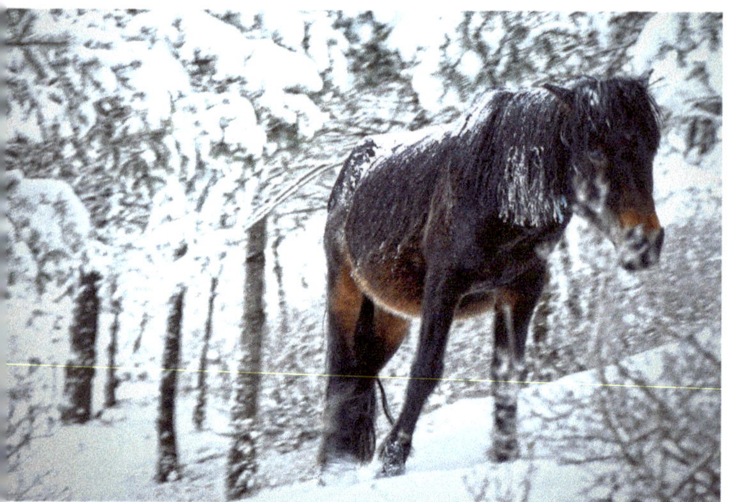

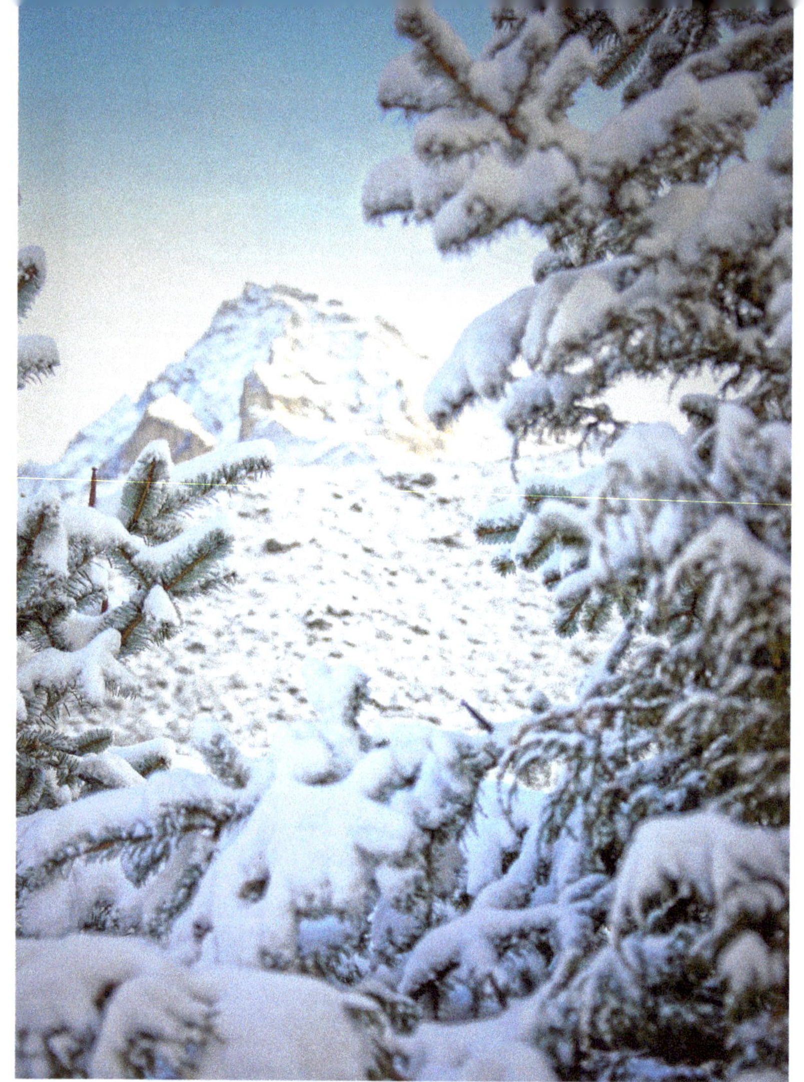

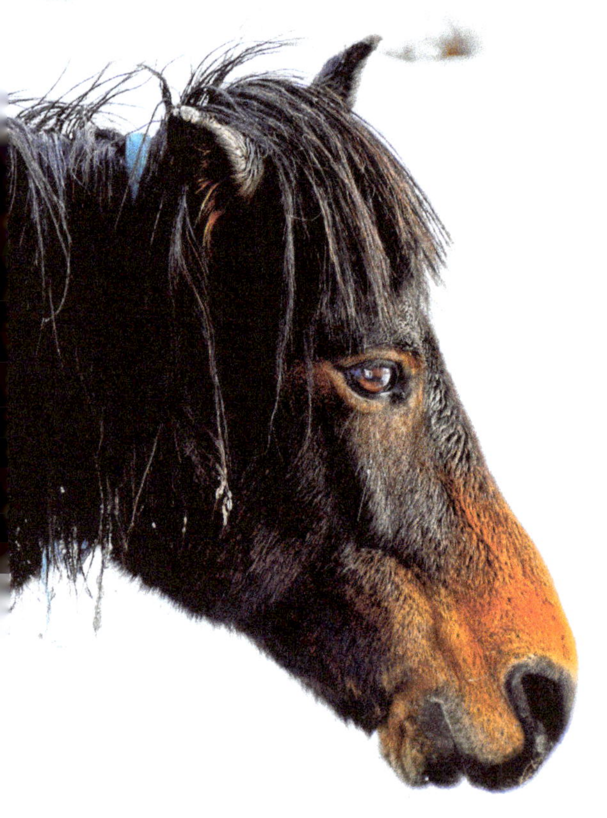

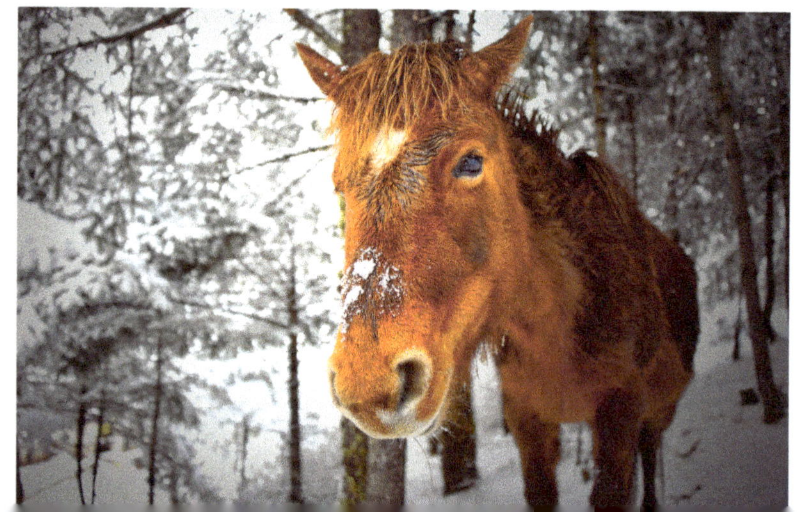

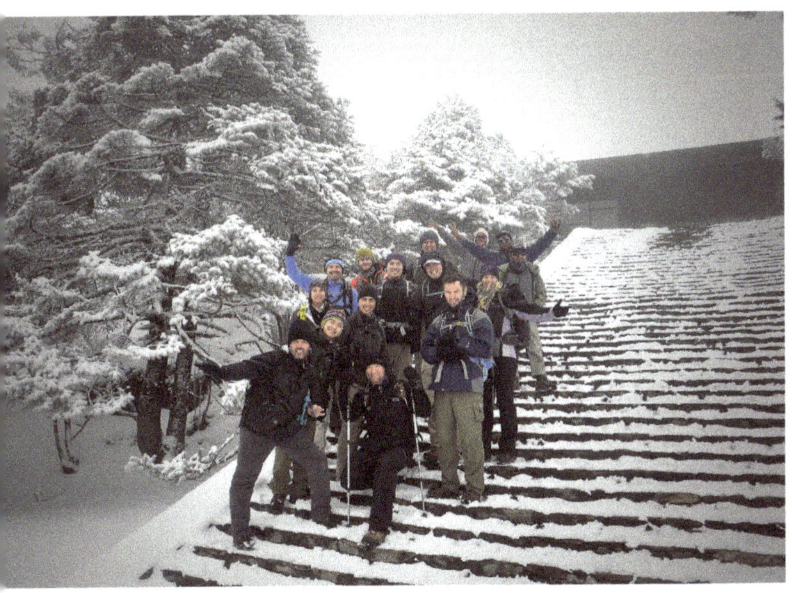

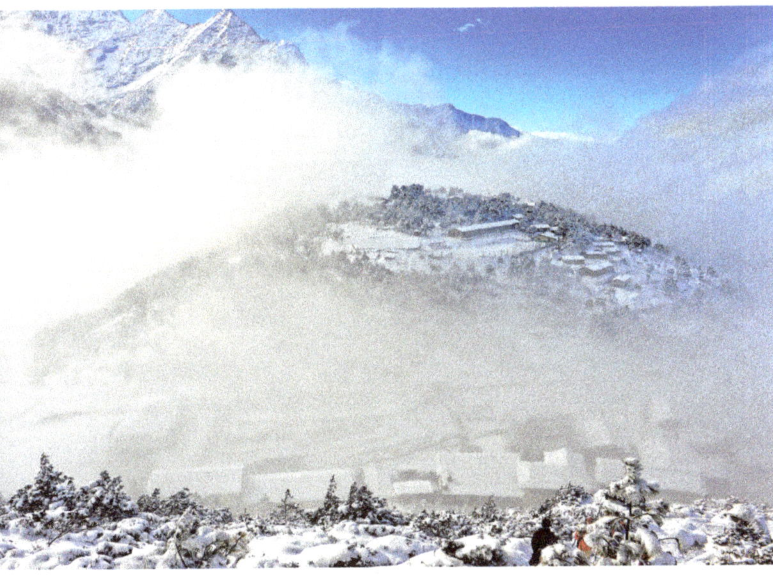

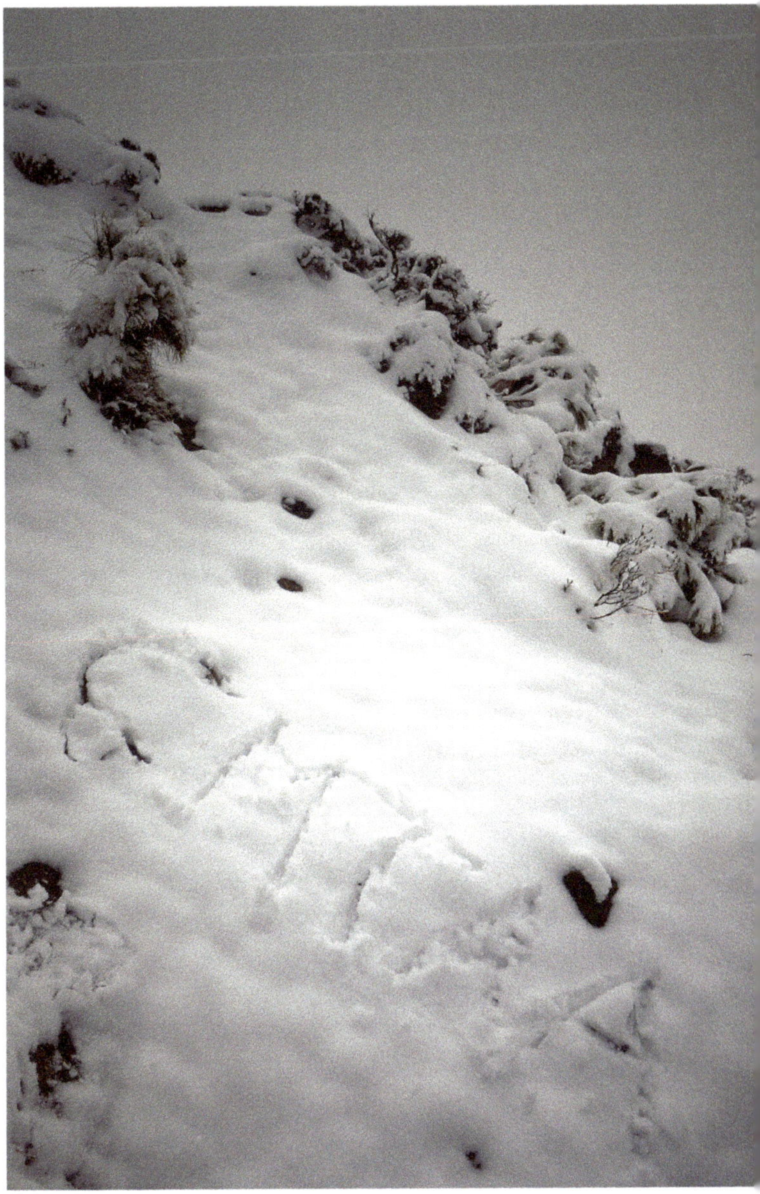

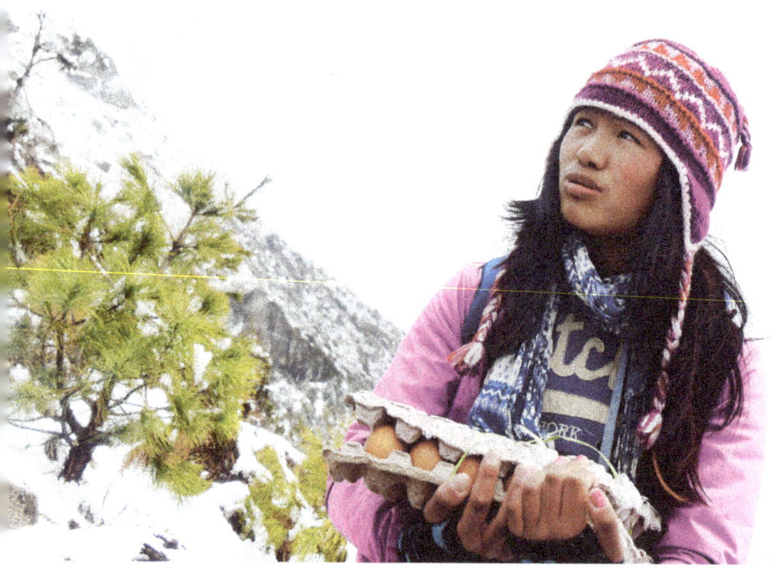

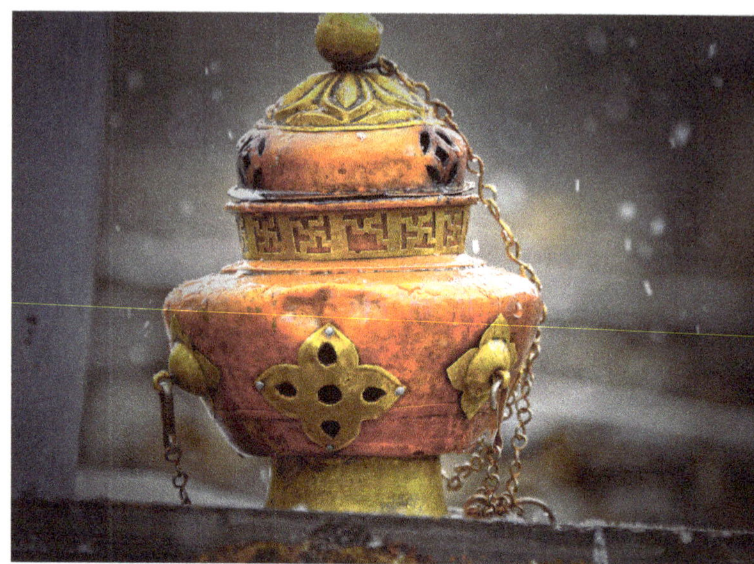

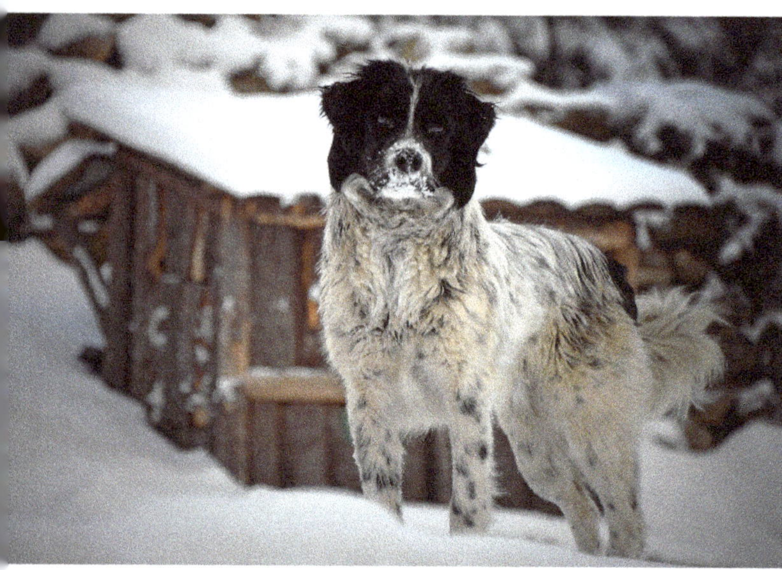

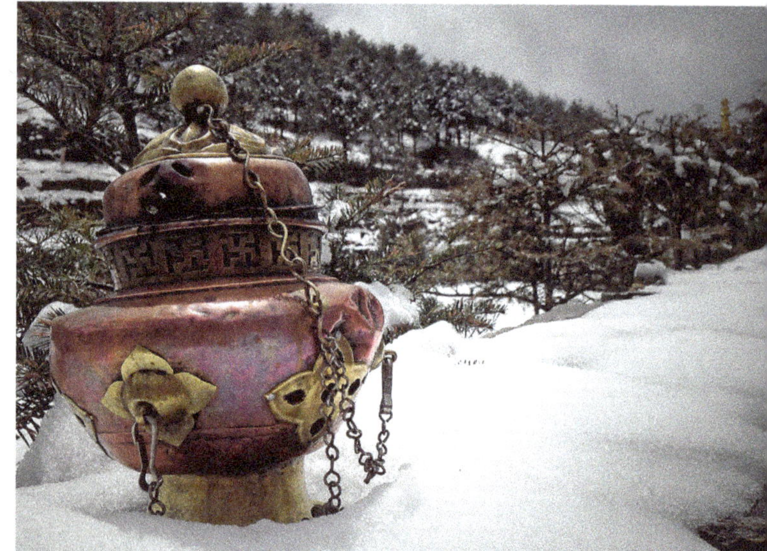

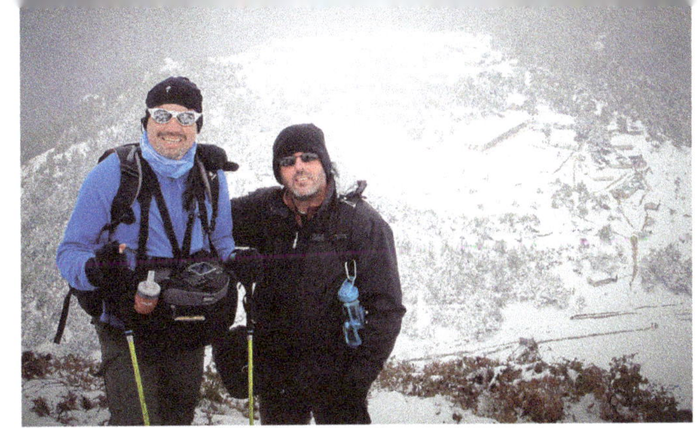

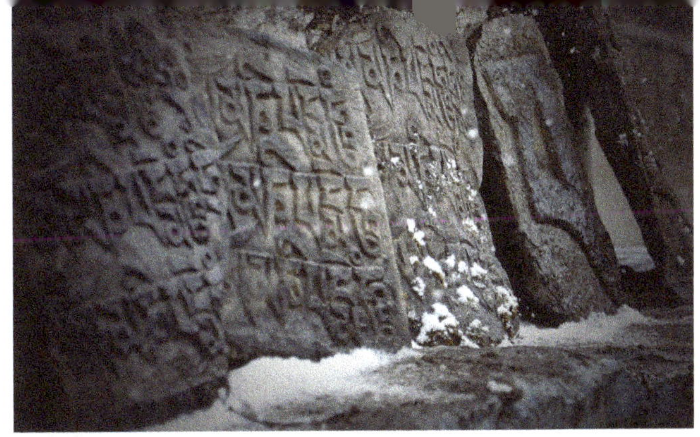

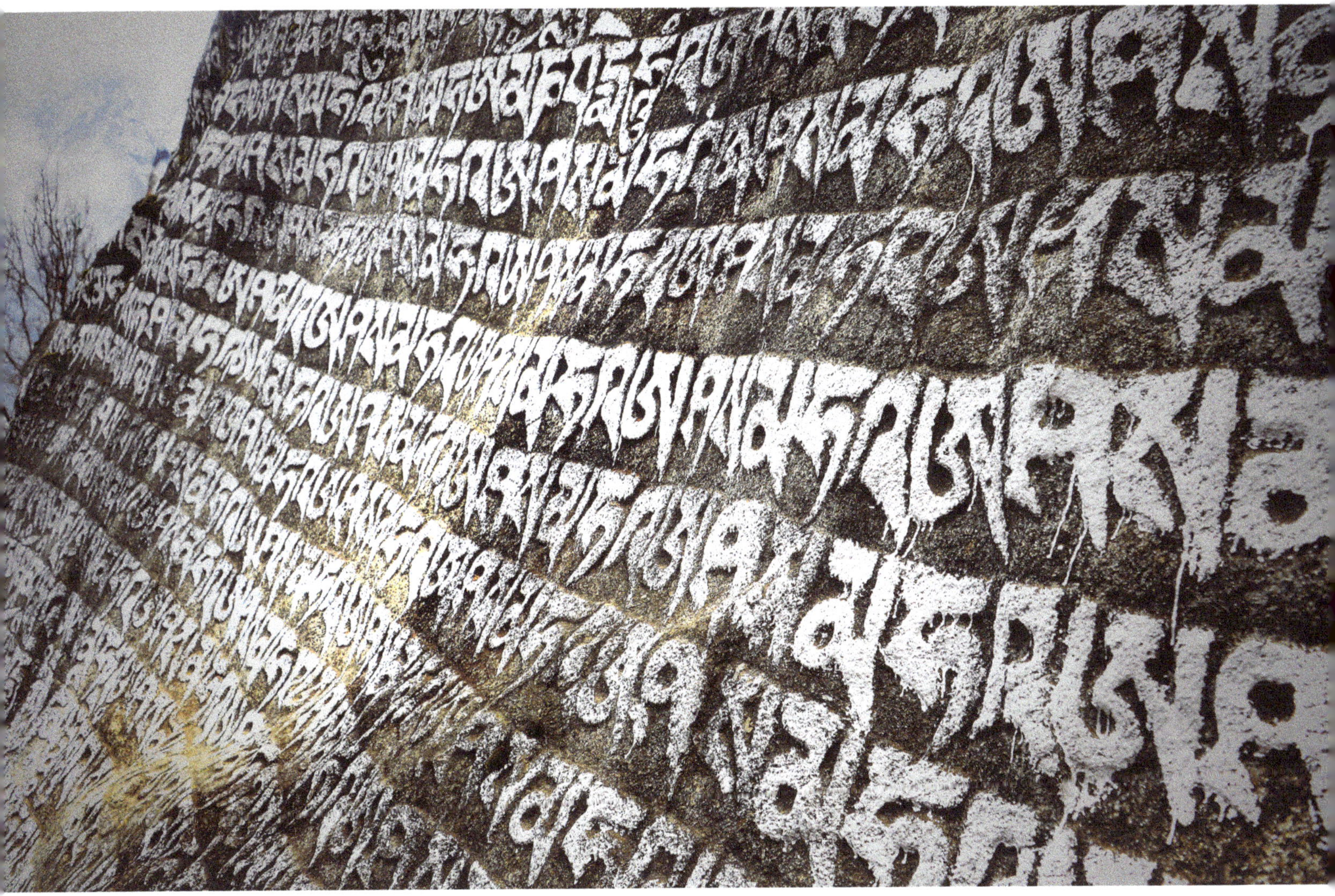

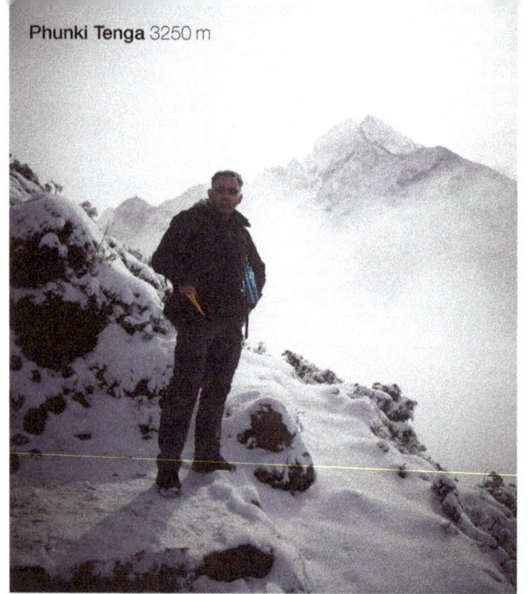

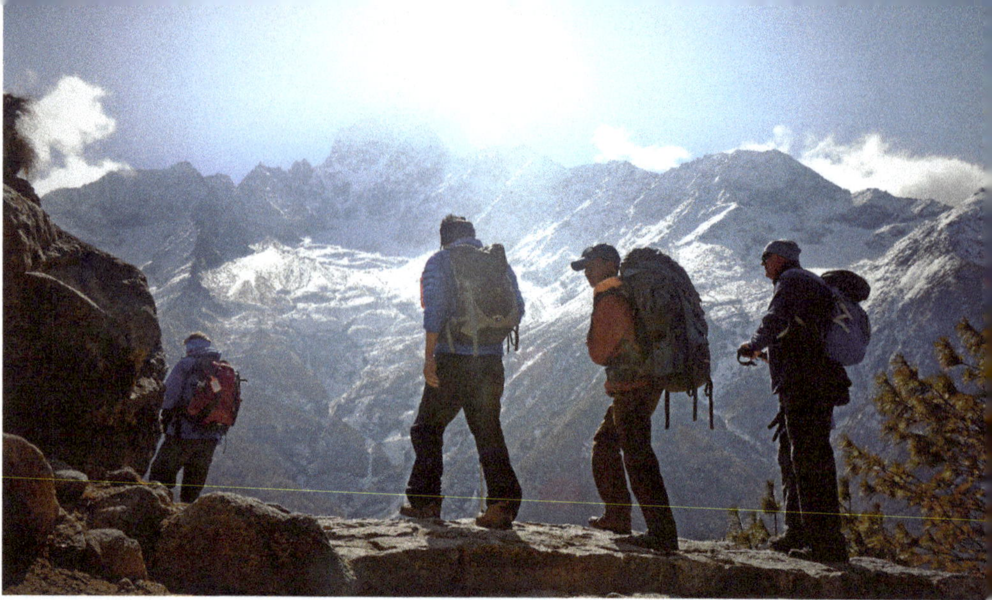

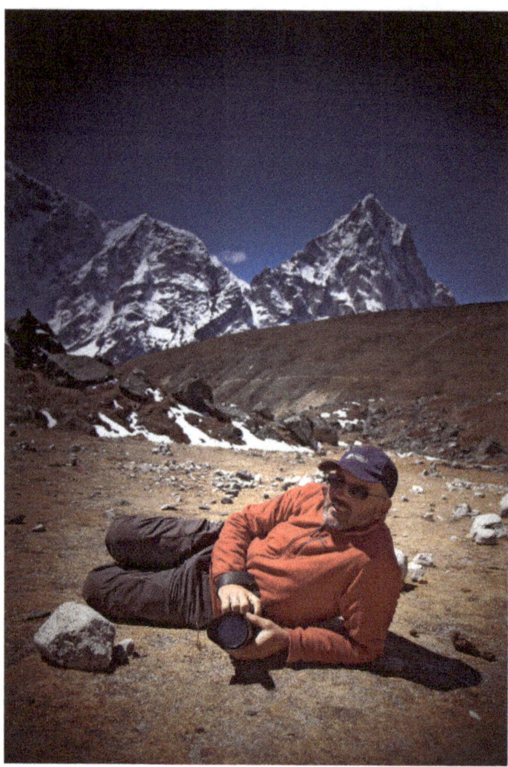

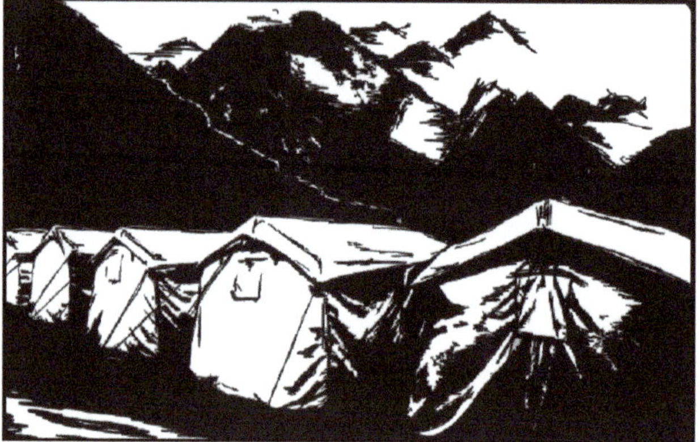

Our tents are so bright, all grouped like a town

After a long day of walking, all I need is to lie down

But we are told not to snooze in the arvo oh so bright

As our heads will suffer headaches due to our high mountainess height

Just let me lie down, I need so to nap

But the sherpas warn us daily that this feeling is a trap

With our Dianox all taken the headaches now do pass

As the higher we now go the clear heads will now last

But the tablets make you pee, not once, two or three

All through the night I'm up to go do a wee

Now this might be fine at home now and then

But running to the loo in your trackies is no fun at minus 10.

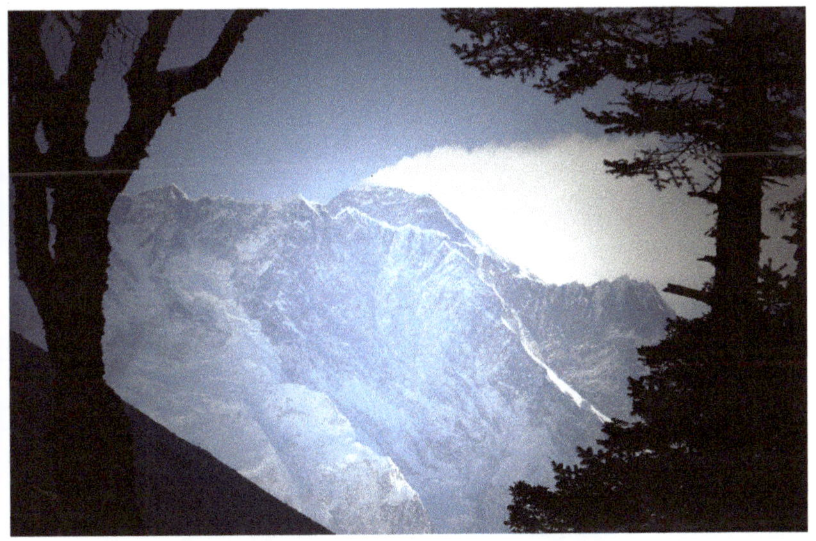

I remember the first few days of the trek we were all eager beavers seeing who could spot Mt Everest first, thinking it was one of the many mountains we first saw. Well turns out after many false guesses and days of trekking you kind of forget that you are even there to see it at all or that it might peek out at some stage when you least expect it. There is so much else filling your senses on the trek that you are just totally consumed by Nepal in all its glory. On about day 3 during a normal drink stop we are casually informed to look out through some trees nearby … and there it is, Mt Everest standing tall, taller then all the rest.

You can tell she's the Queen of the Himalayas just by its ability to catch the clouds, turning them from round fluffy shapes into a stretched white mist from its tip to the horizon. It is also a different colour to the other mountains we have seen up till now. Its black dark rock stands it out from the pack, allowing it to then be easily identifiable each time you see it till Base Camp and back. I will always remember that first viewing of her and also the last. I do remember being a little sad knowing that I was looking for the last time on this trek and once I turned away to keep walking, it could be quite a while till I saw it again.

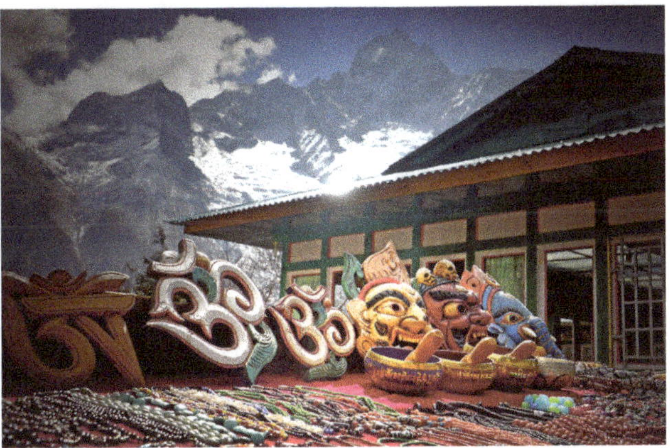

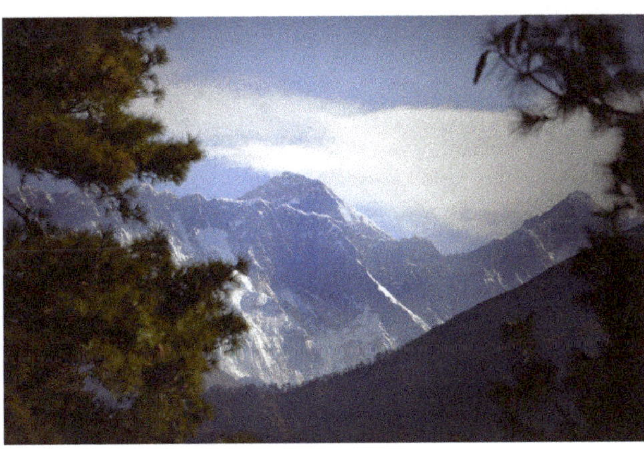

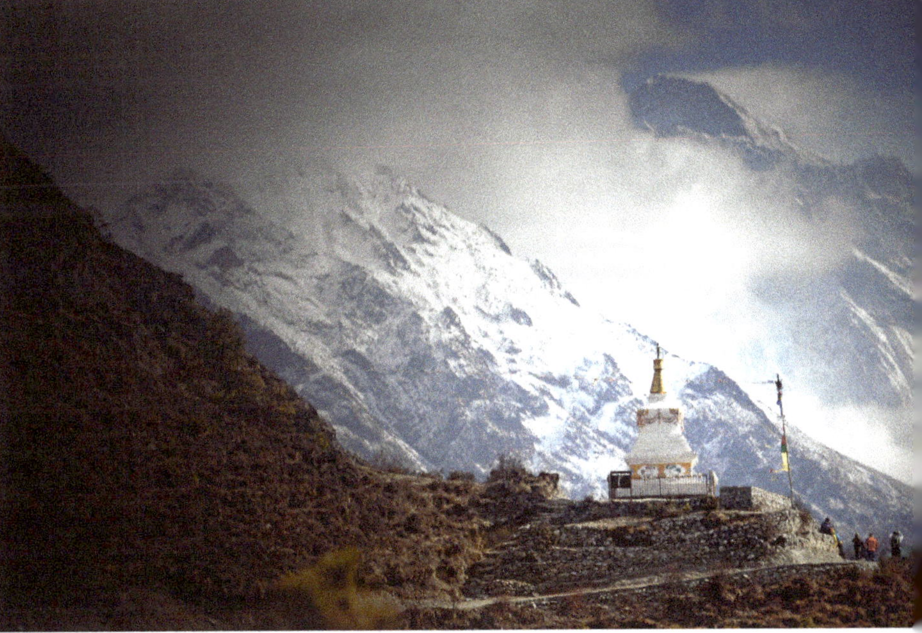

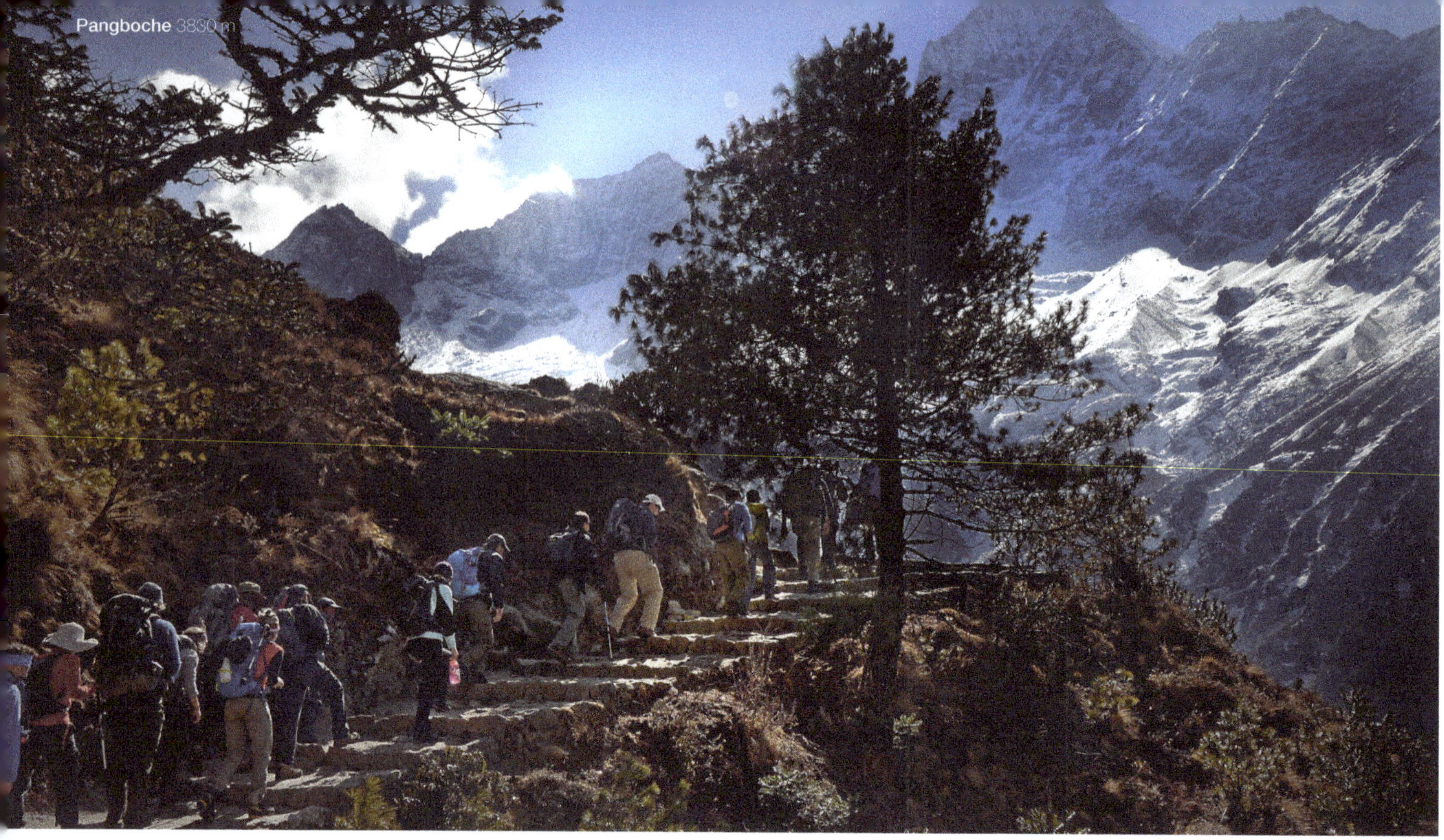

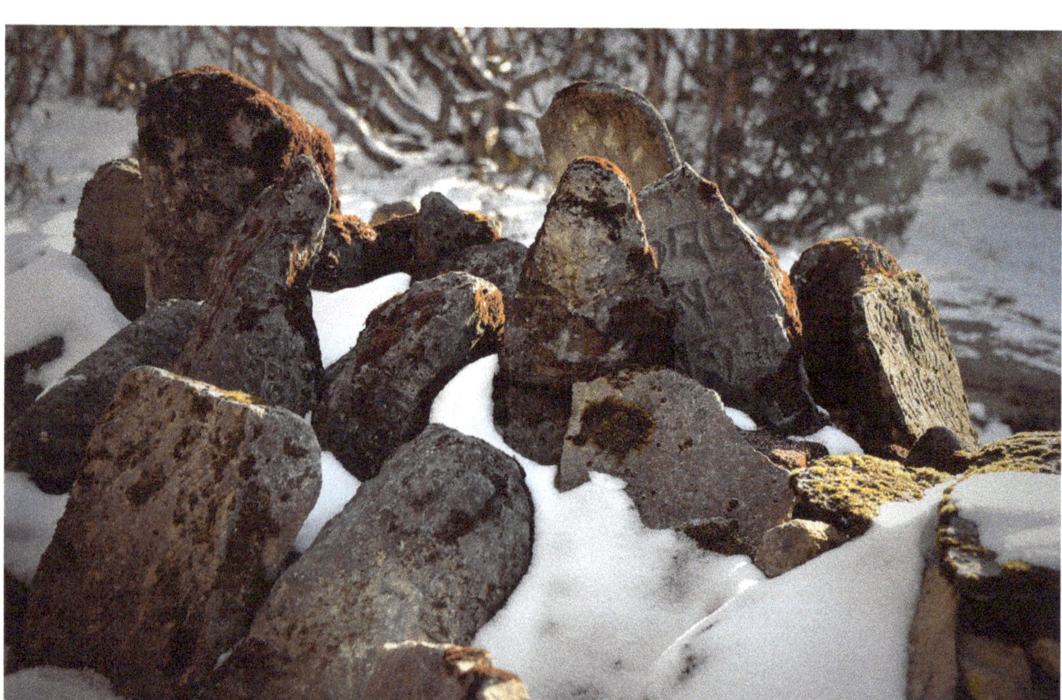

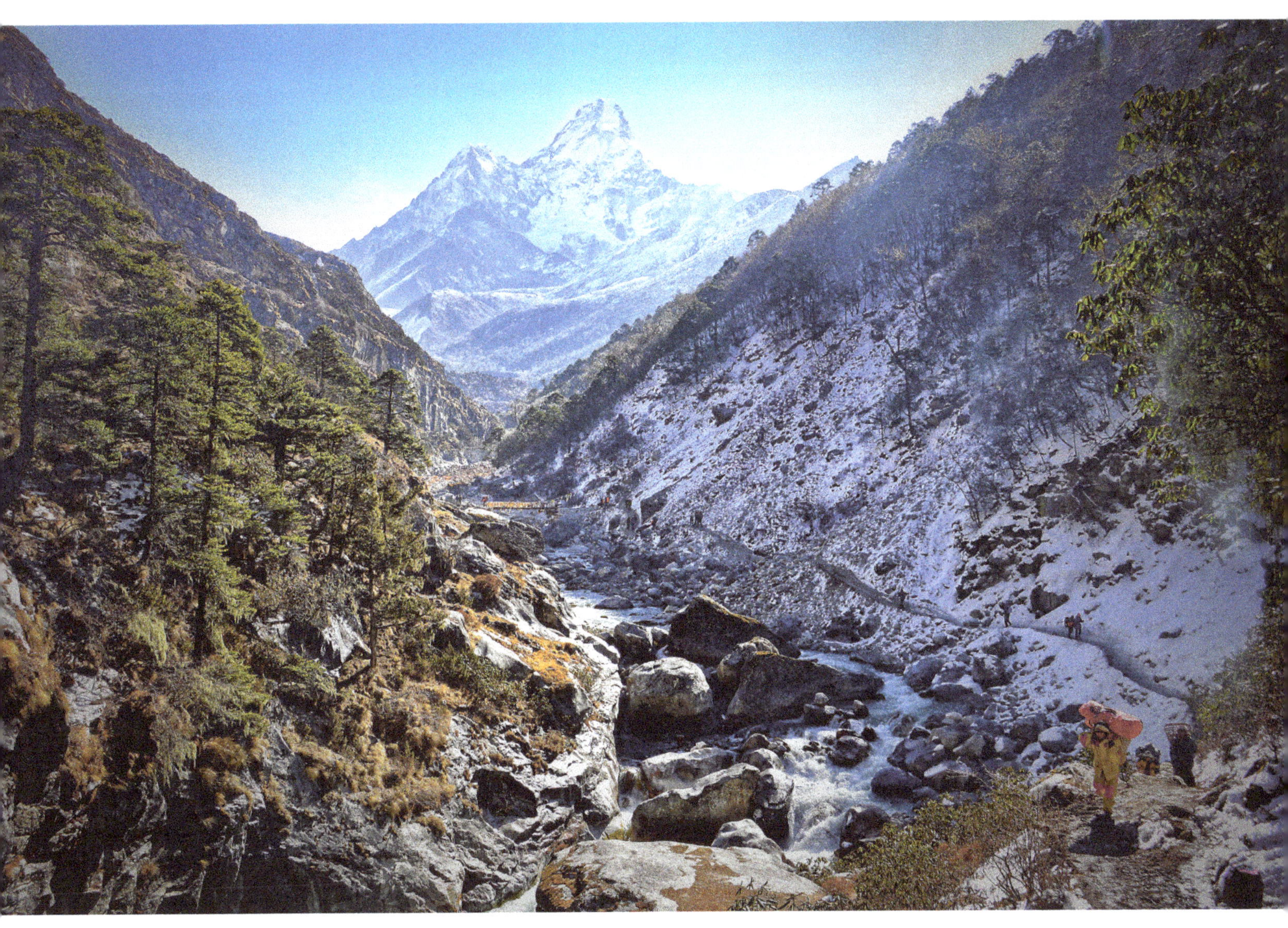

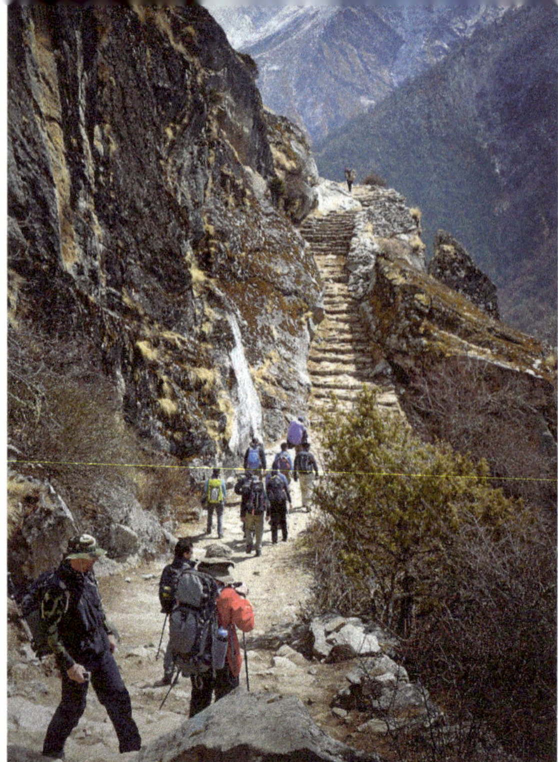
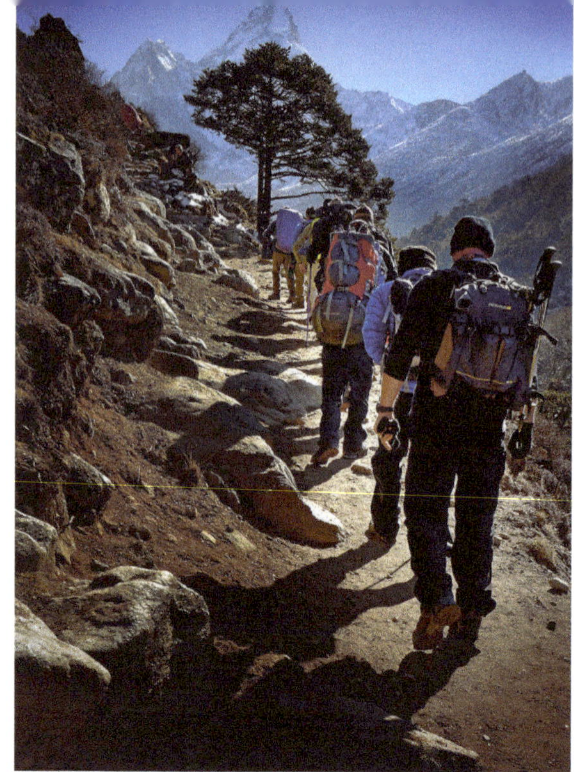
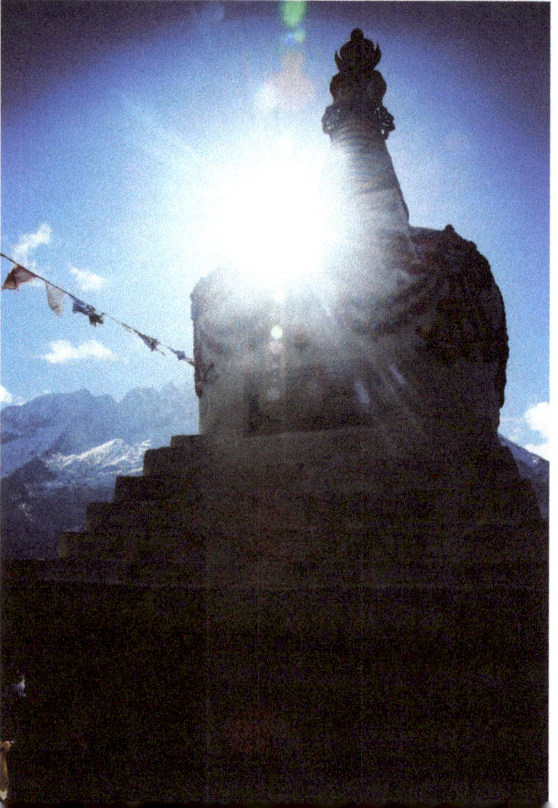
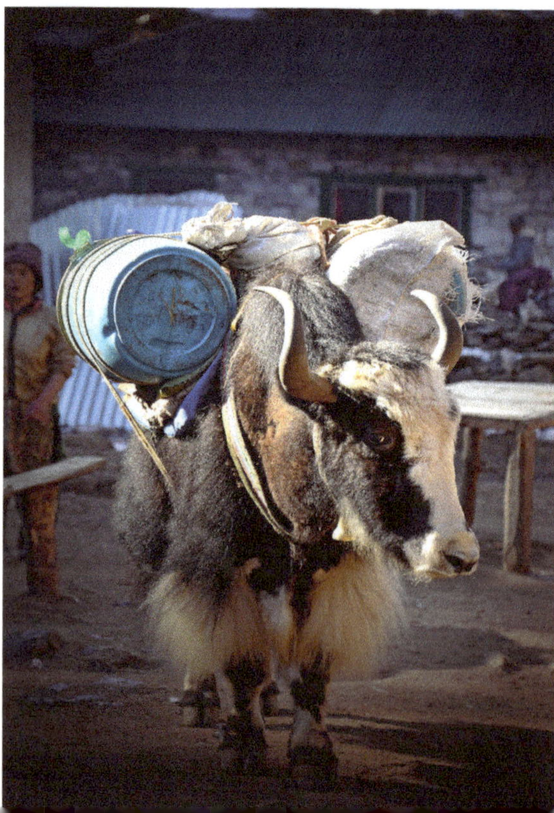

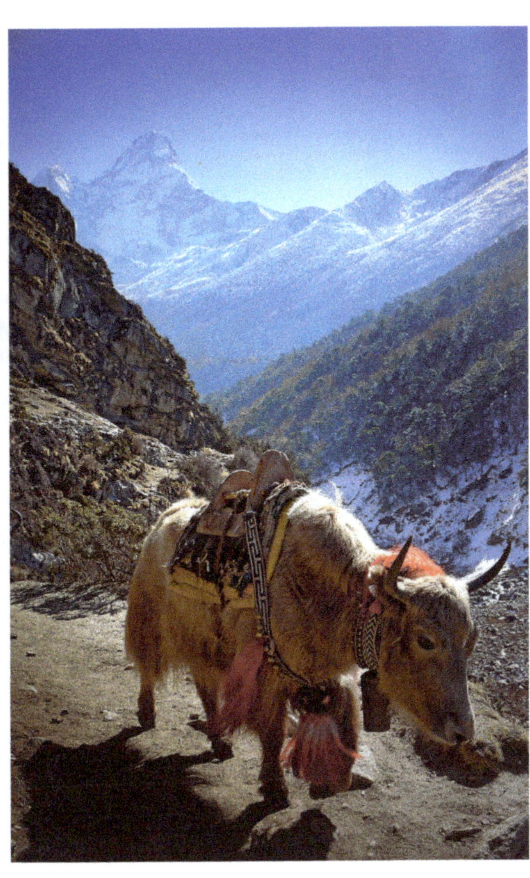

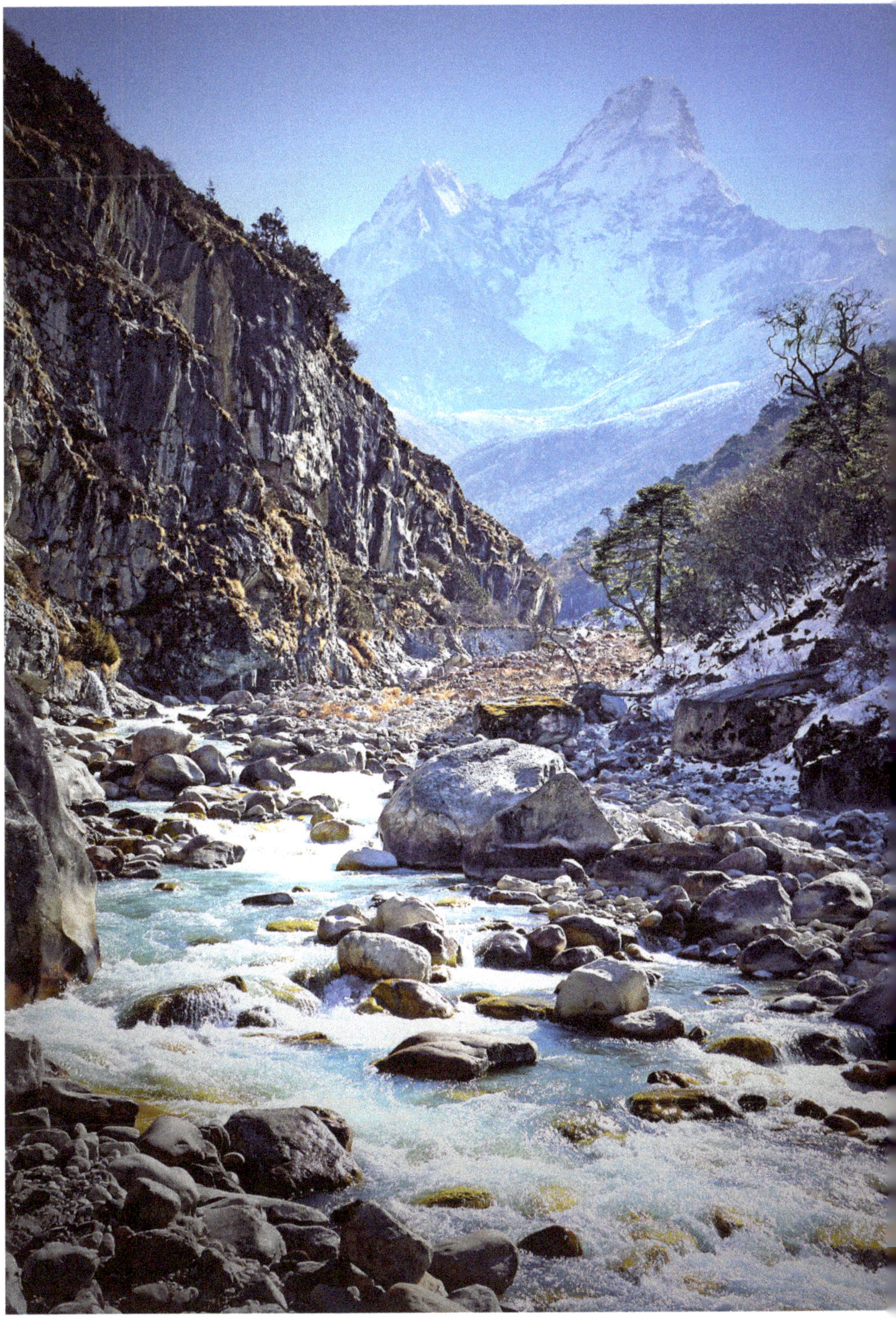

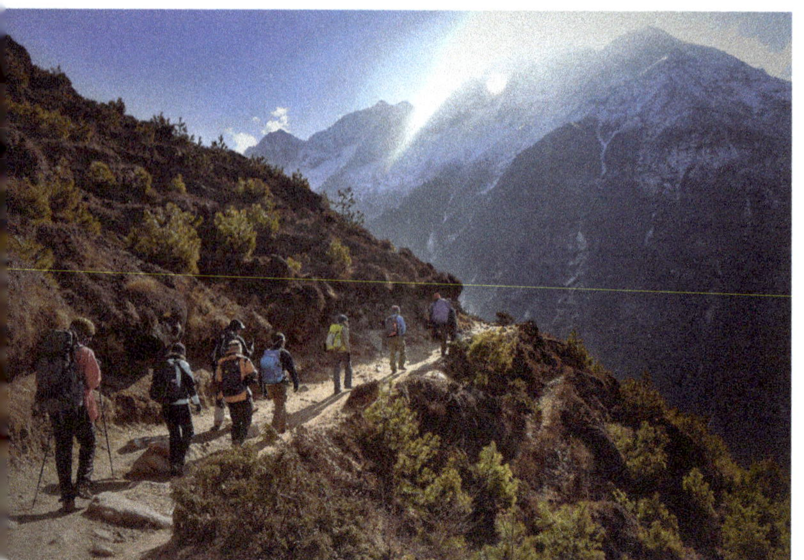

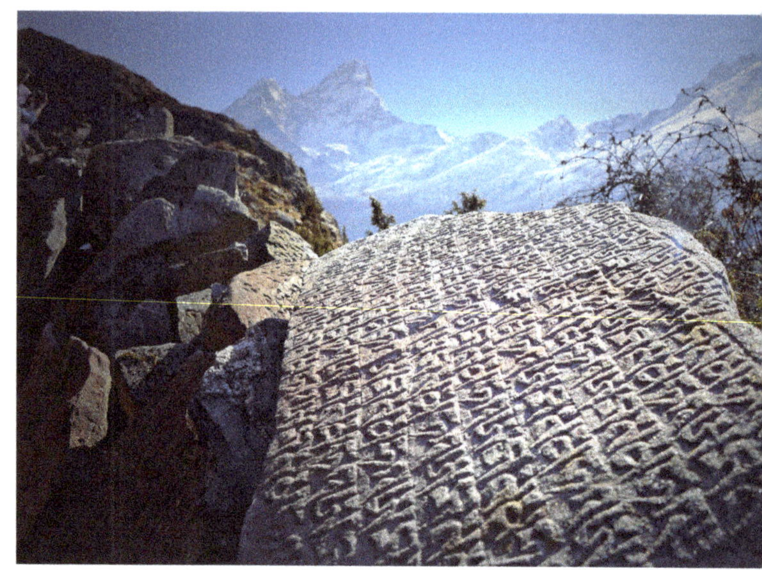

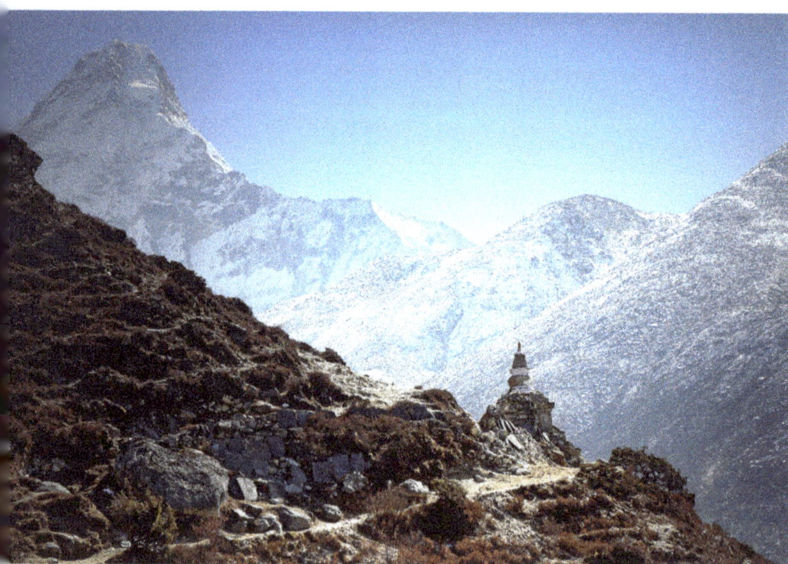

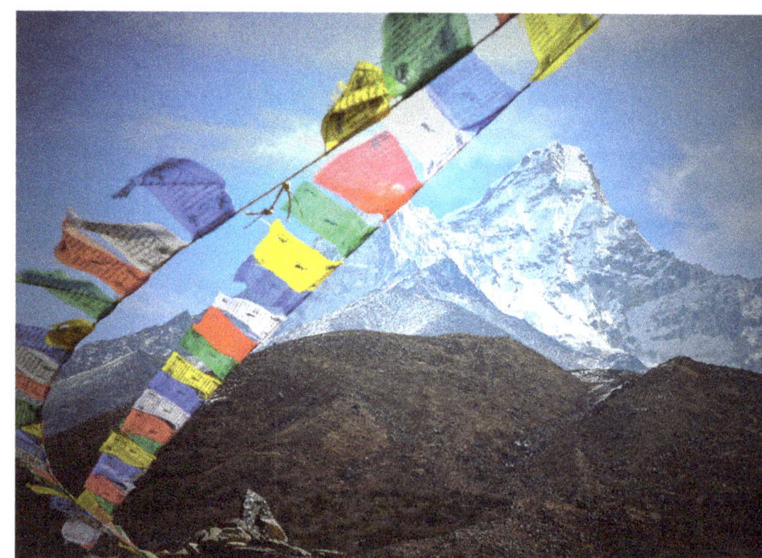

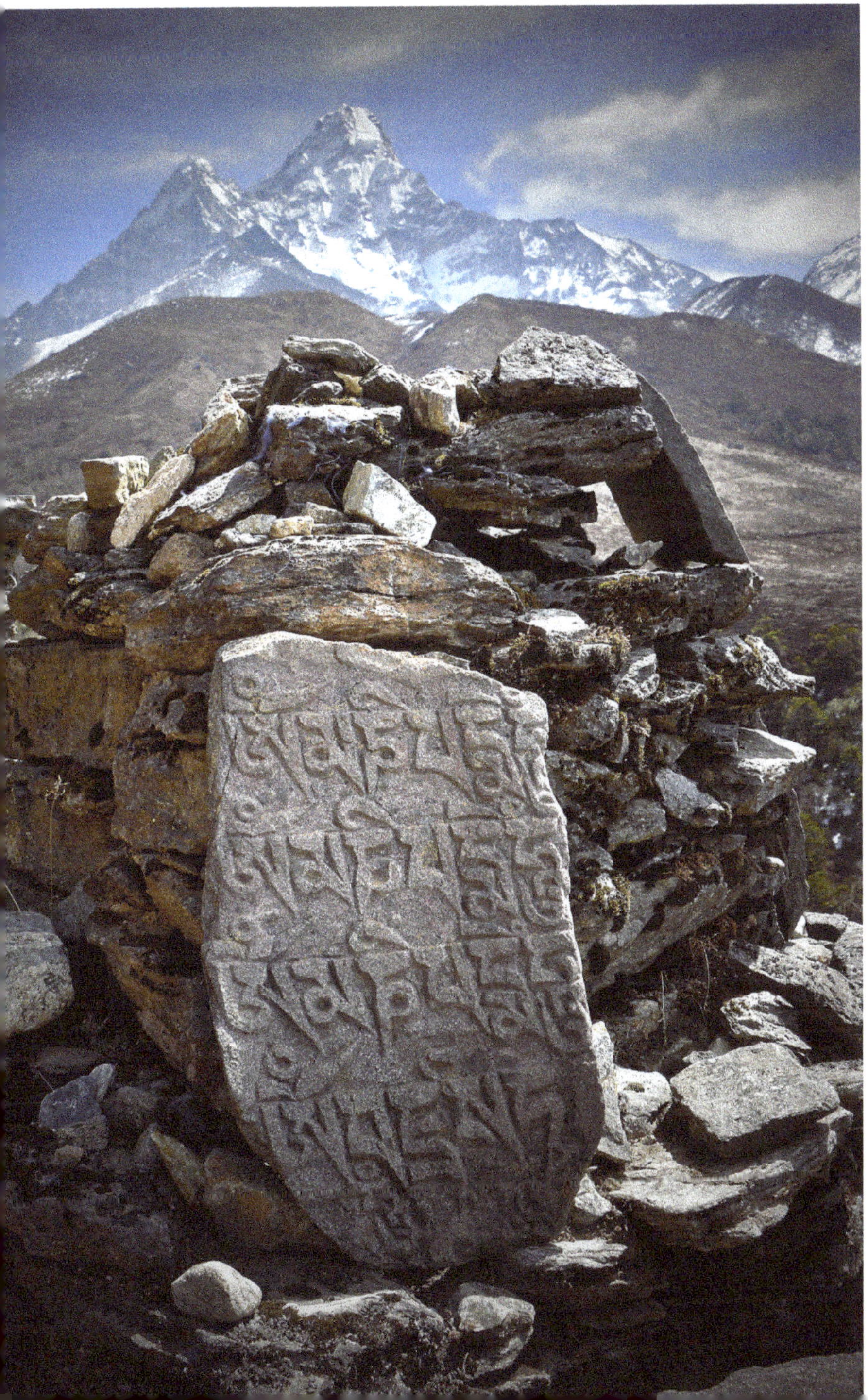

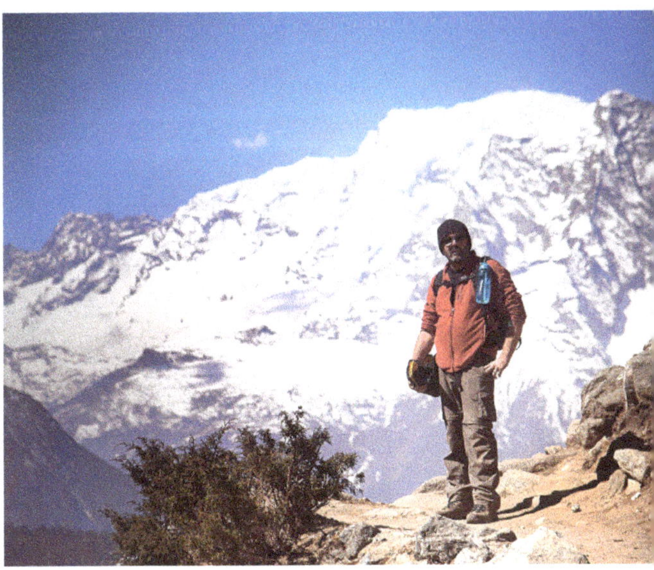

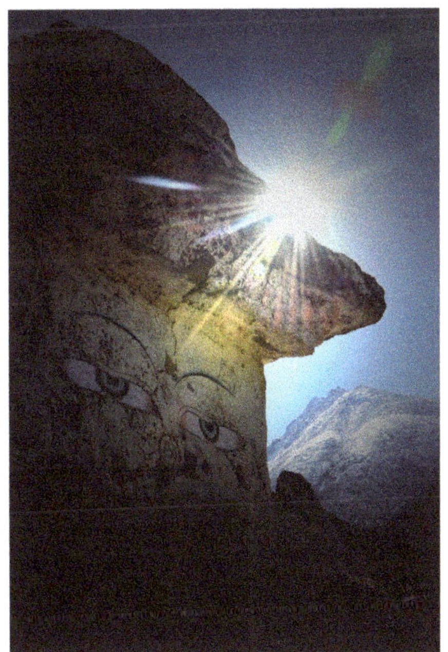

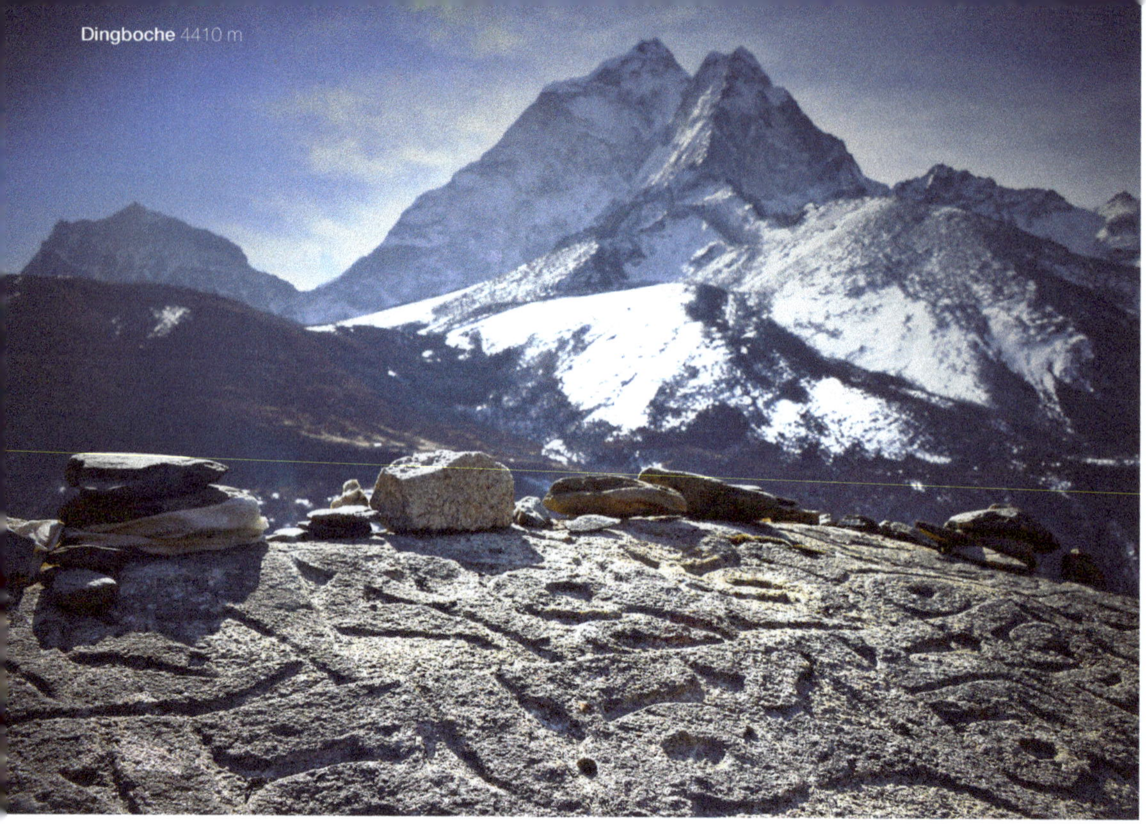

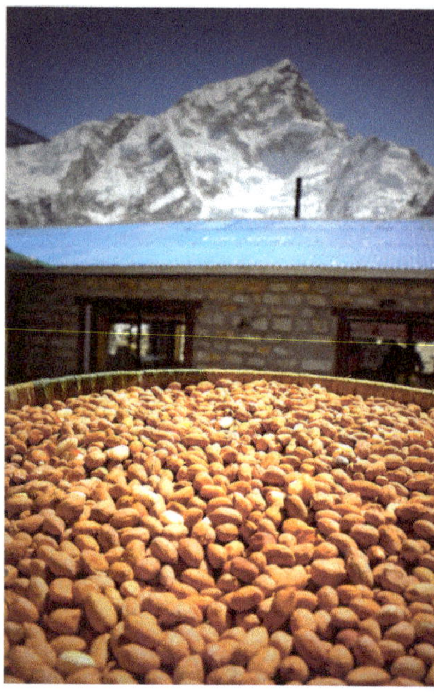

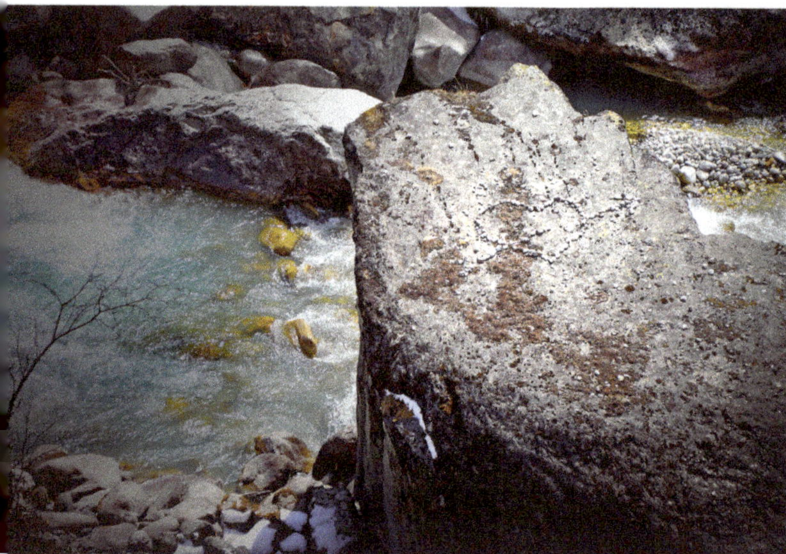

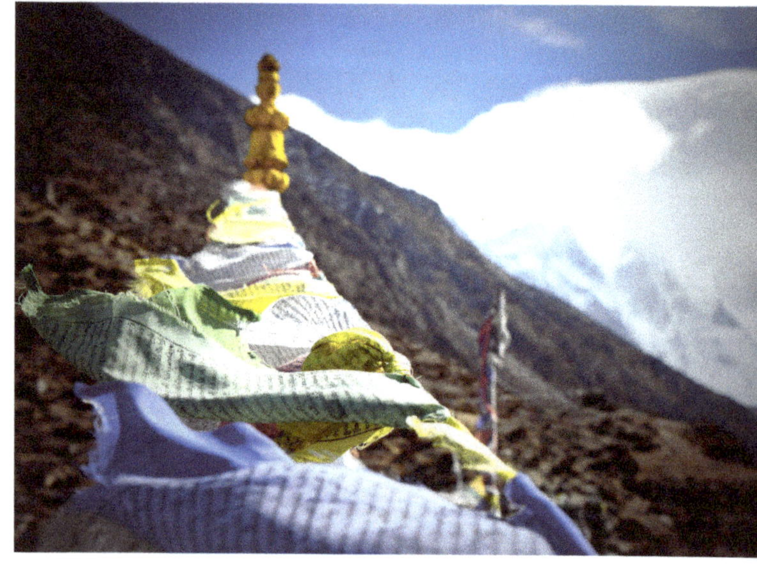

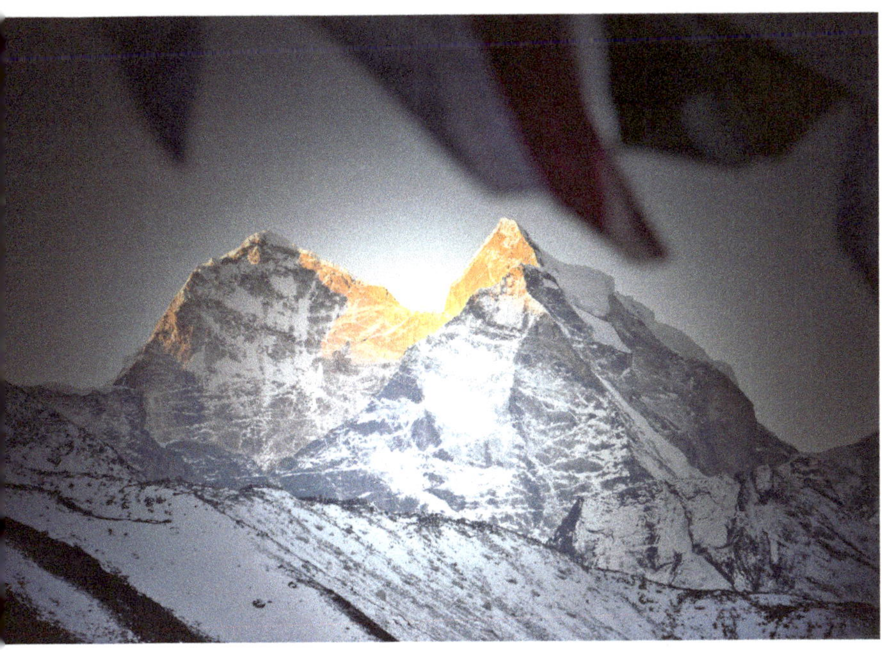

Another rest place and acclimatisation day. The first thing we all noticed was the French bakery and we all drooled at the thought of good coffee and cakes. Sadly, it was just okay, but still nice to sit and relax with the yaks out the window. Dingboche seems quite a large town as you look down on it but after a wander-around, there really isn't much there at all, which is surprising. Average coffee, high internet rates, solar showers and the usual crappy shops and attractions make for a good spot to rest where you can do absolutely nothing.

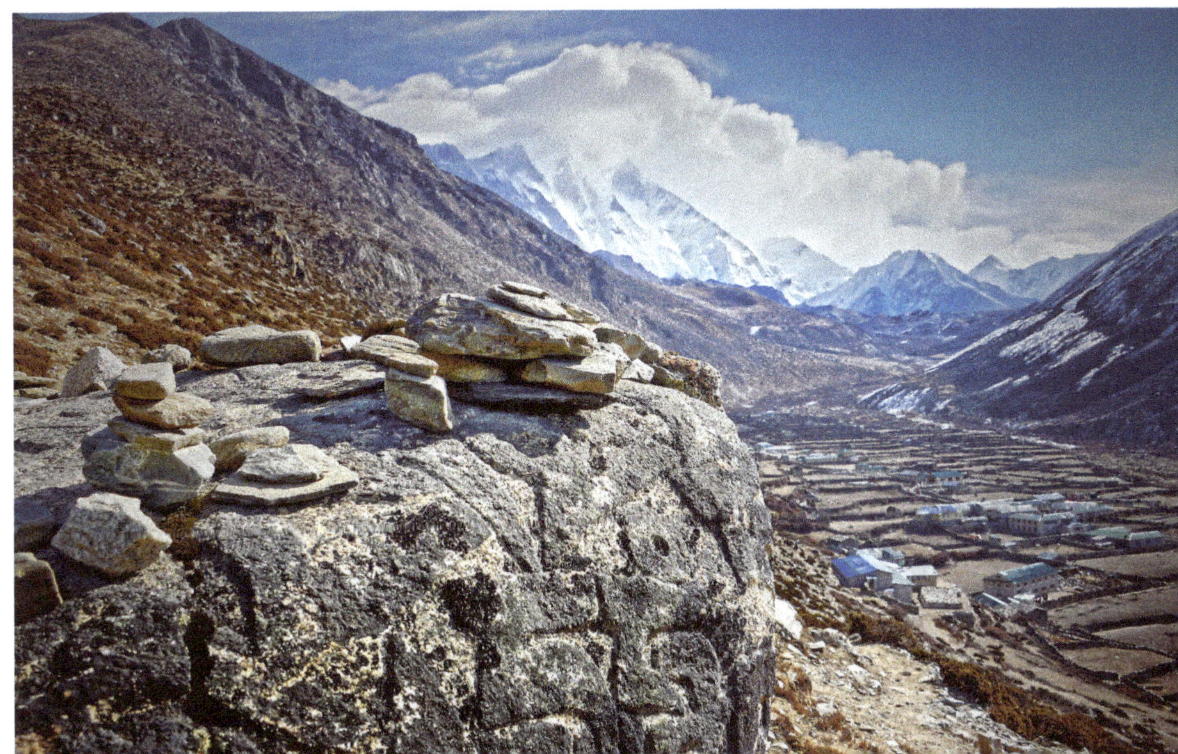

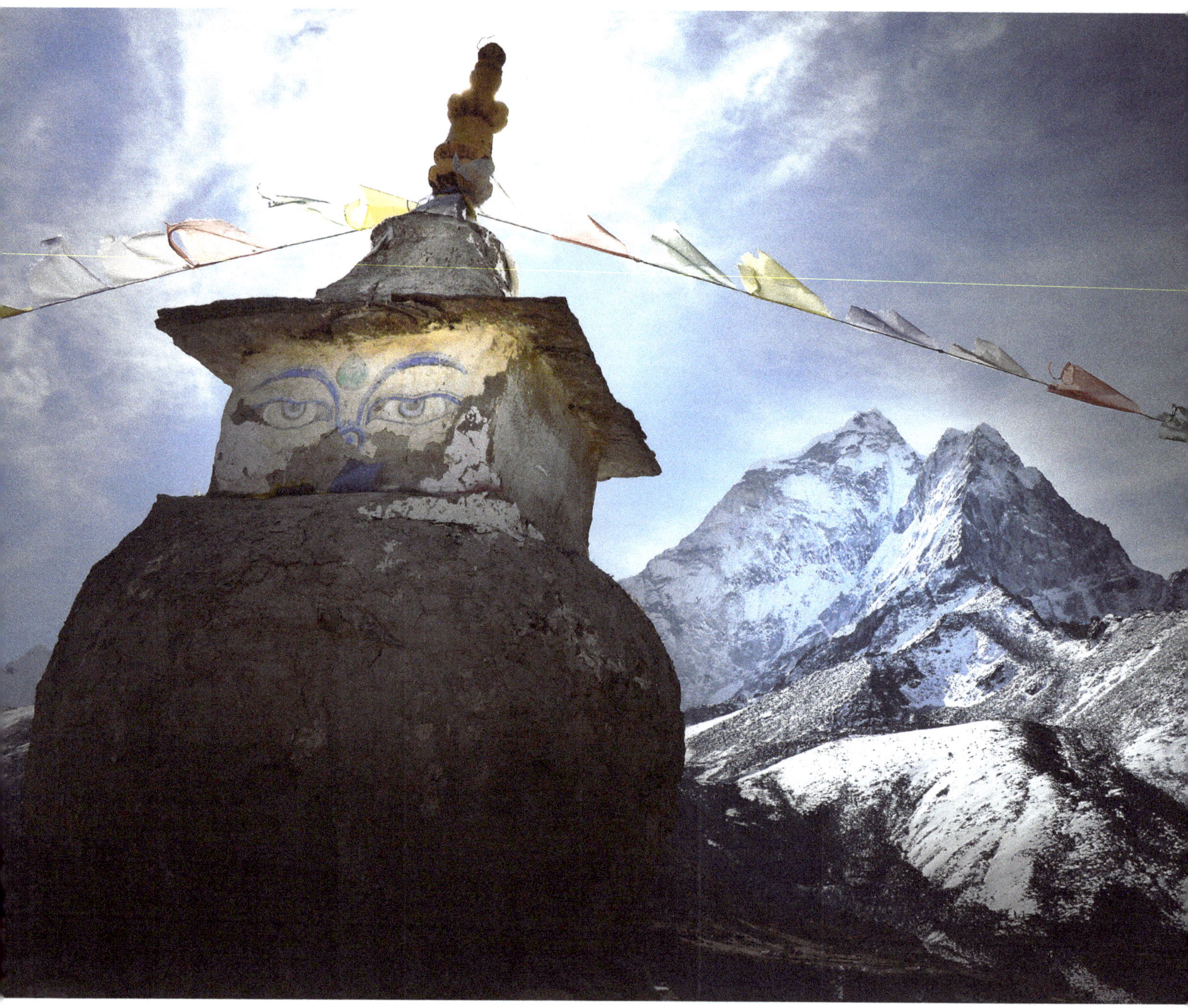

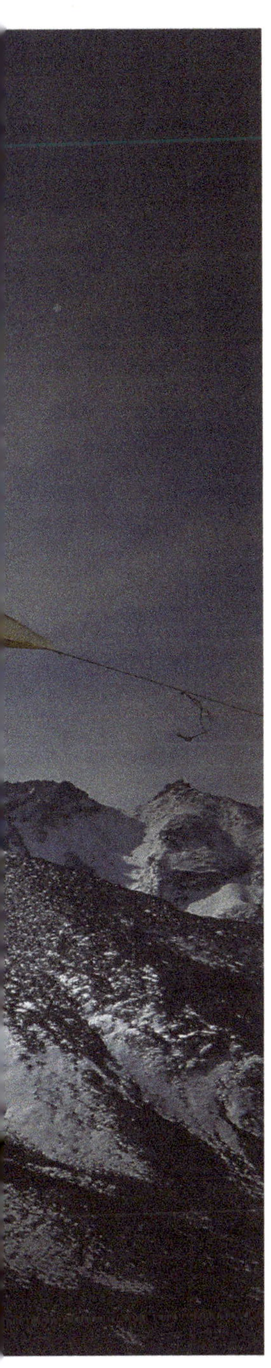
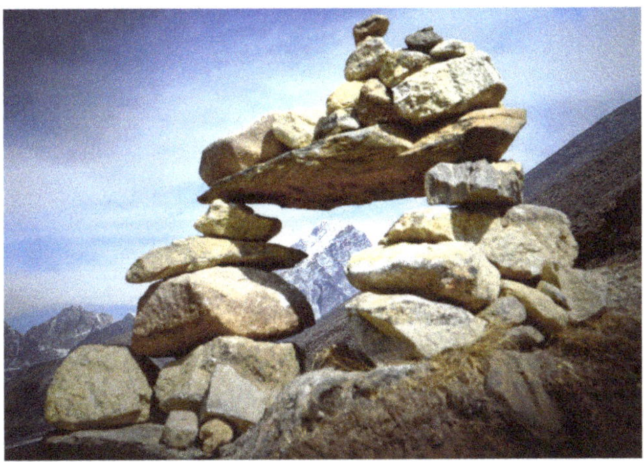
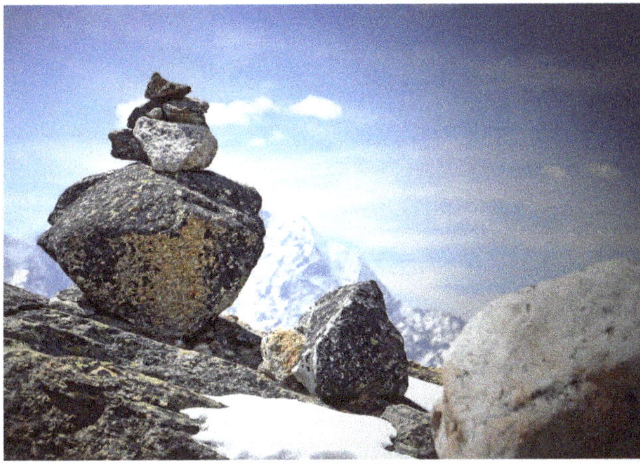
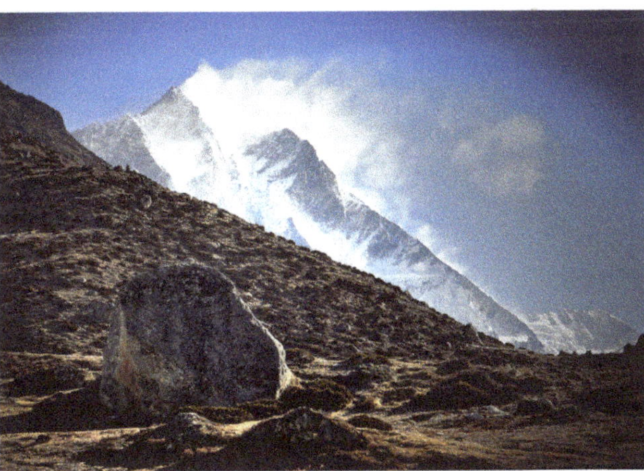
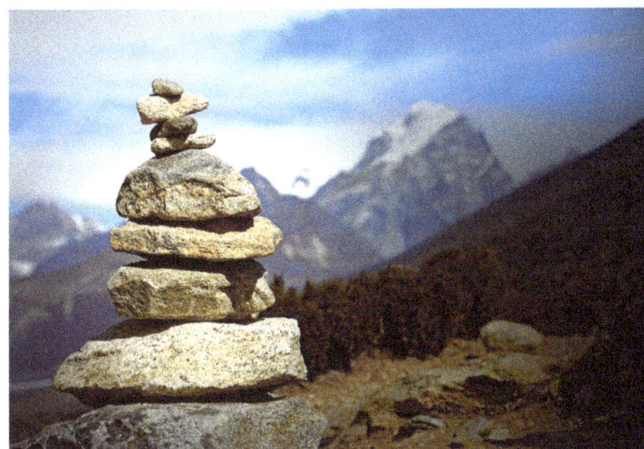

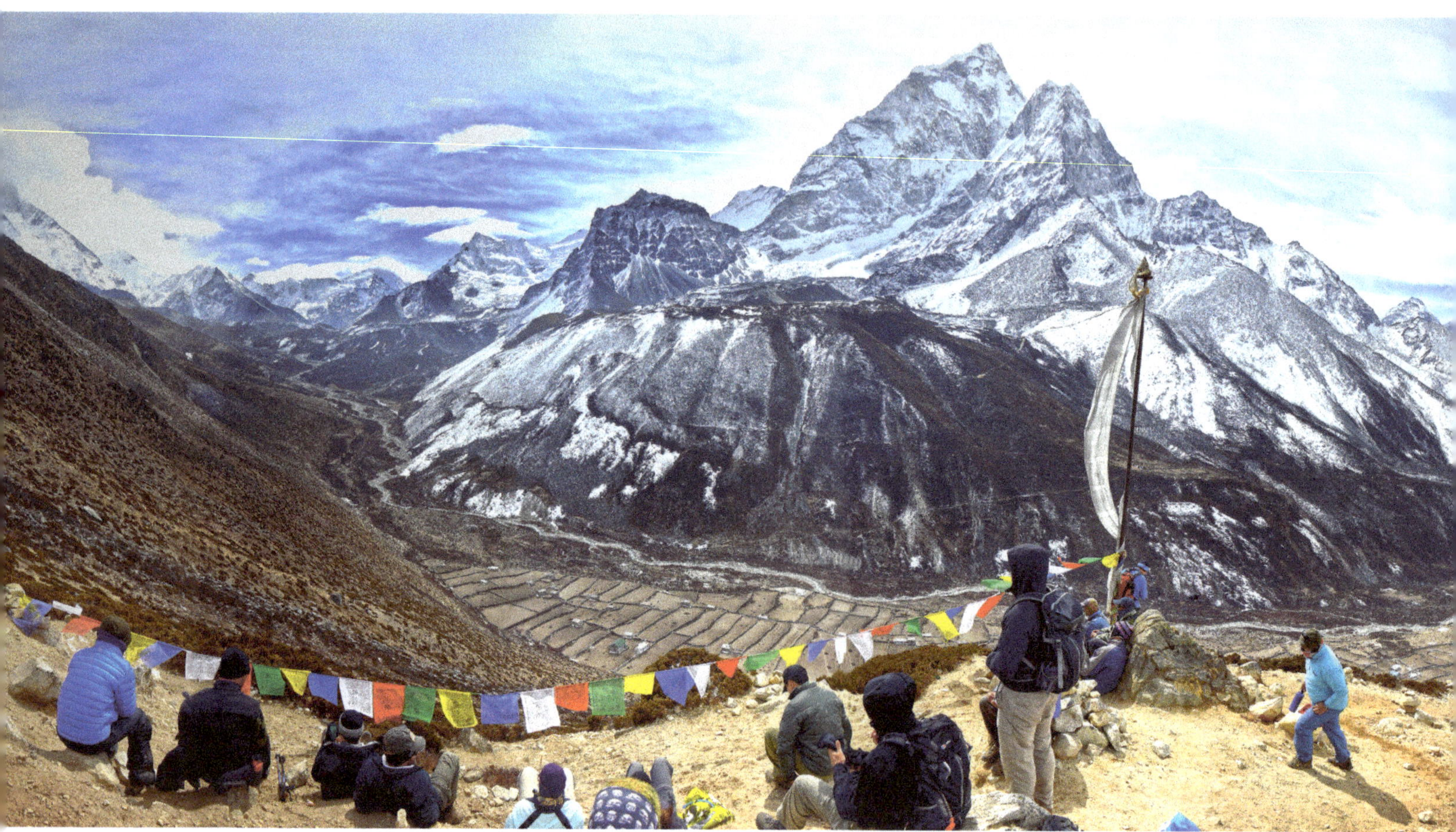

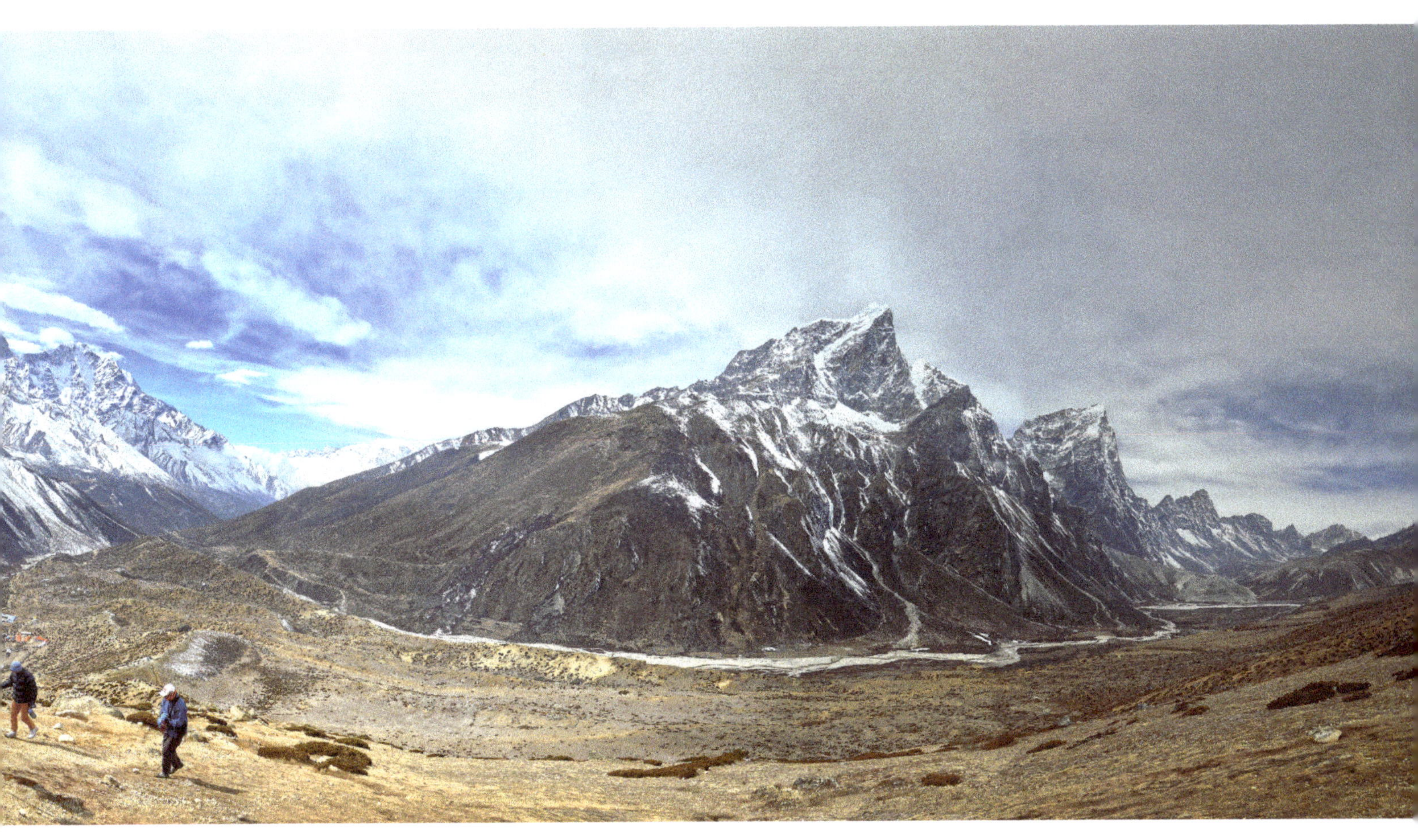

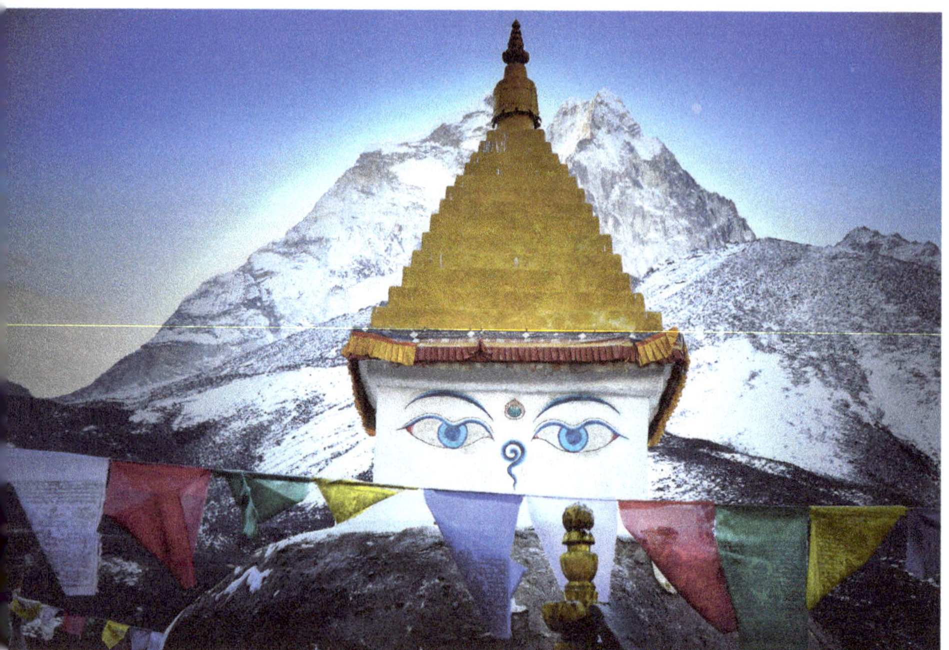

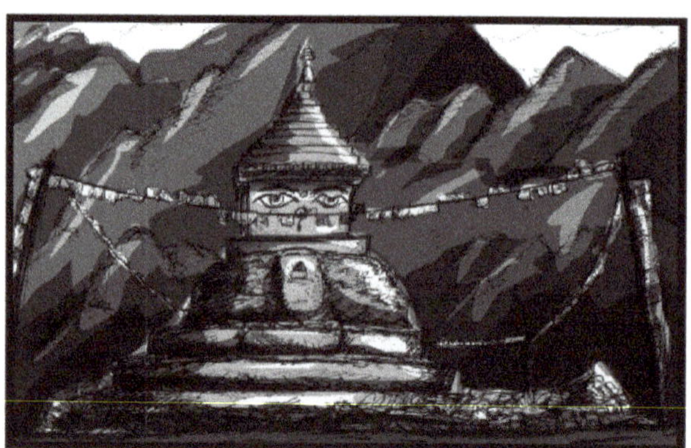

In the freezing winds the proud stupa stands
His eyes watching over these barren mountainess lands
The fog comes in low as the day passes by
But by the morning its crisp with a clear bright blue sky.

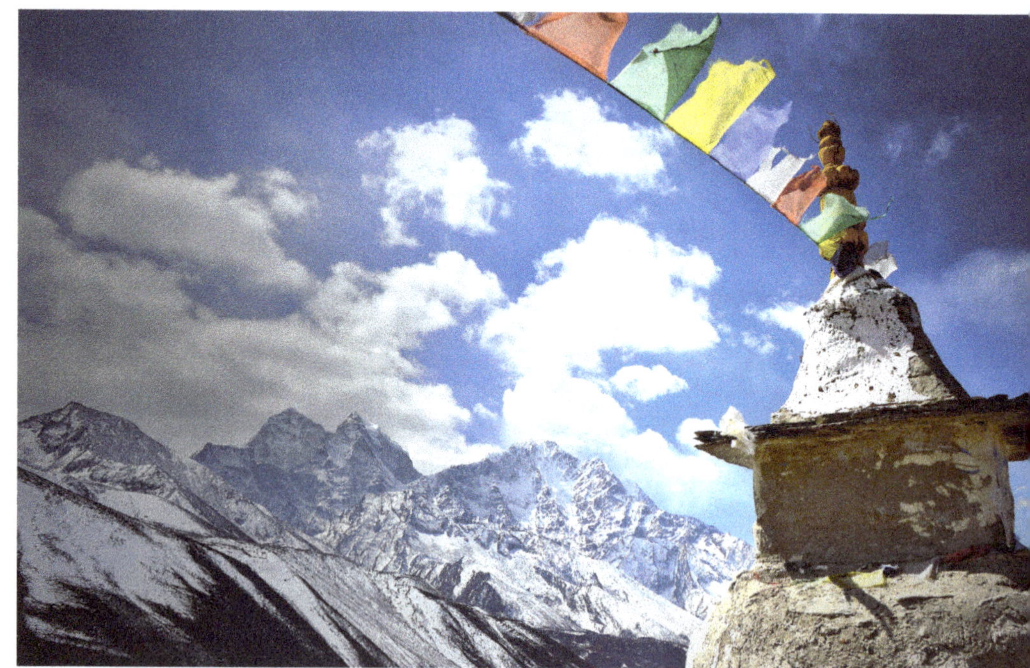

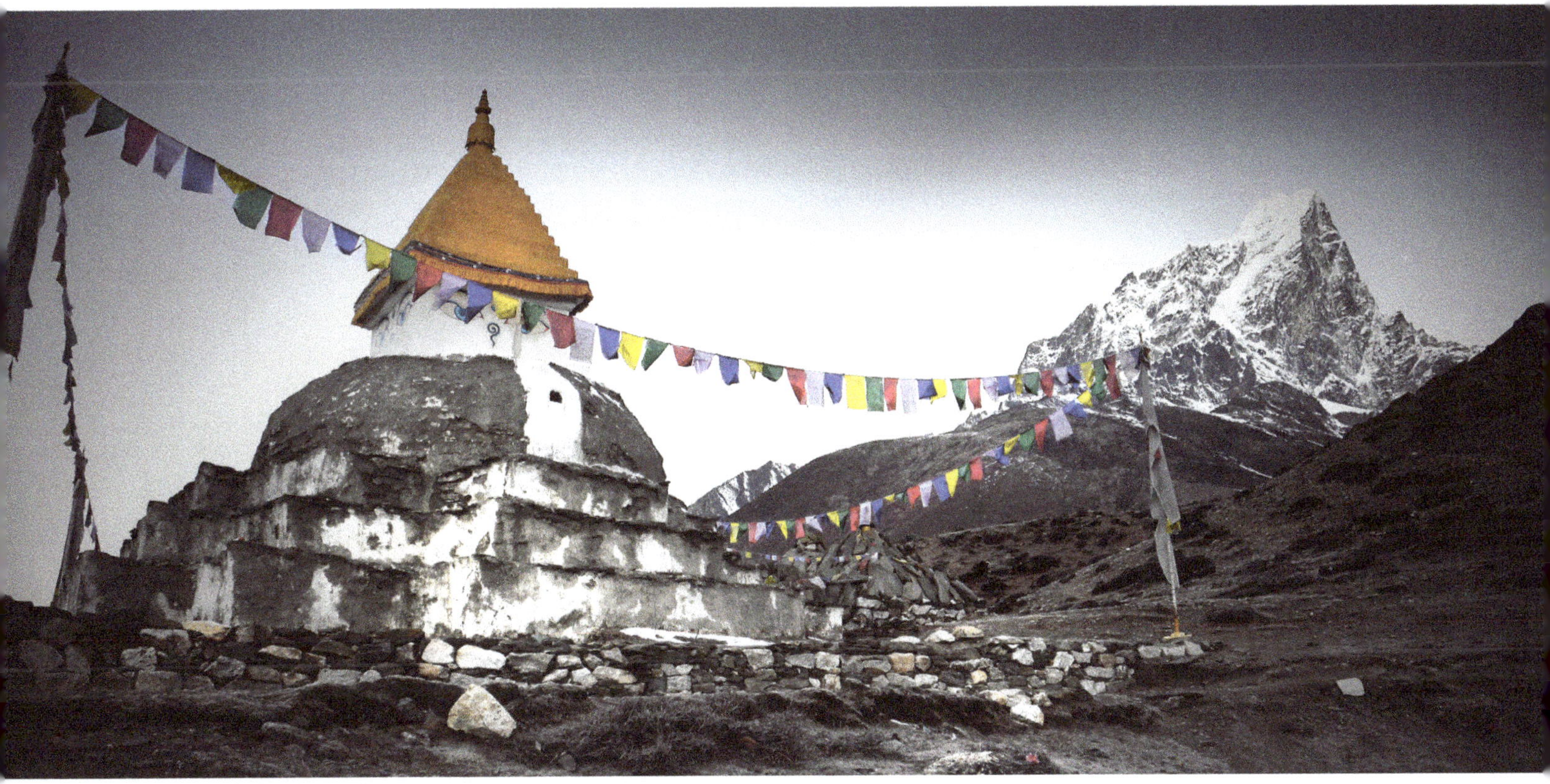

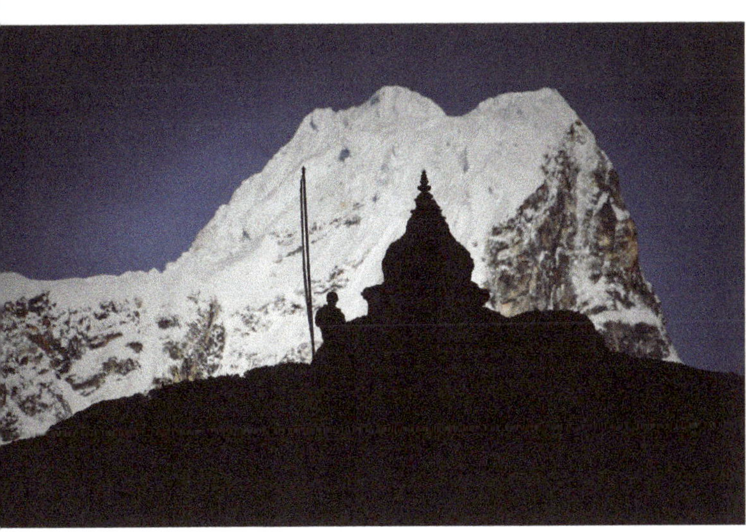

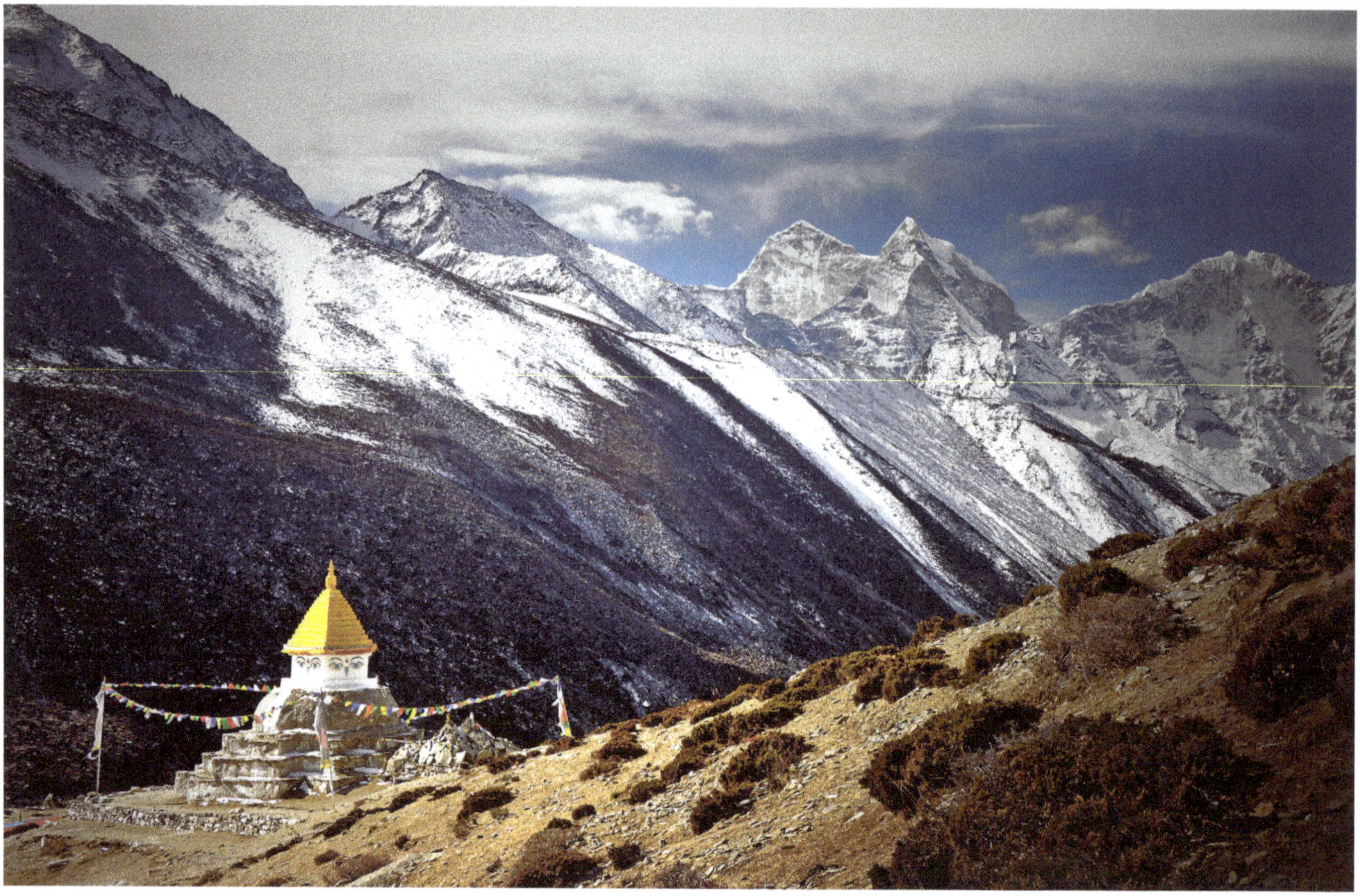

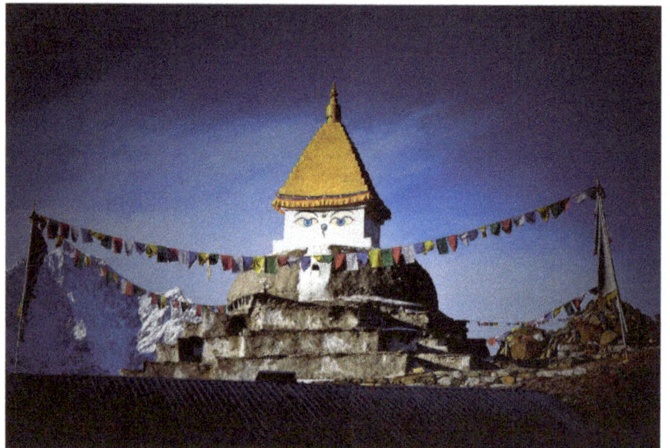

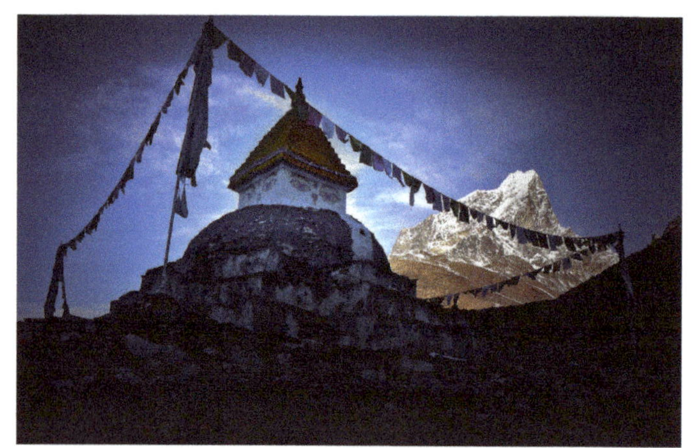

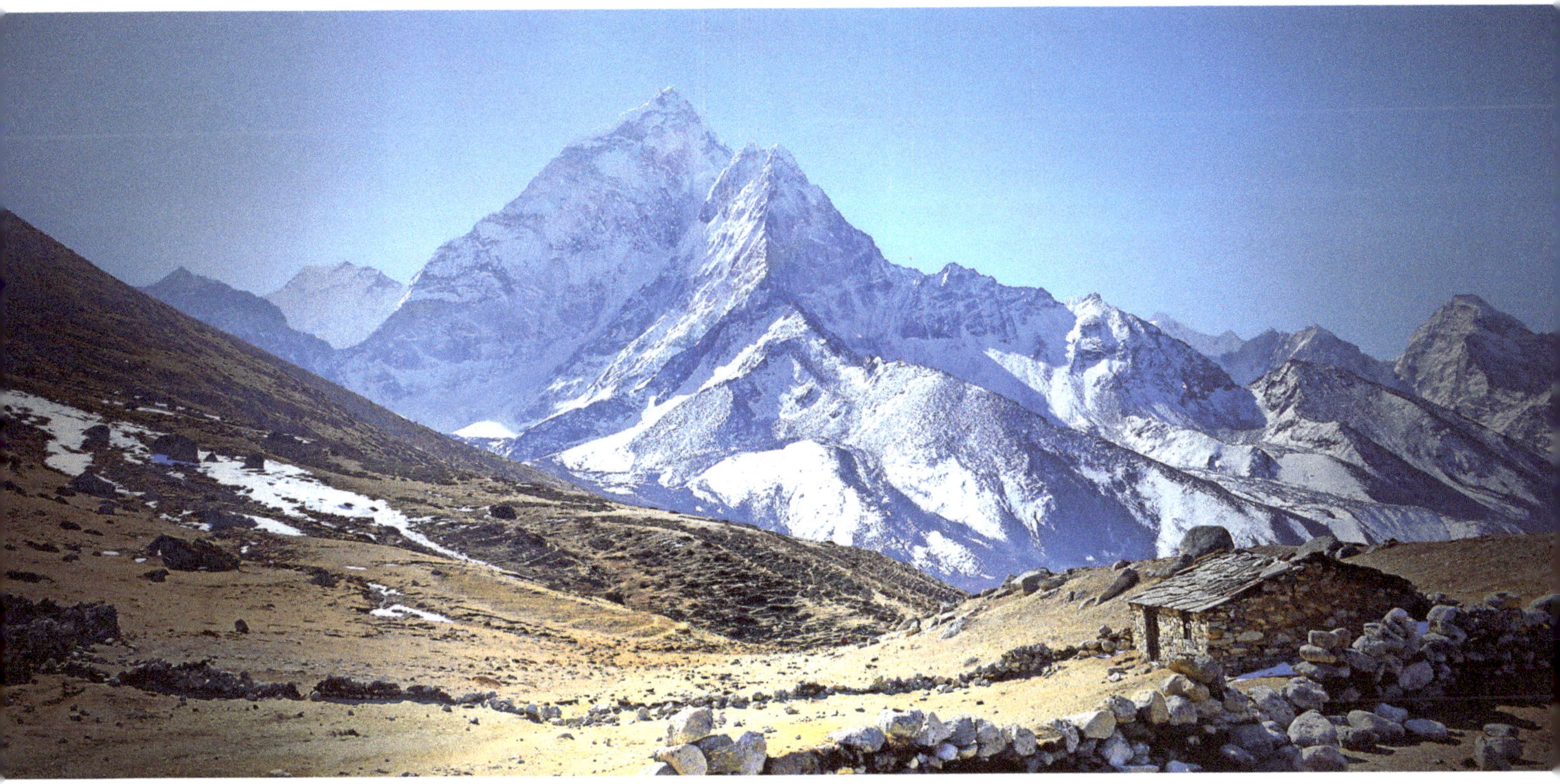

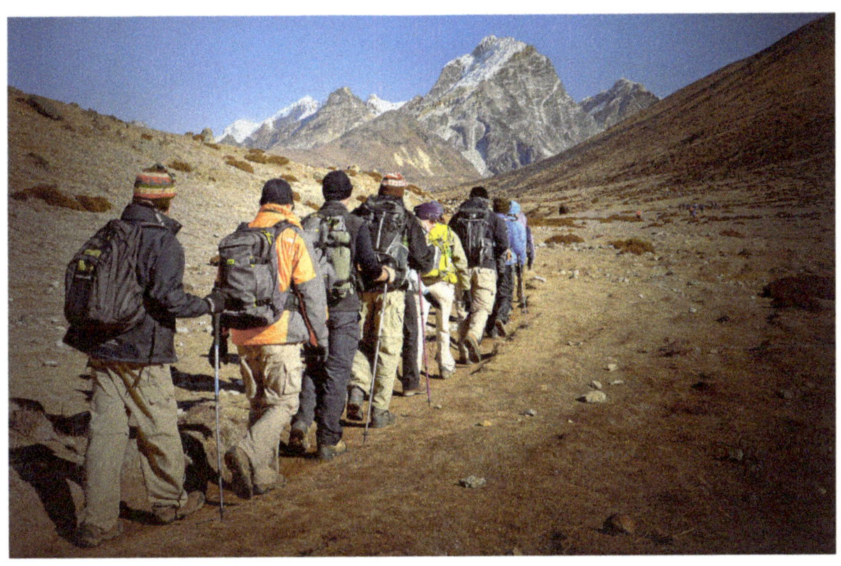

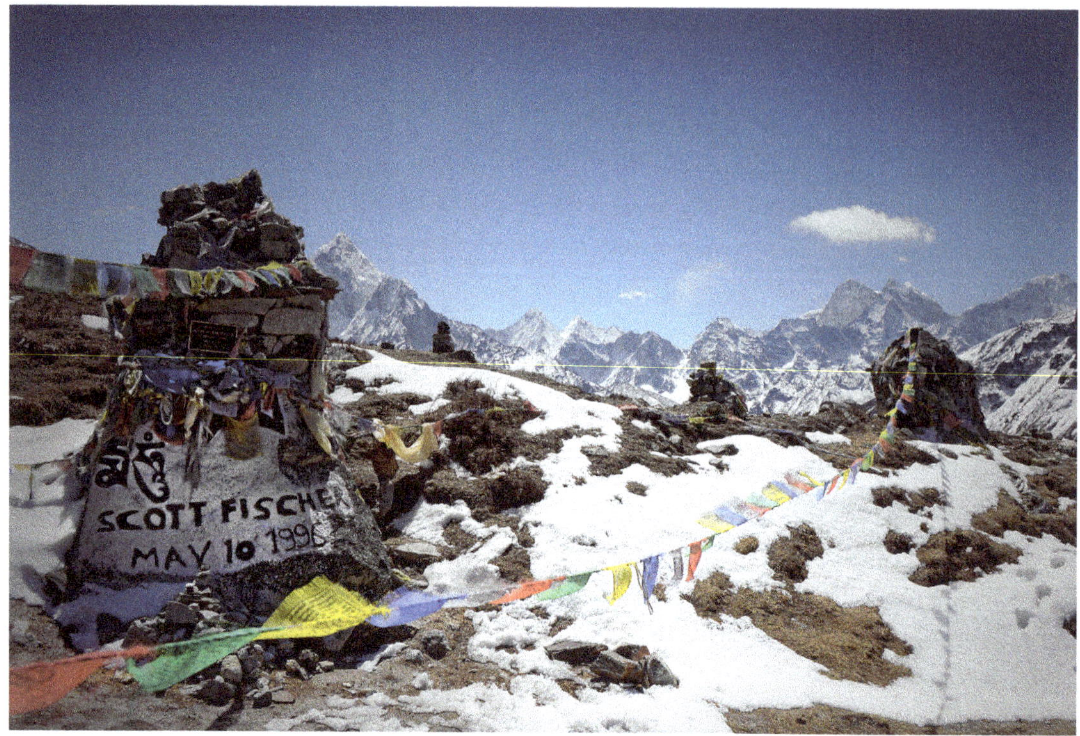

Memorials to those lost on Mt Everest

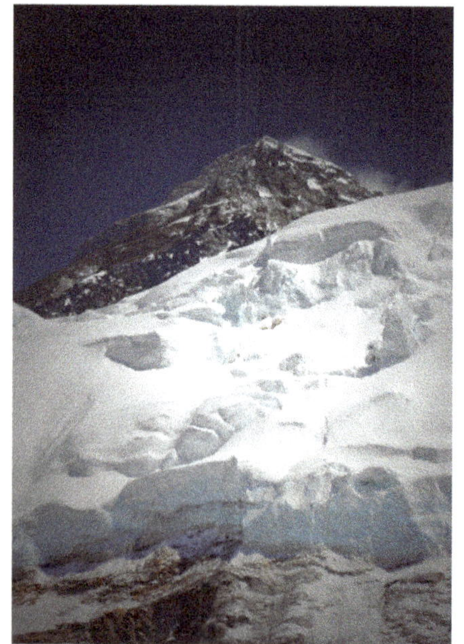

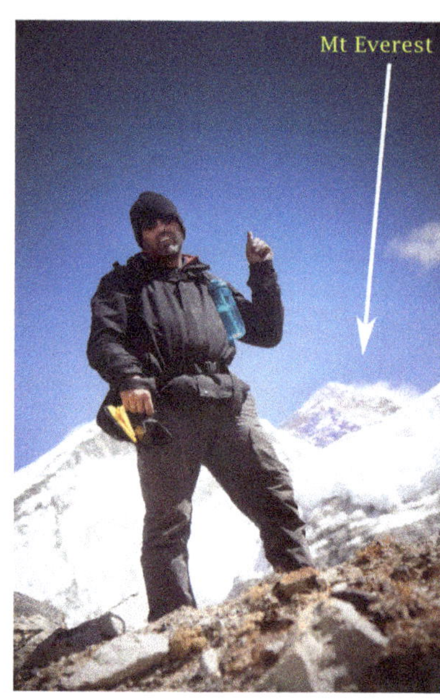

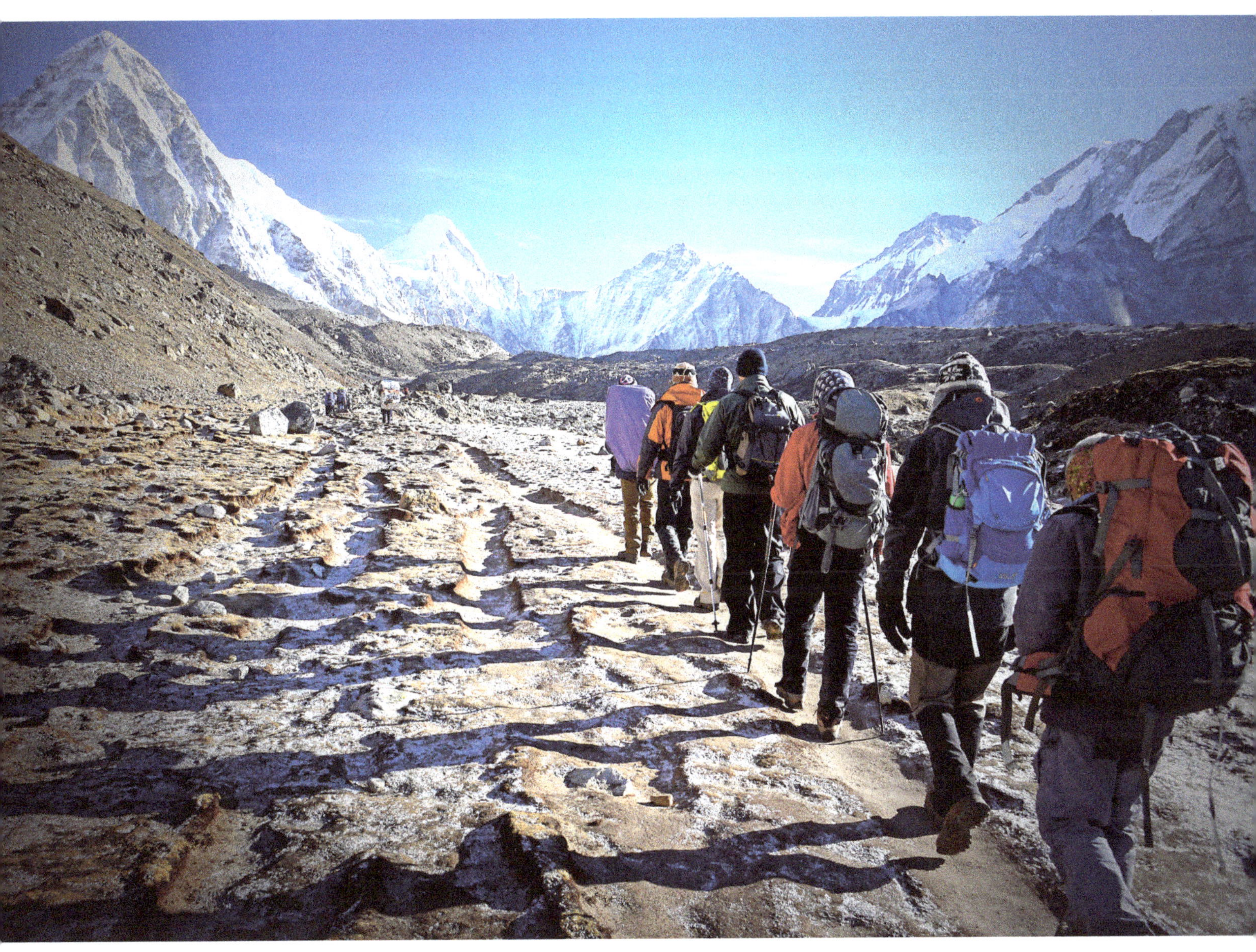

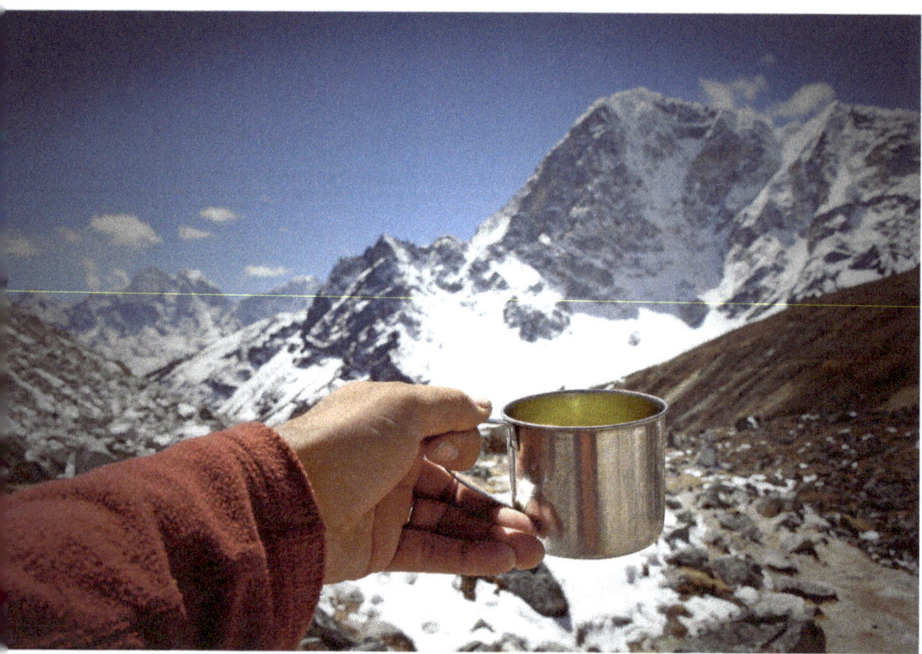

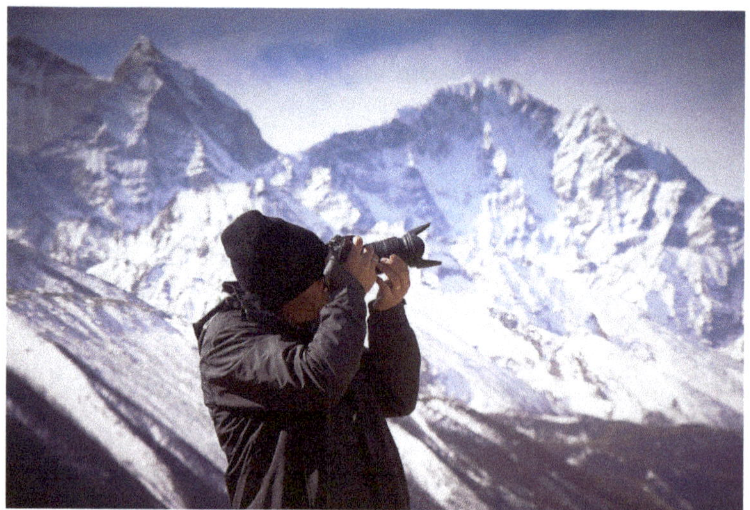

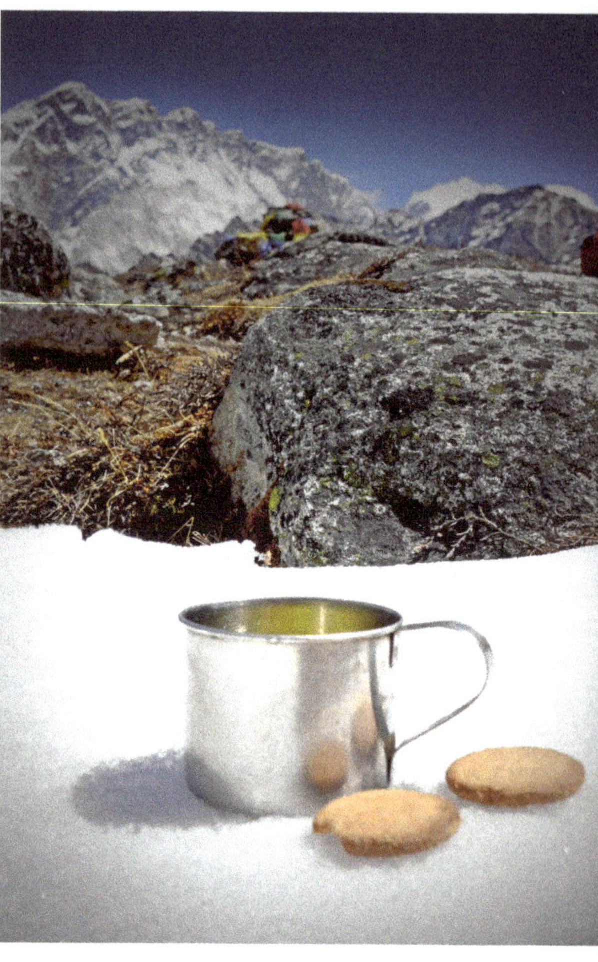

Warm pineapple juice and biscuits

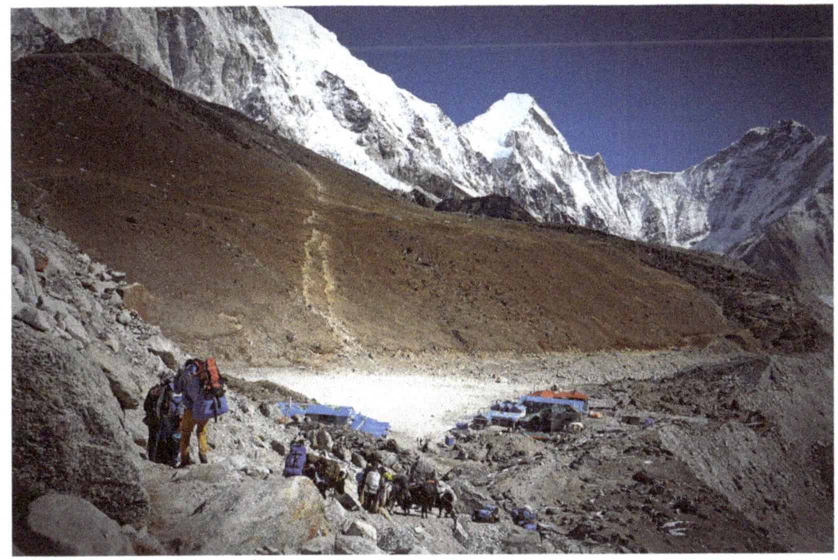

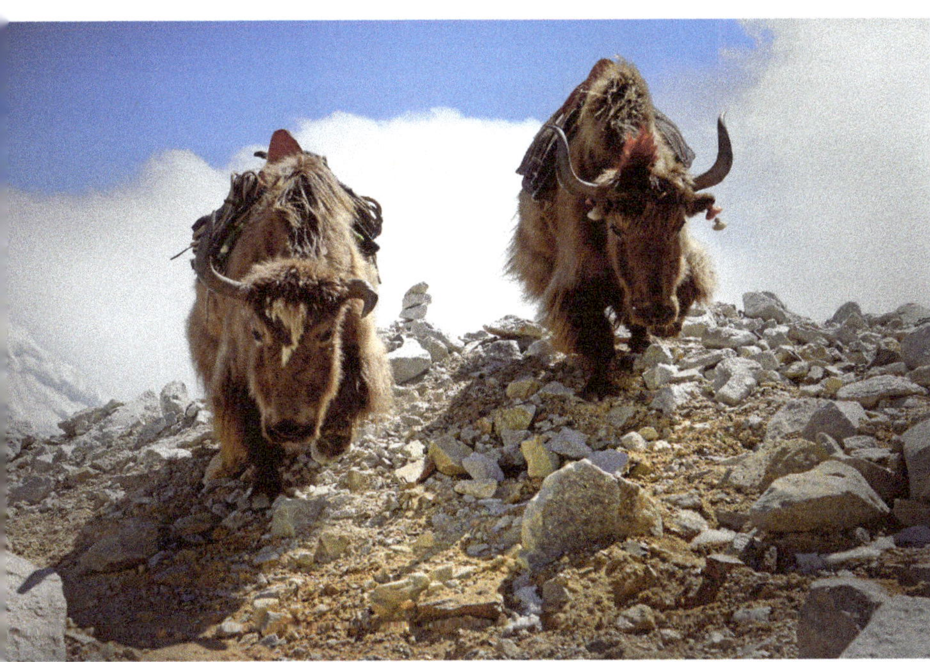

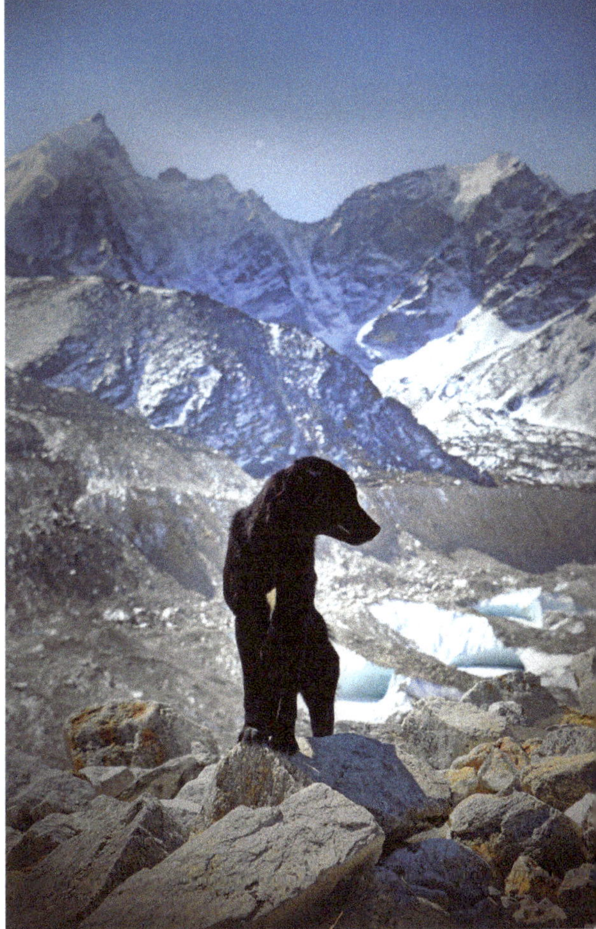

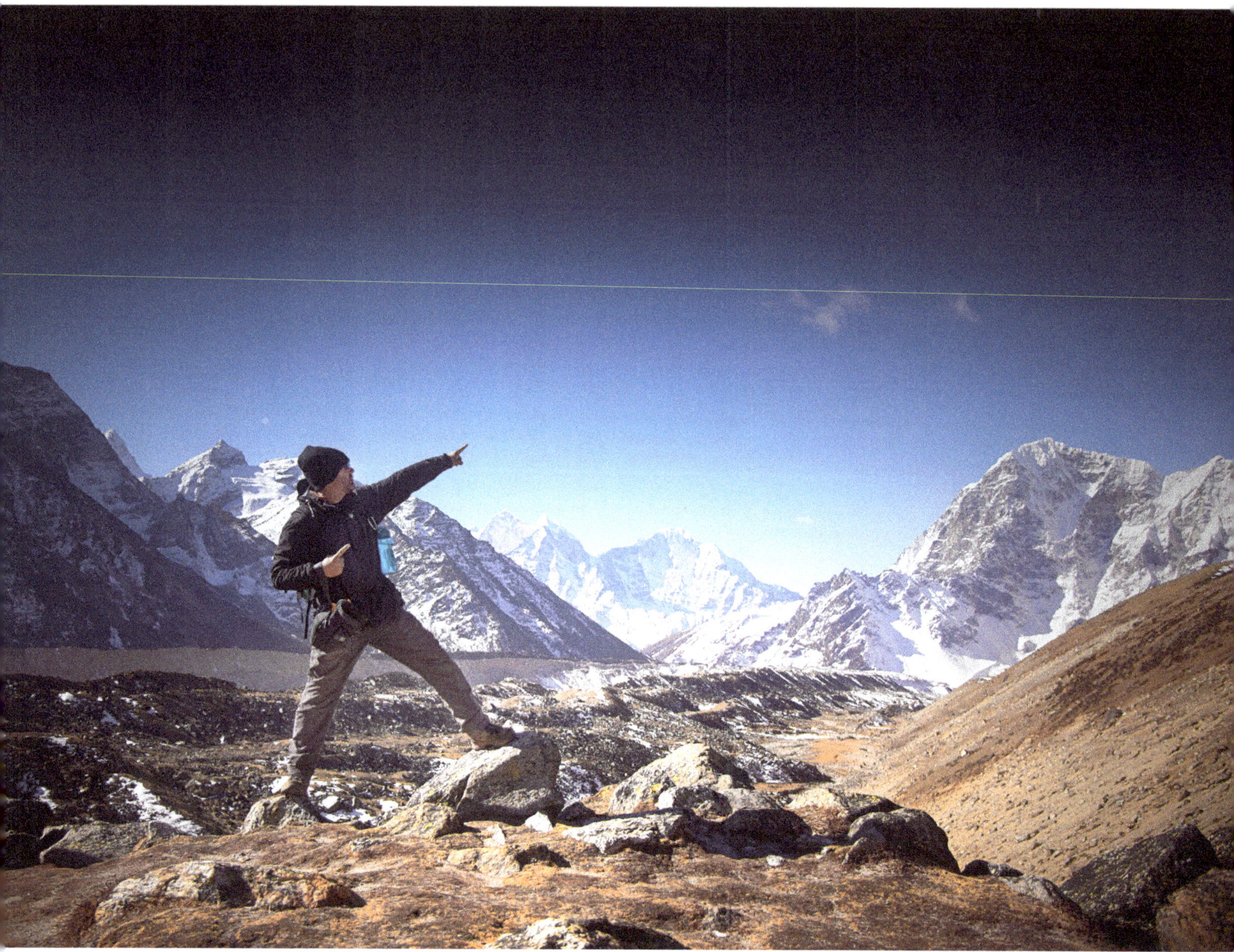

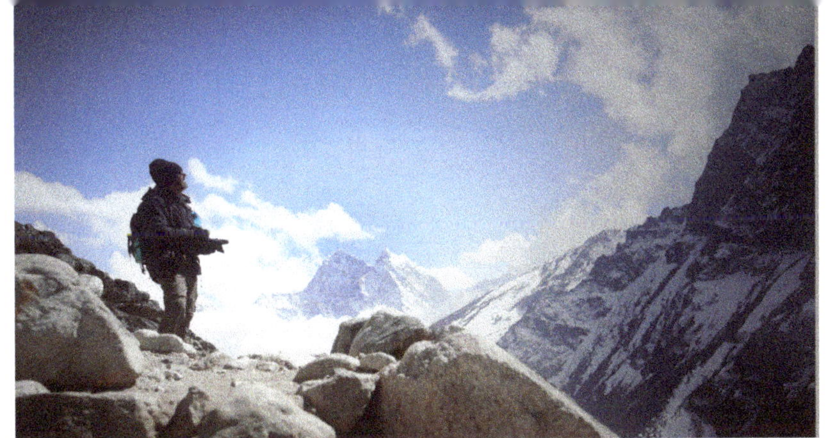

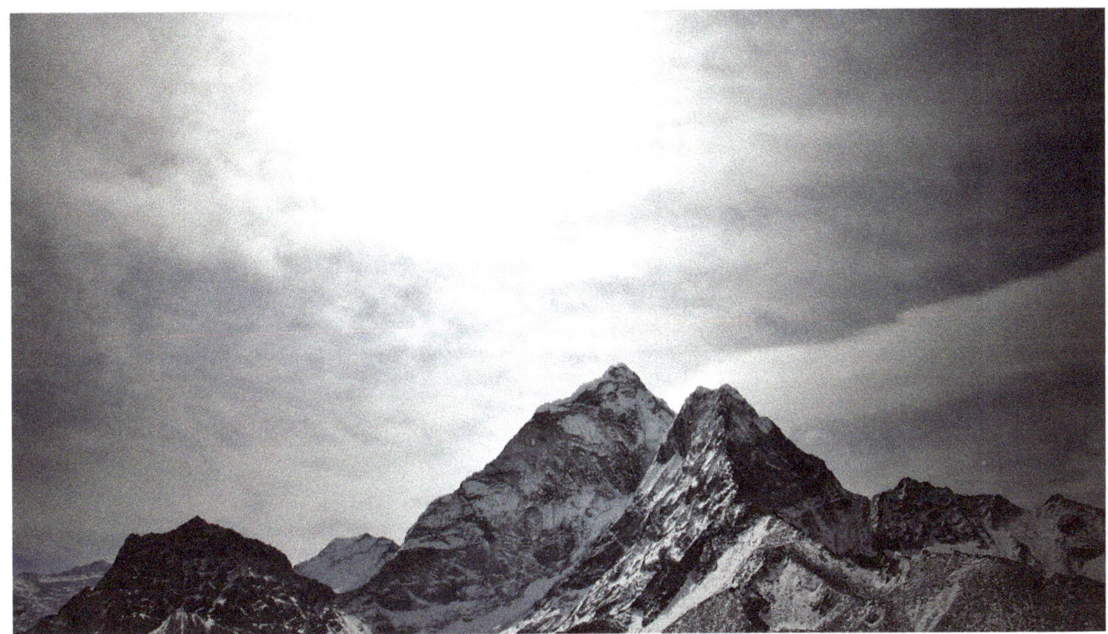

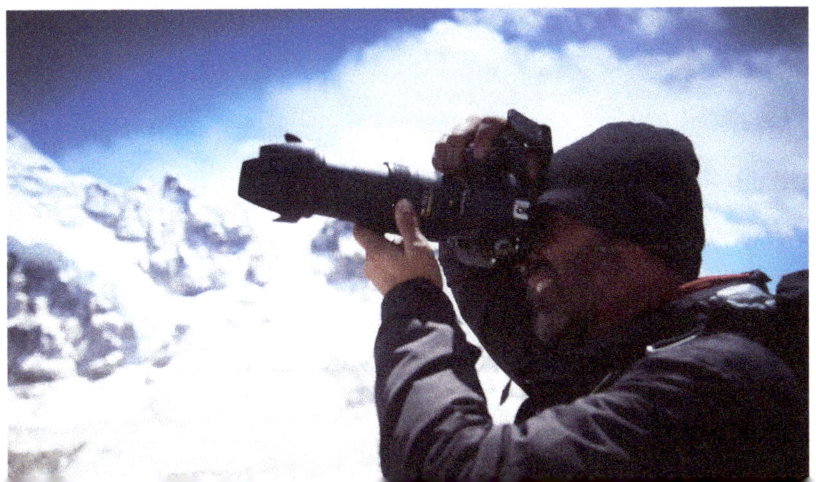

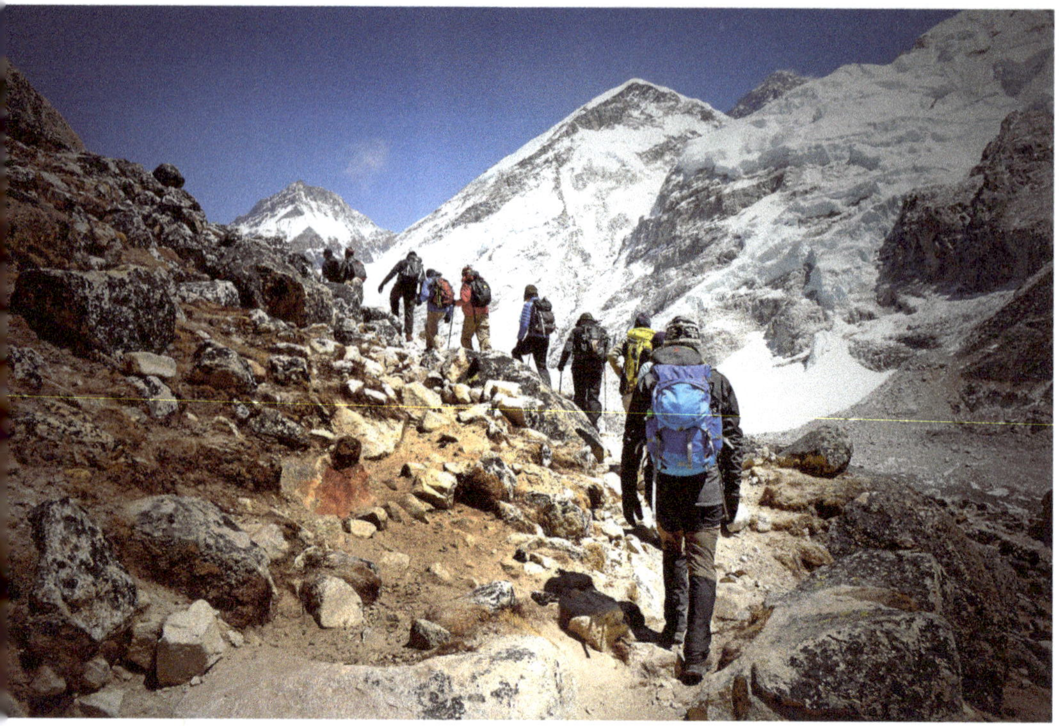

Walking into Gorak Shep after four hours of trekking down the steep rocks into a tiny ramshackle village we all knew it was not only our lunch place but also the last stop before reaching EBC later that afternoon. It was also our accommodation that night after the six hour return trek to EBC. At over 5,100 meters, it is a tough place to sleep and relax. Gasping for air at night combined with the cold made it a restless night. I asked Roy, our head sherpa, why it's such a tough day – eleven hours trekking getting to EBC and back, then staying only one night at Gorak Shep. I thought it could be easier if we stayed two nights and broke it up a bit. His reply was that people don't rest well at Gorak and it would make it even tougher on them with the altitude. He had seen trekkers not cope before, so the hard day has to be done. Now, after staying there, up all night with the effects of the Dianox tablets (taken to cope with altitude), waking myself up gasping and then a nine hour walk back to Lobuche, I can fully understand his argument.

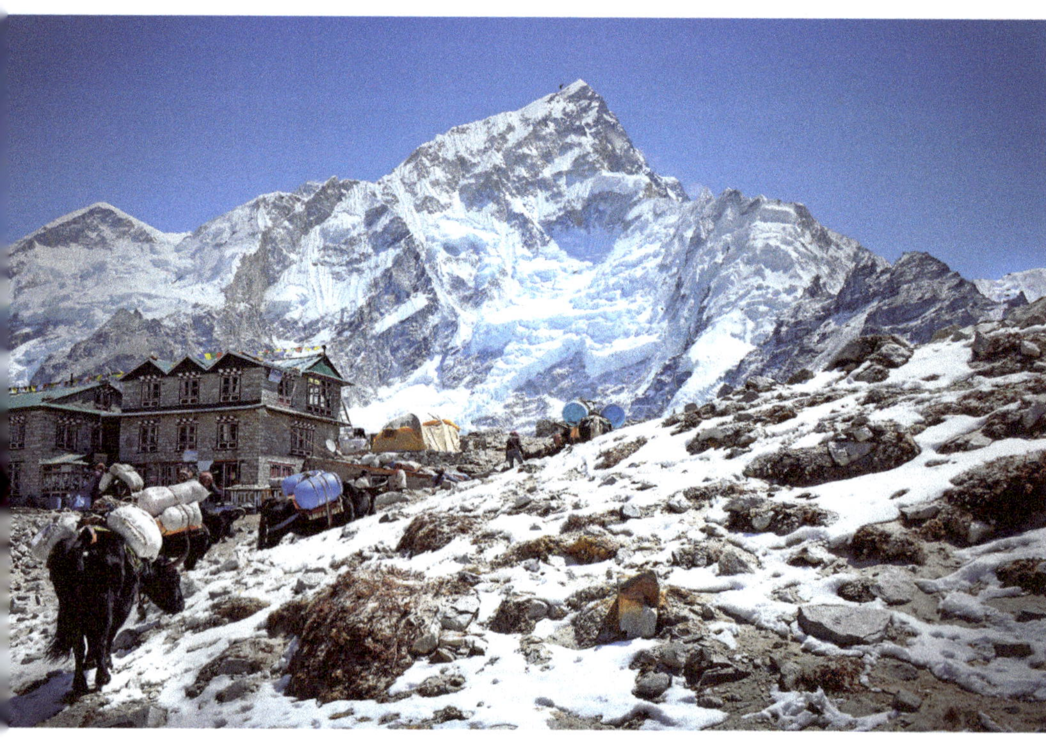

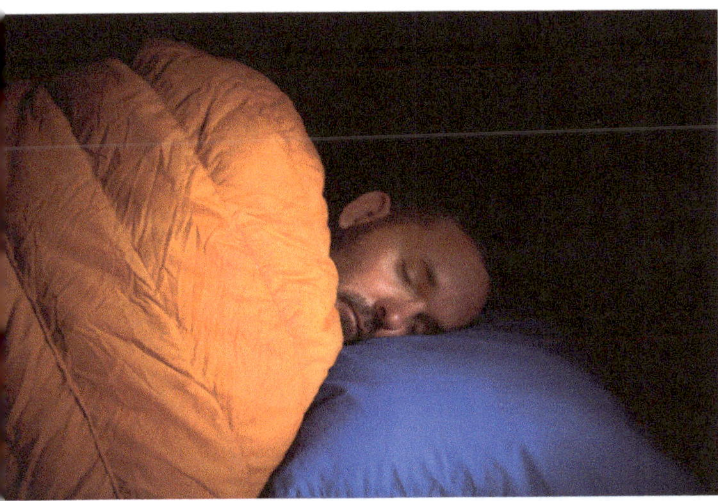

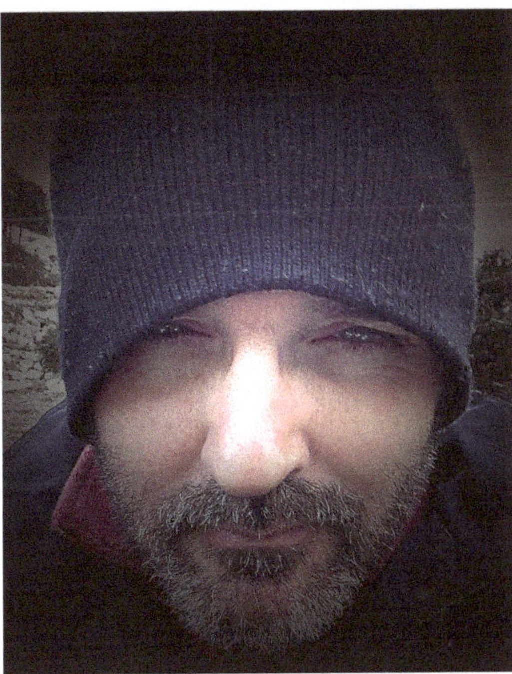

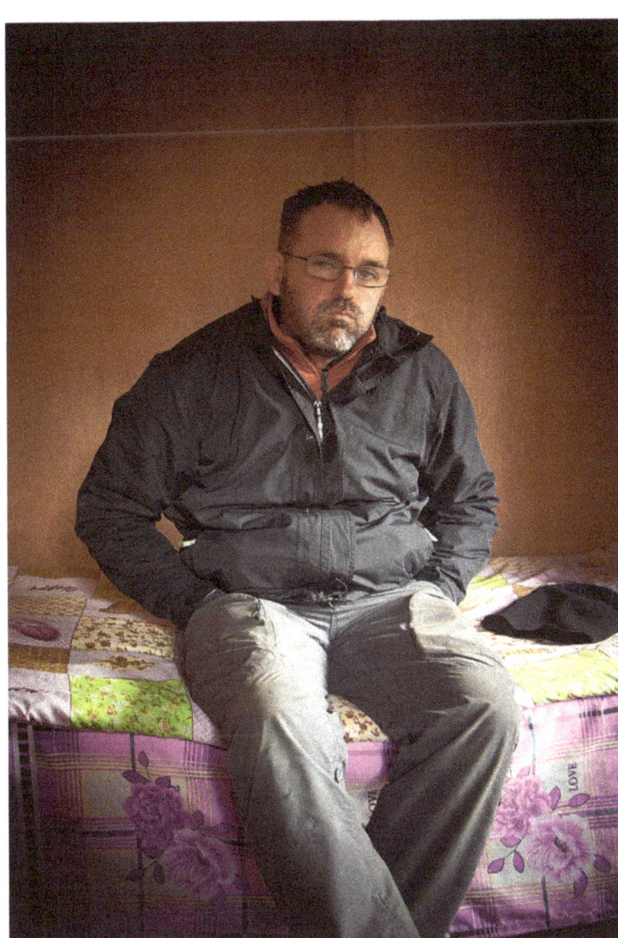

Feeling a little tired

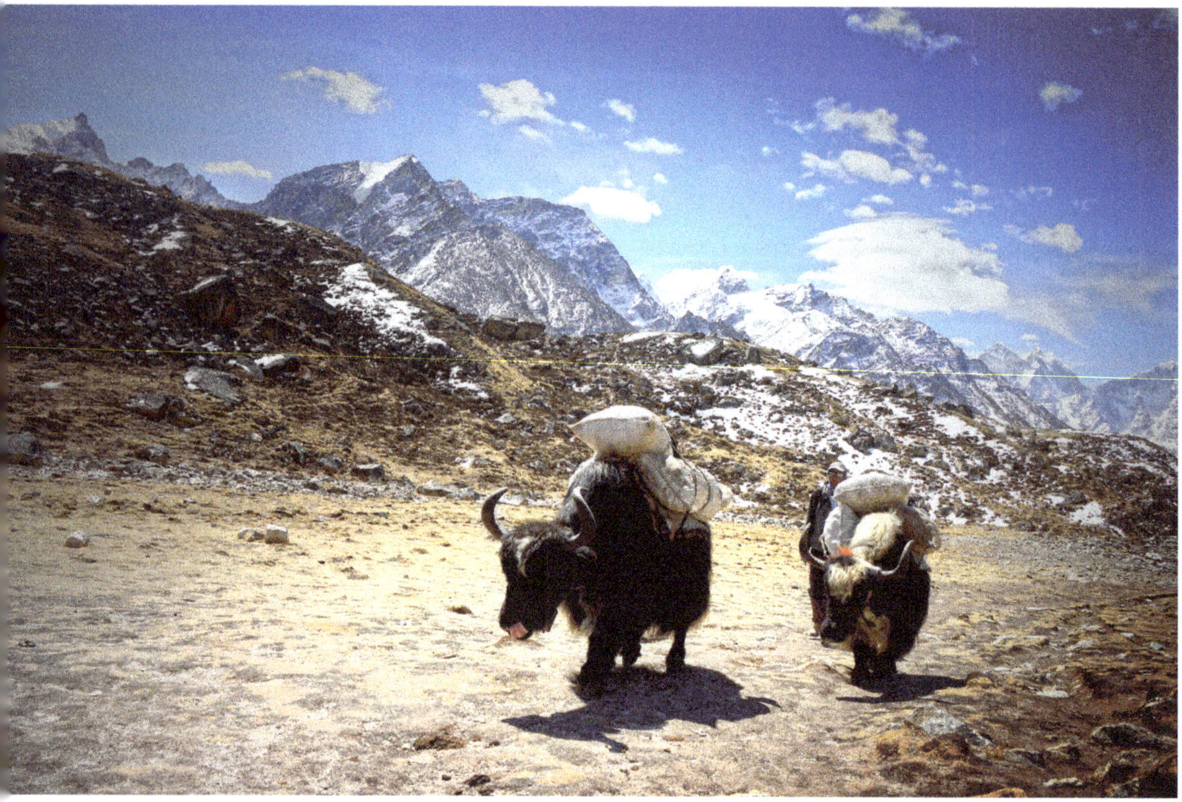

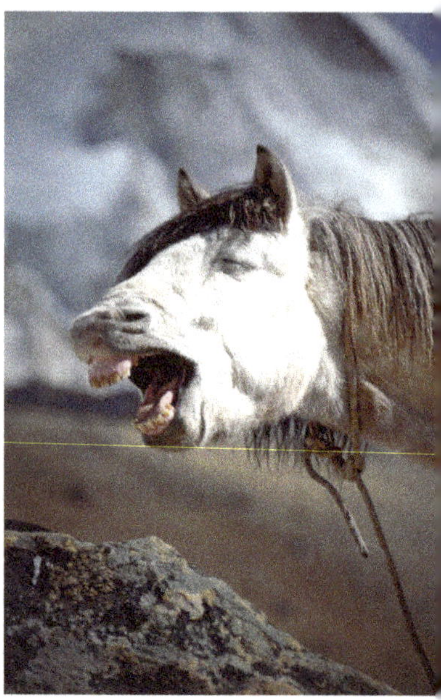

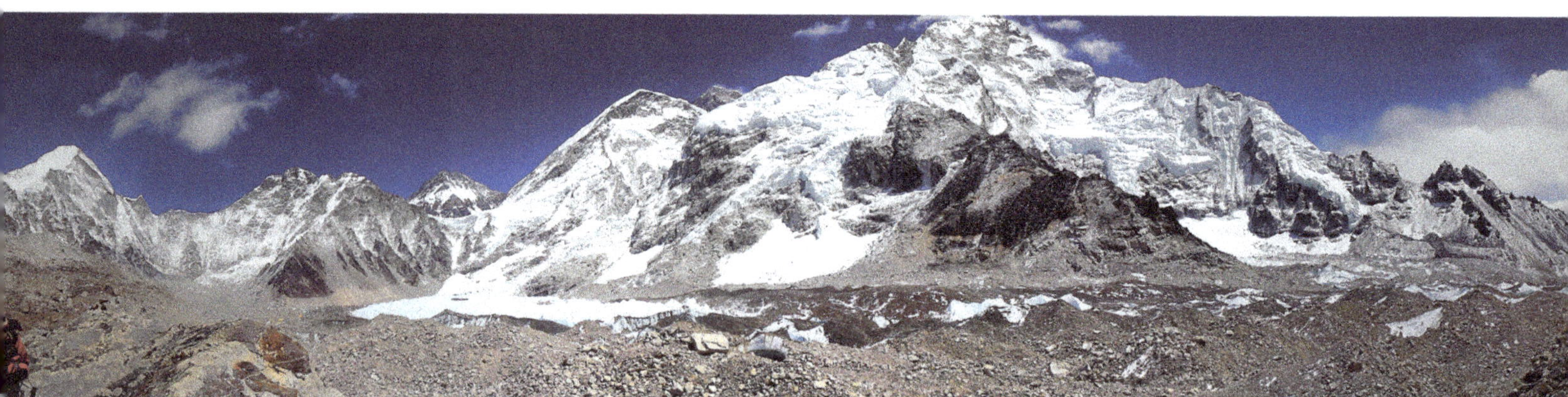

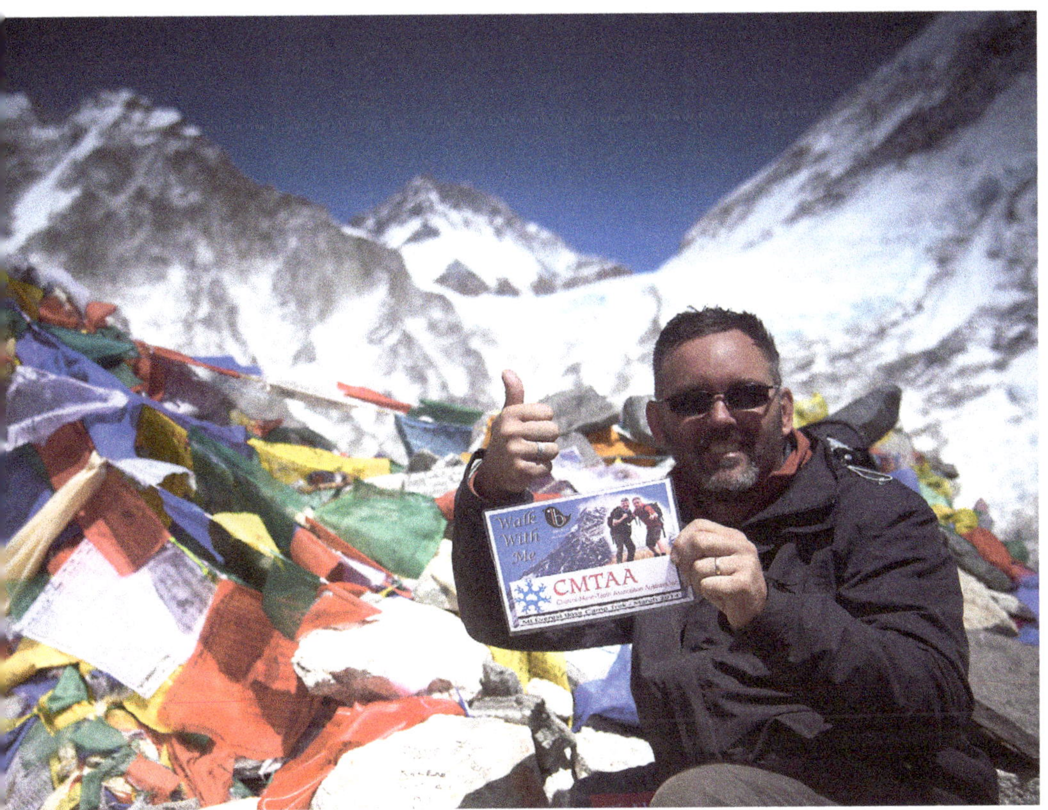

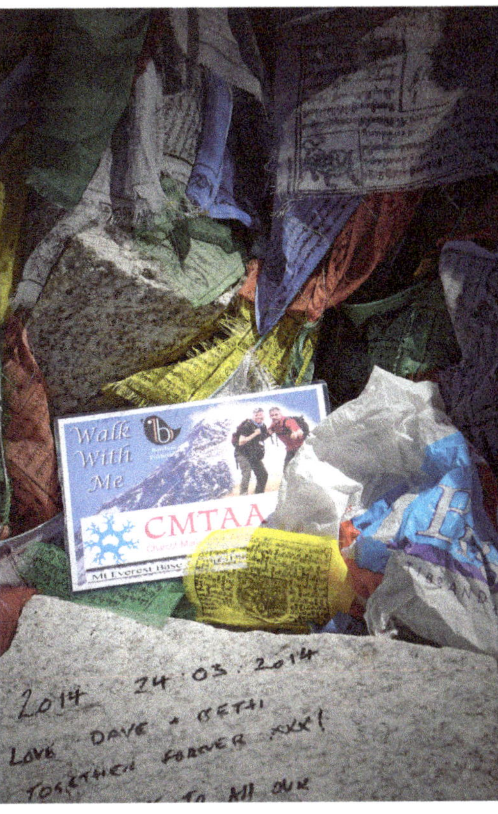

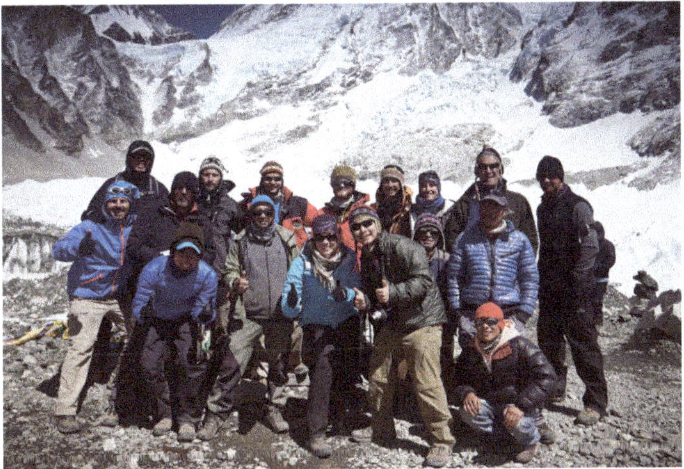

I made it!

After eleven days walking for up to nine hours up and down massive mountains, freezing nights in tents, and Nepalese food not quite sitting right, you would expect to get somewhere other than a pile of rocks covered in prayer flags and without a view of Mount Everest itself, but that's the case with Base Camp. It's an amazing feeling reaching there after all the adventure, but the twenty minutes you spend there goes all too quick. You apparently need time to head back to Gorak Shep before the afternoon winds pick up and weather sets in. We all do a group hug, I say my CMT speech to video, we take our group photos and have a quick look around, grab a rock or two maybe, and then we hear ZOOM ZOOM by our Sherpas and off we're go again. As much as it is brief it is still the highlight of the trek, the reason we went, but you soon realize it's not the destination, it's the journey.

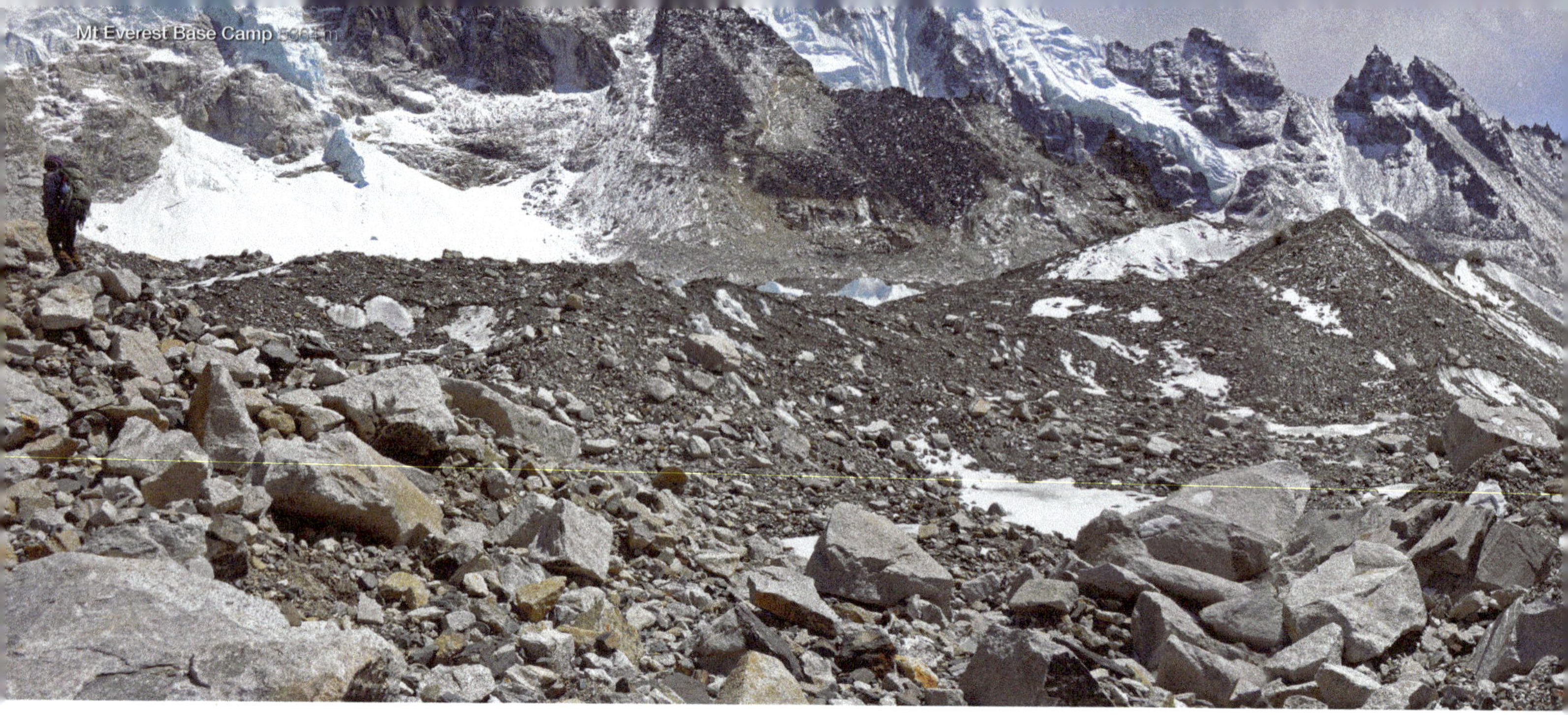

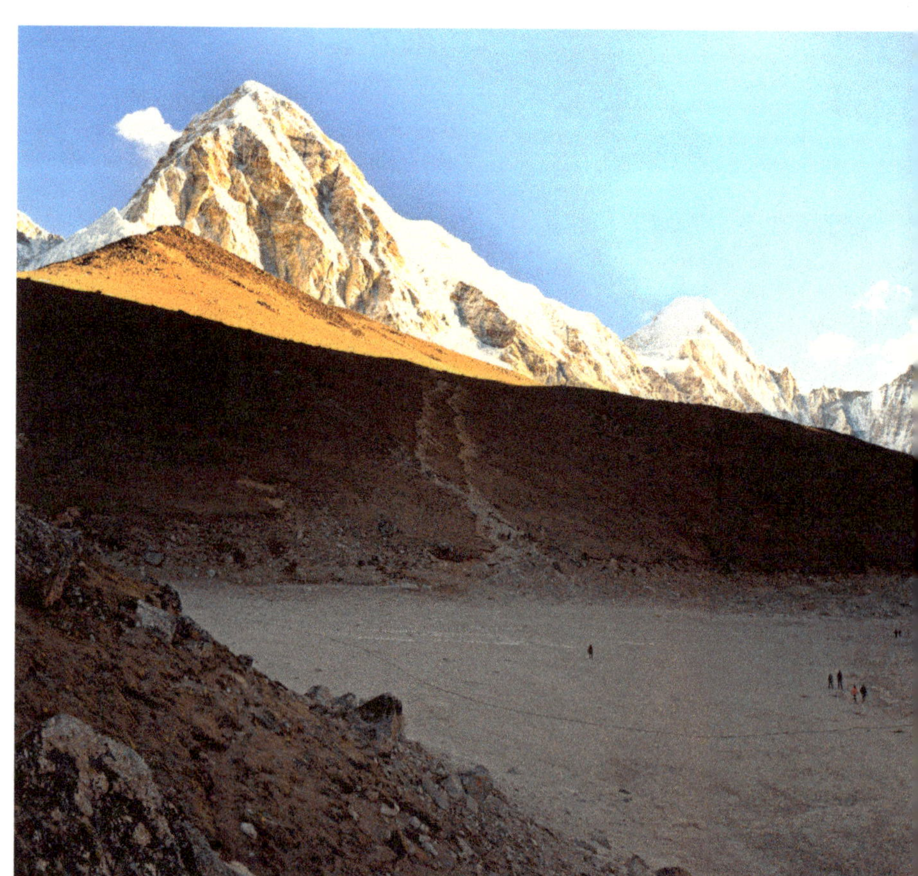

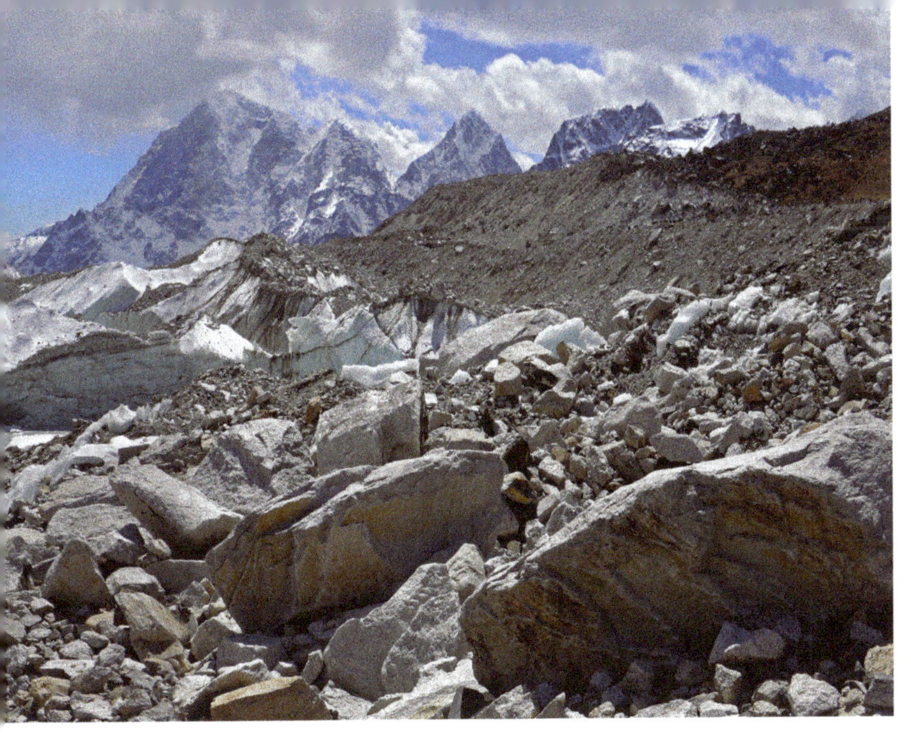

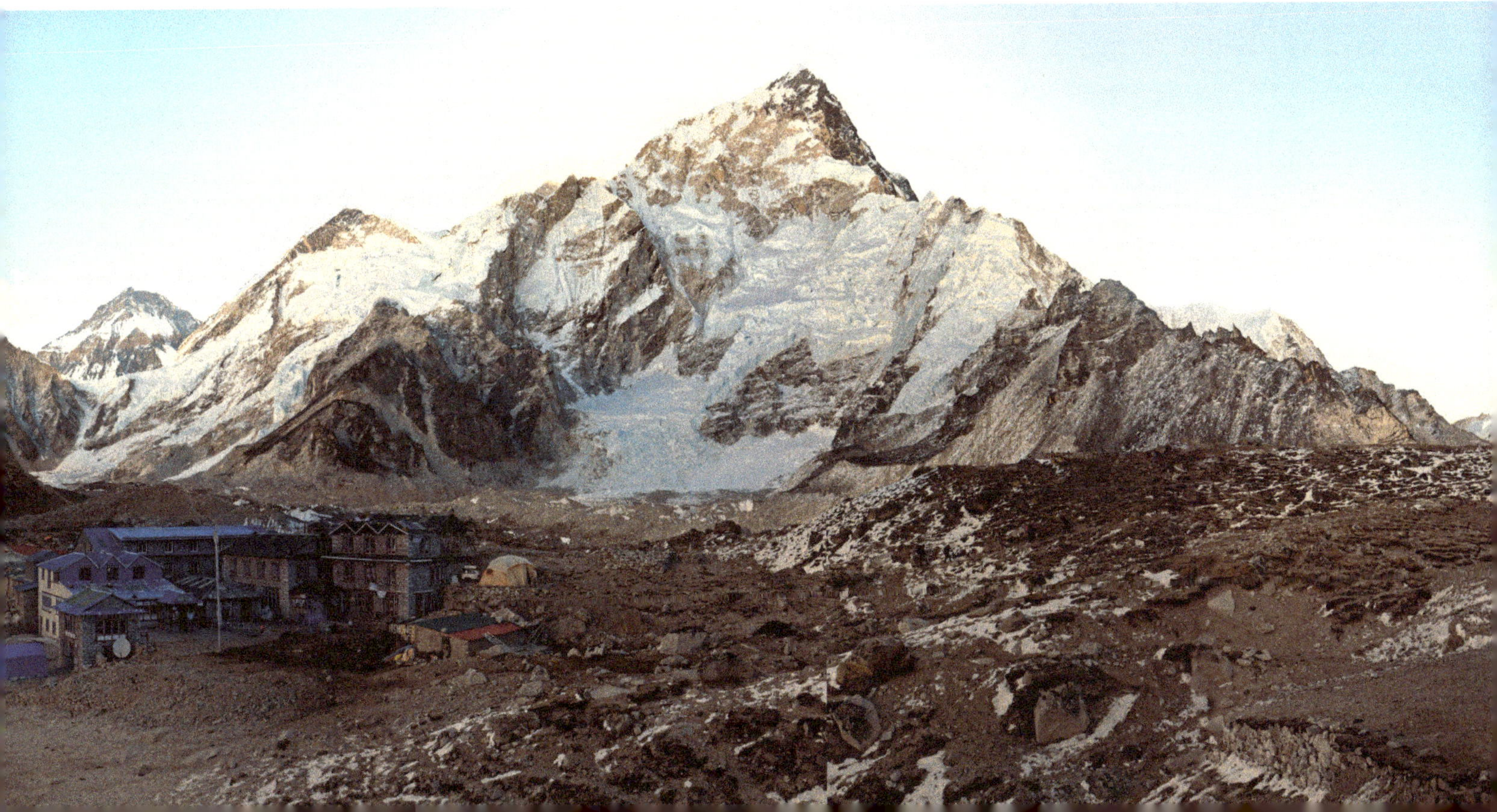

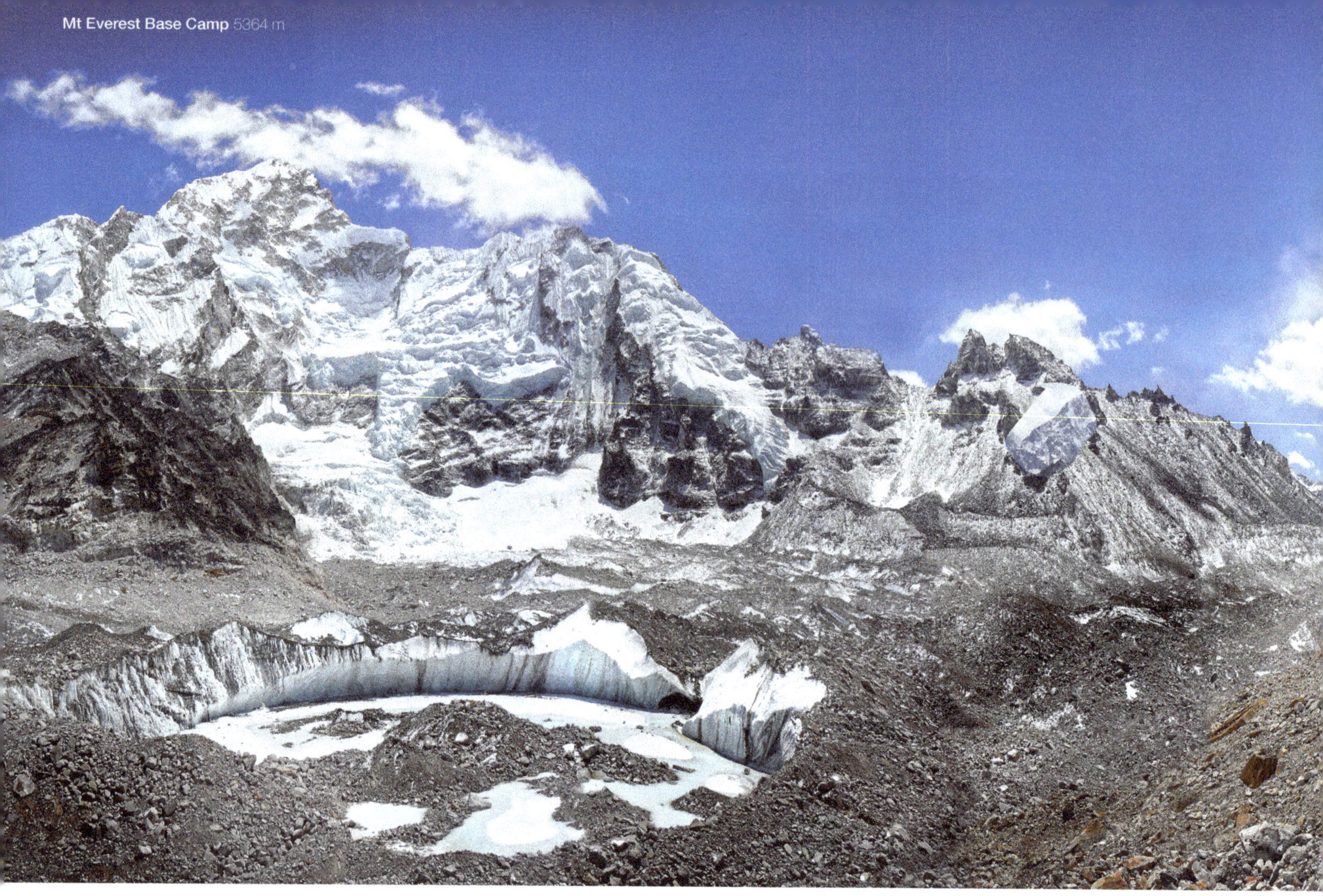

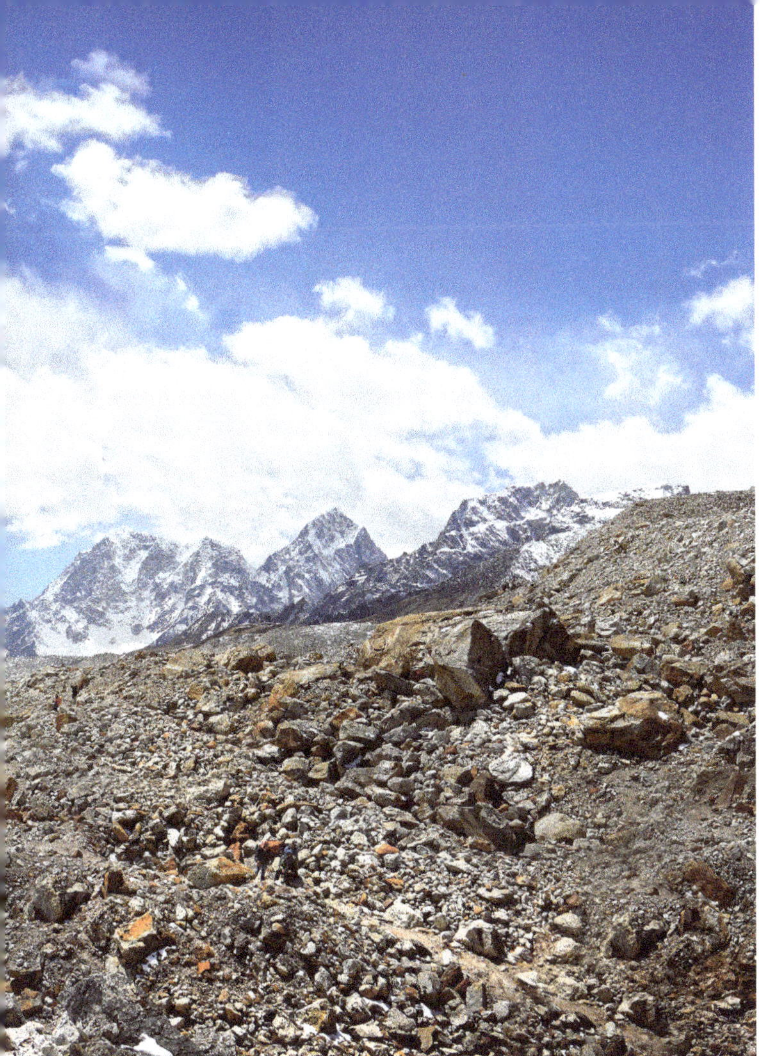

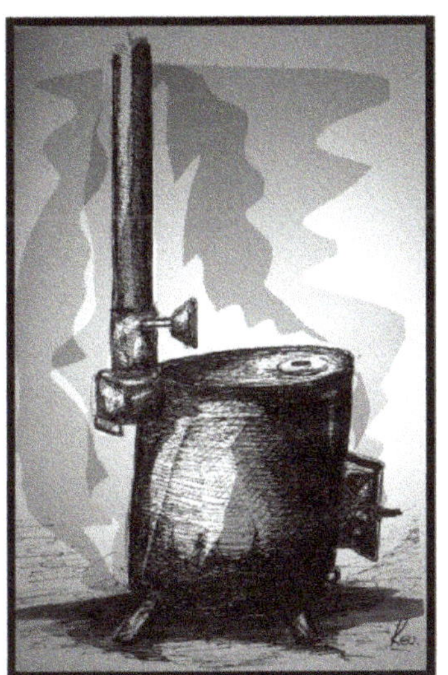

In the centre of the room the potbelly does stand

The life saving heater, warming up all of our hands

We eat in its warmth, its radiance and glow

To the sound of melted Everest snow in the river down below.

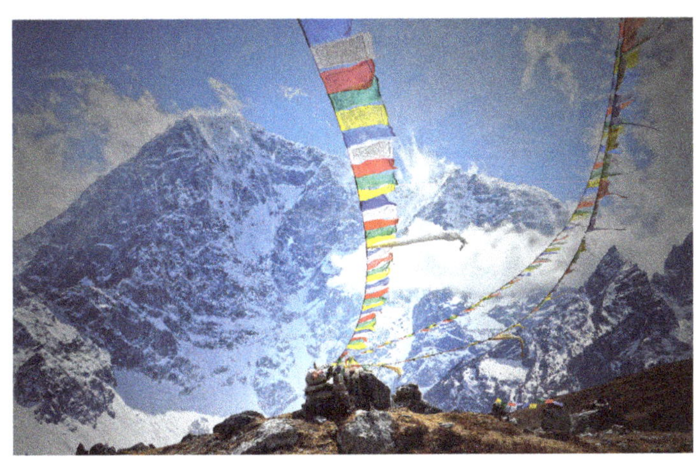

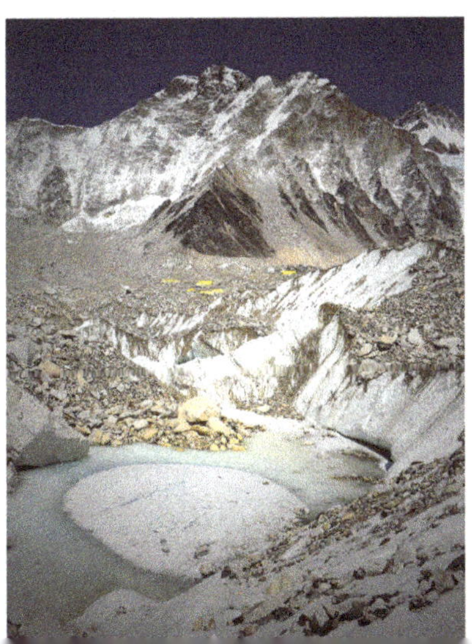

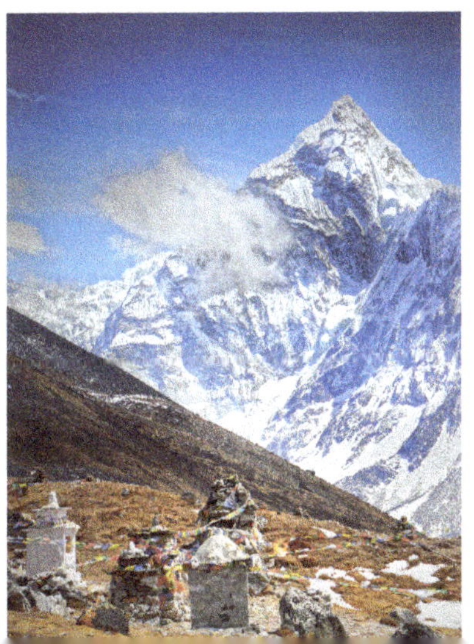

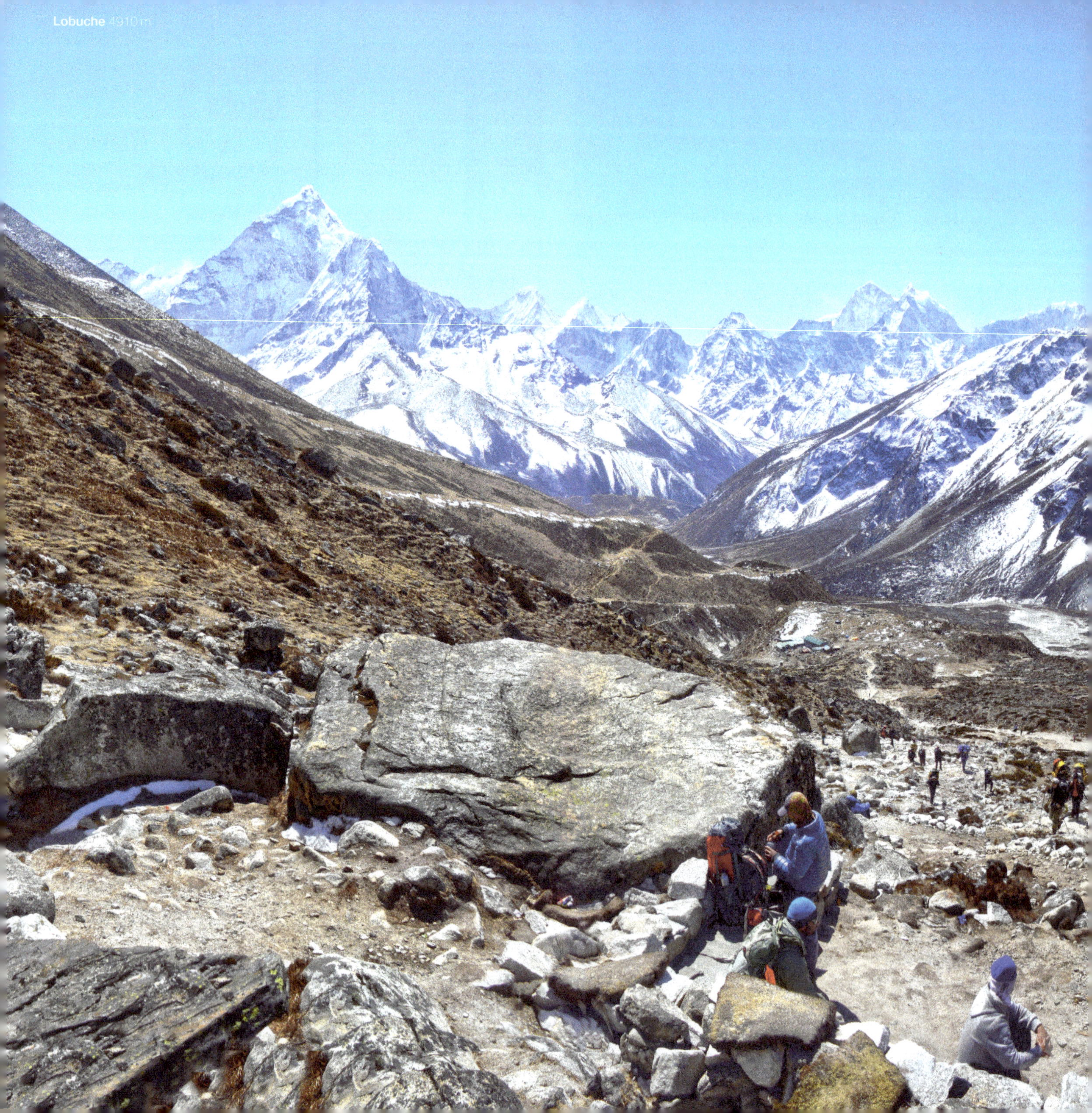
Lobuche 4910m

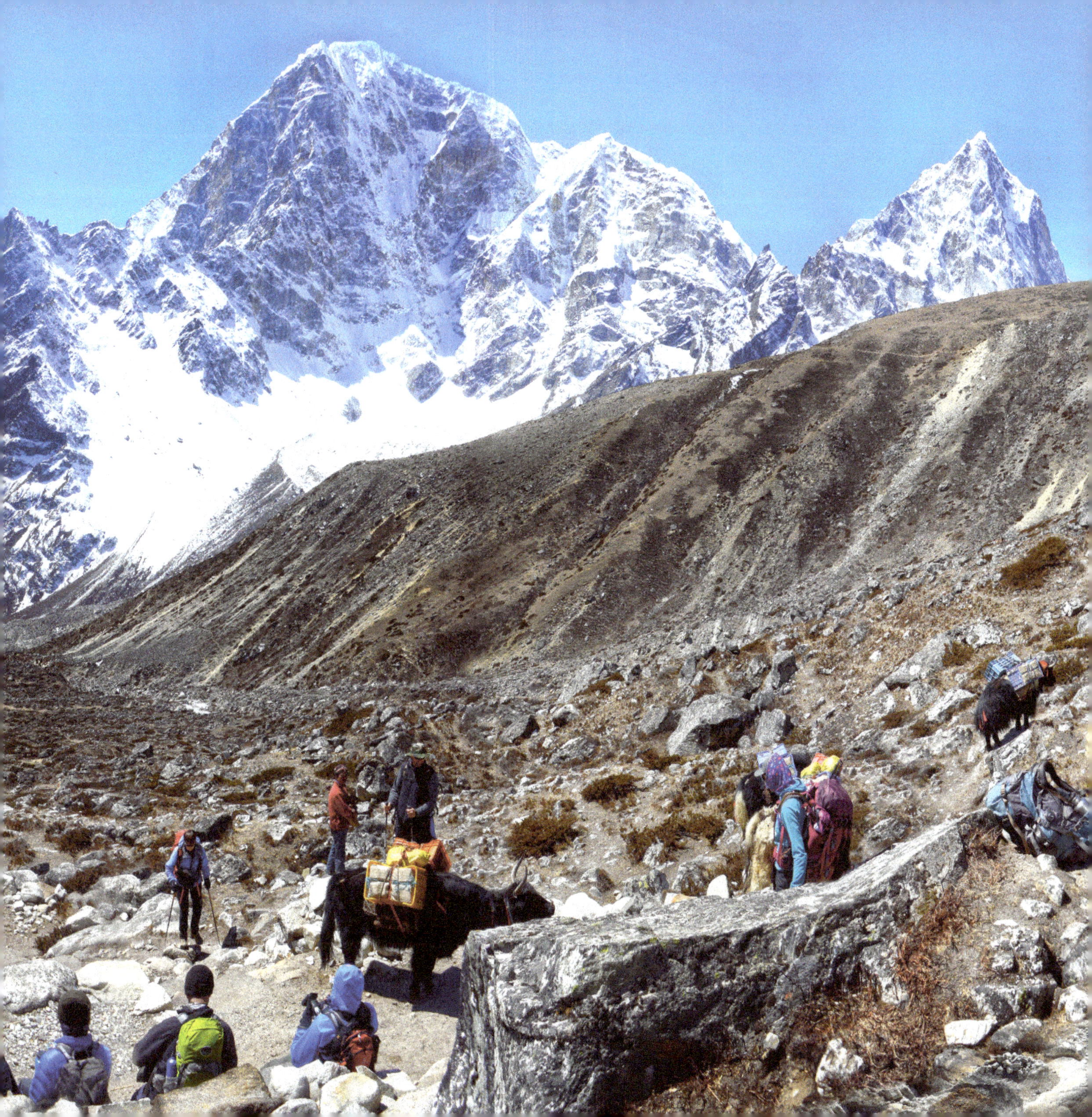

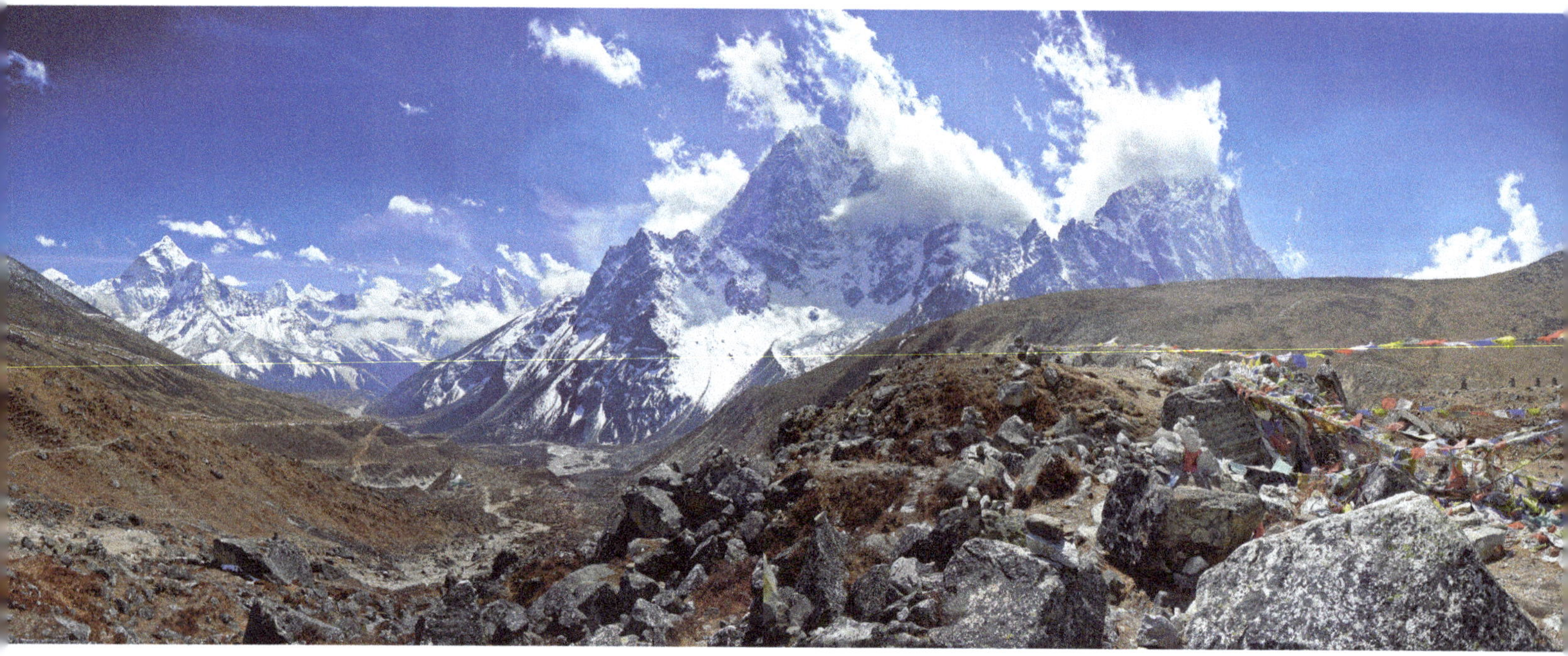

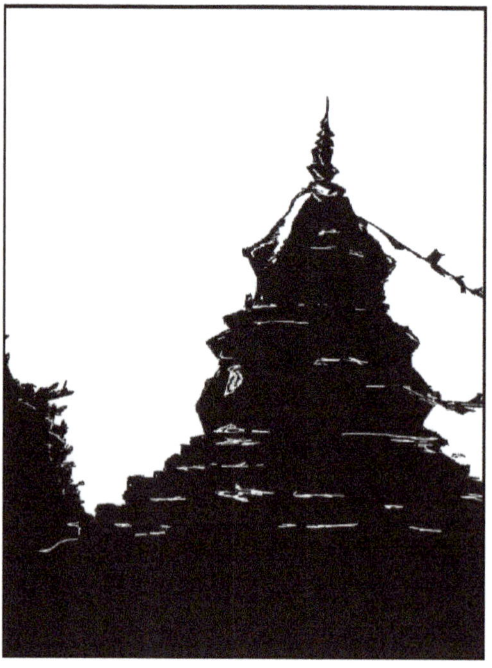

On the trail all you see is mountains and some towns

But now and then you see a stupa if your head's not looking down

They dot the entire trail and there's only one way to pass

Always go around them to the left and your luck will still last

With prayer flags flapping fast as the wind howls right by

There's always a stupa perched on a cliff way up high

Surrounded by stones stacked in piles or beside

Engraved with poems of peace, amazingly carved out with pride

I wish I could read them so I knew what they were

But I struggle with basic English so maybe next tour

Well as we walk to the next rockcliff a stupa comes into view

I never get sick of them even though now I've seen quite a few.

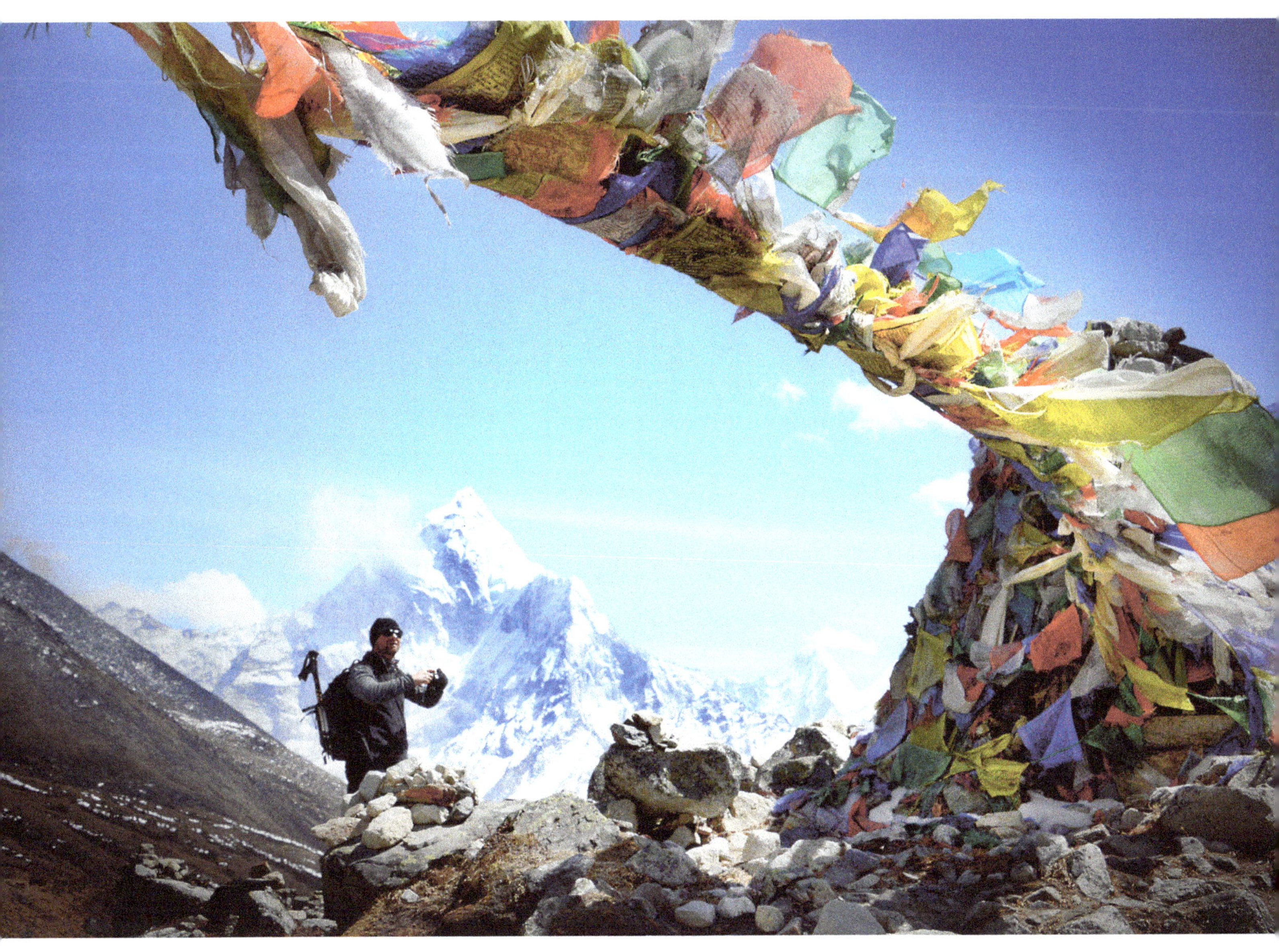

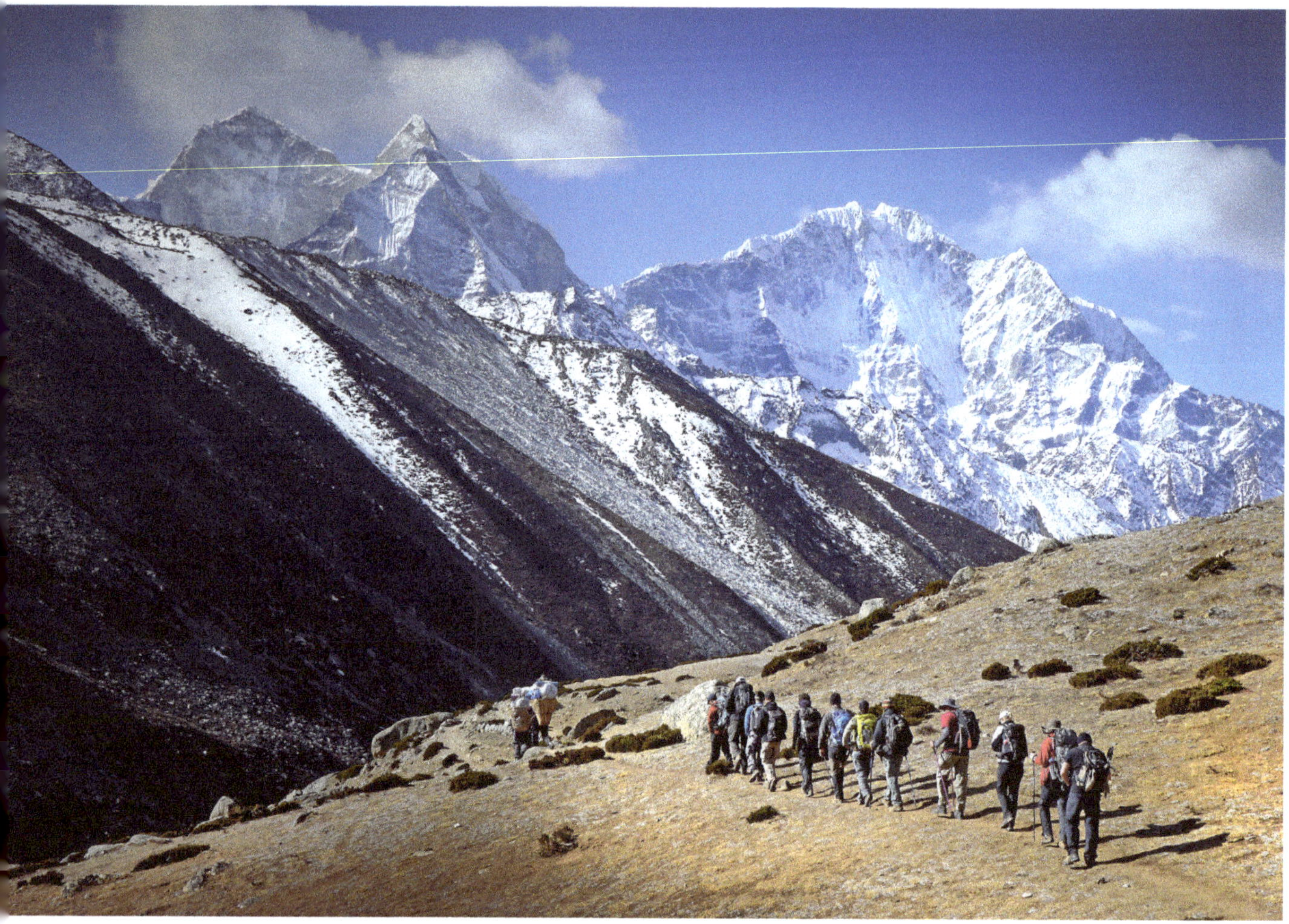

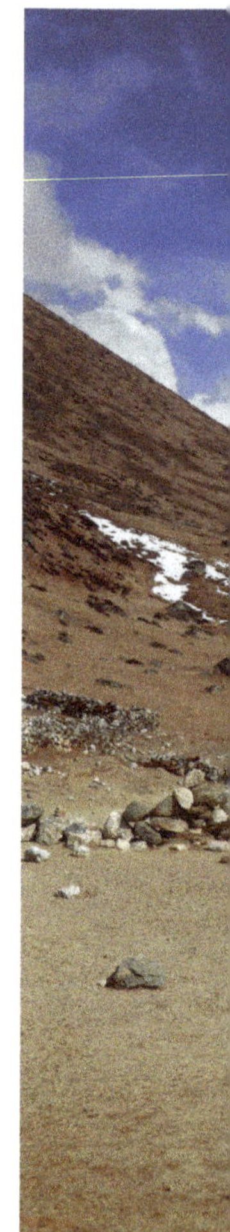

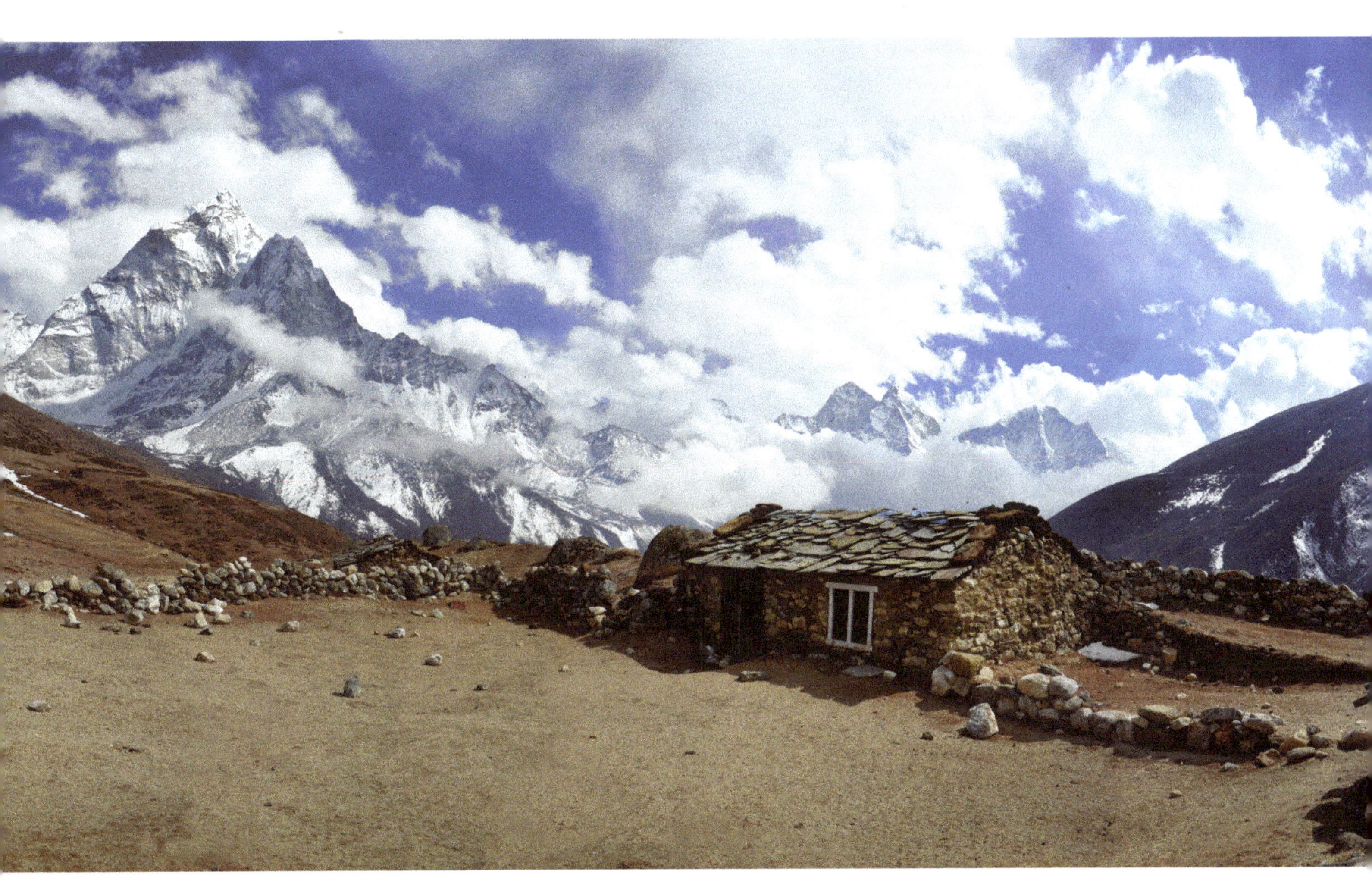

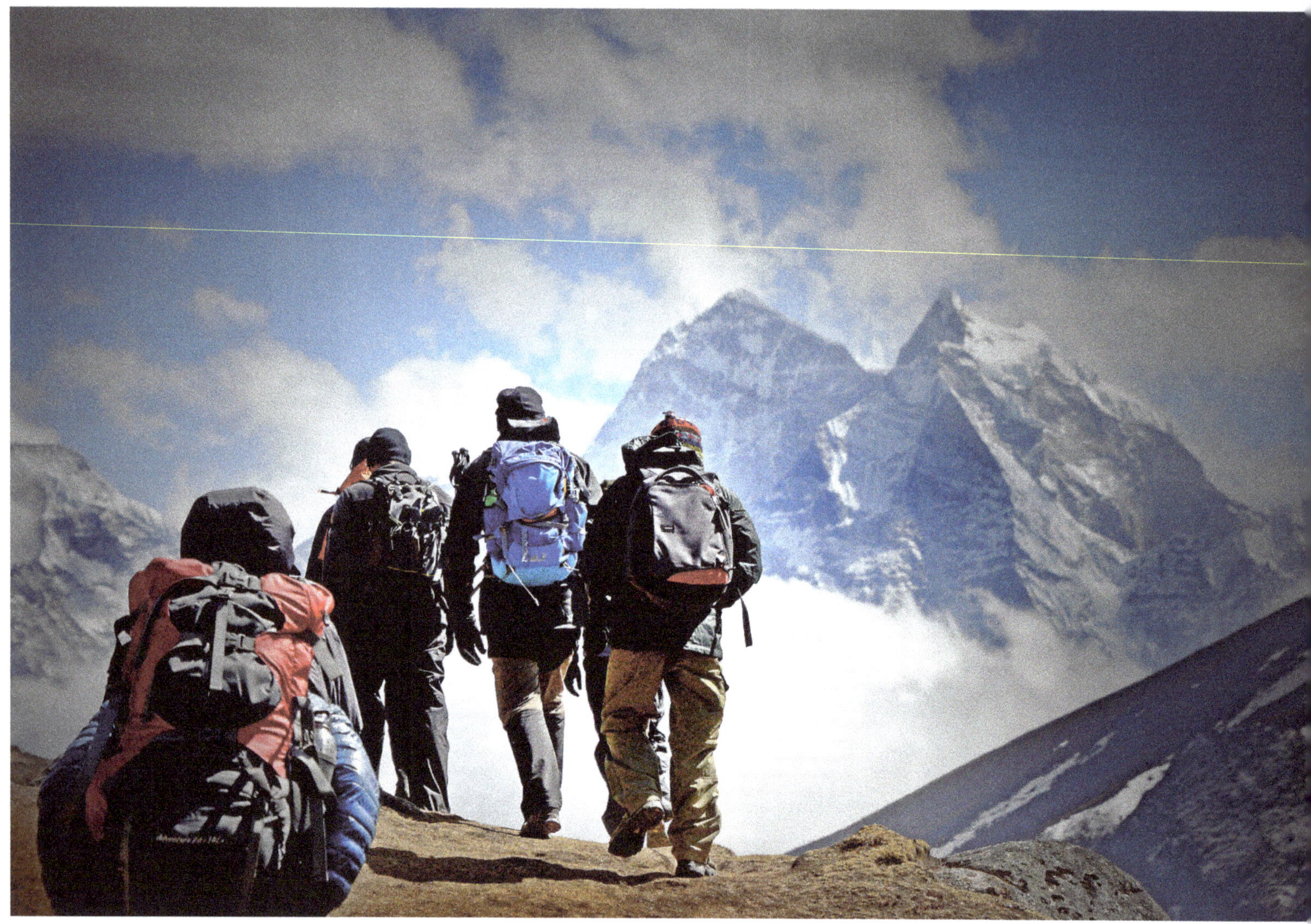

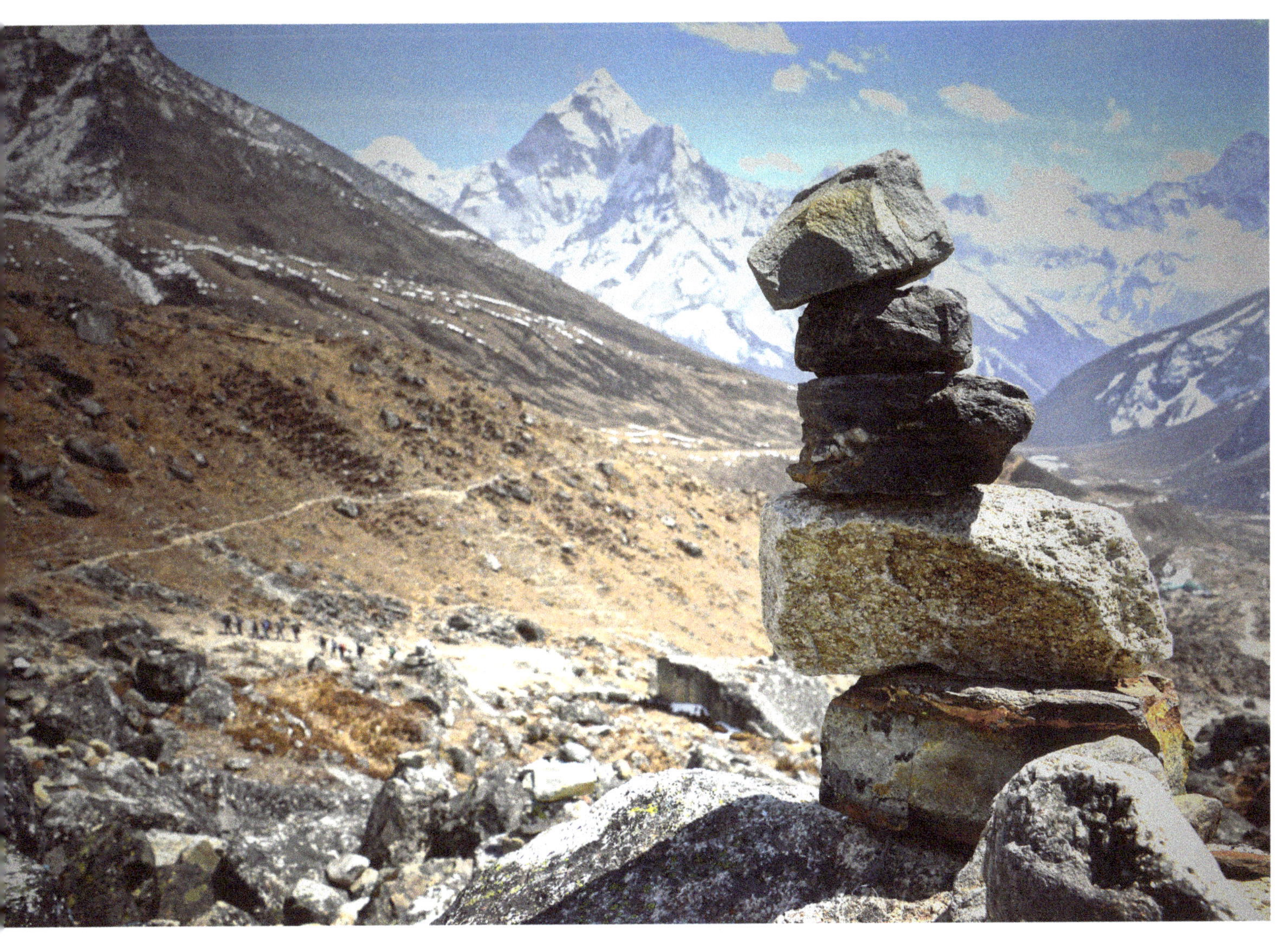

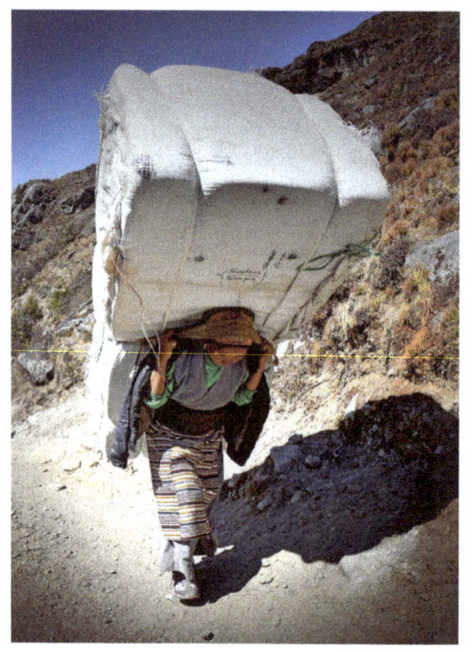

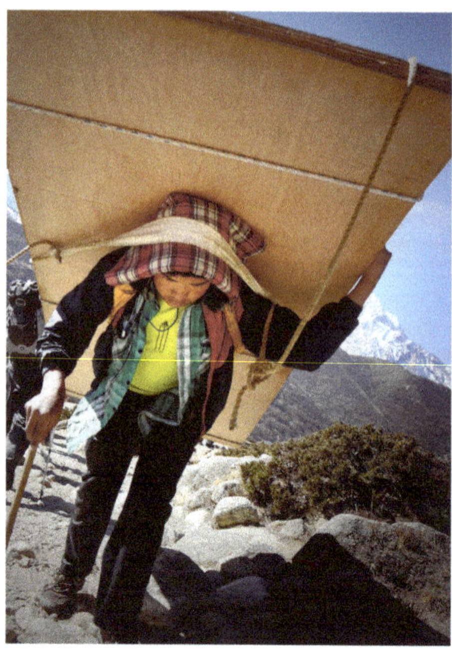

Sherpas – these people are the real superhumans on this planet. Everyday I was amazed at what they were carrying up the EBC trail to restock the towns along the way. My trekking group walked day after day carrying our day packs, and water bottles, struggling up and down those ridiculous mountains for nine hours a day, but as we were stopping and resting, flaking on the ground, these people carried essential goods, wood or food sometimes stacked double their height without a murmur. At one stage we talked to an older sherpa, fifty years old, four foot nothing and asked what the wood he was carrying weighed. He answered 135kg. I was blown away and tried to nudge the pile of wood. Believe me, it weighed what he said. I would have hated just lifting it onto my back and standing there. I have the utmost respect for these people, their strength and ability to do what they do, and was constantly reminded of how weak and pathetic we are in our cushy lives back home. We so don't know the meaning of real hard work until we have done what the Nepalese sherpas do. Superhumans, but always with a smile.

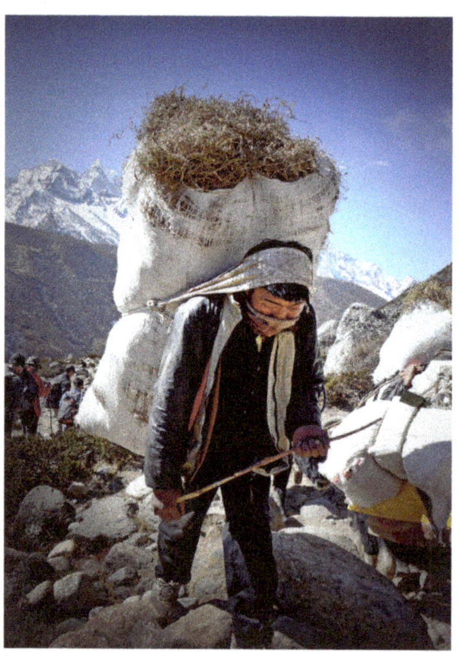

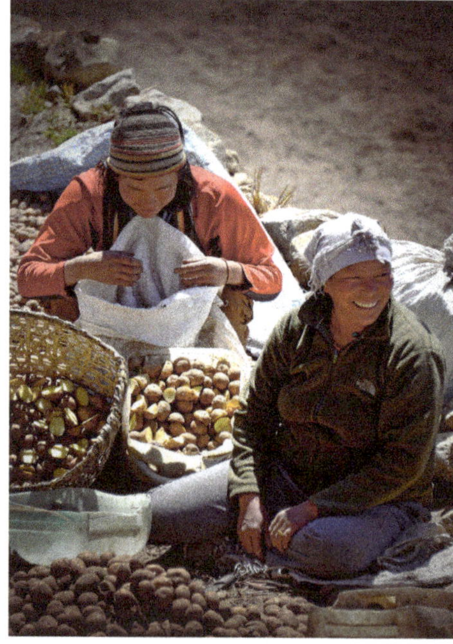

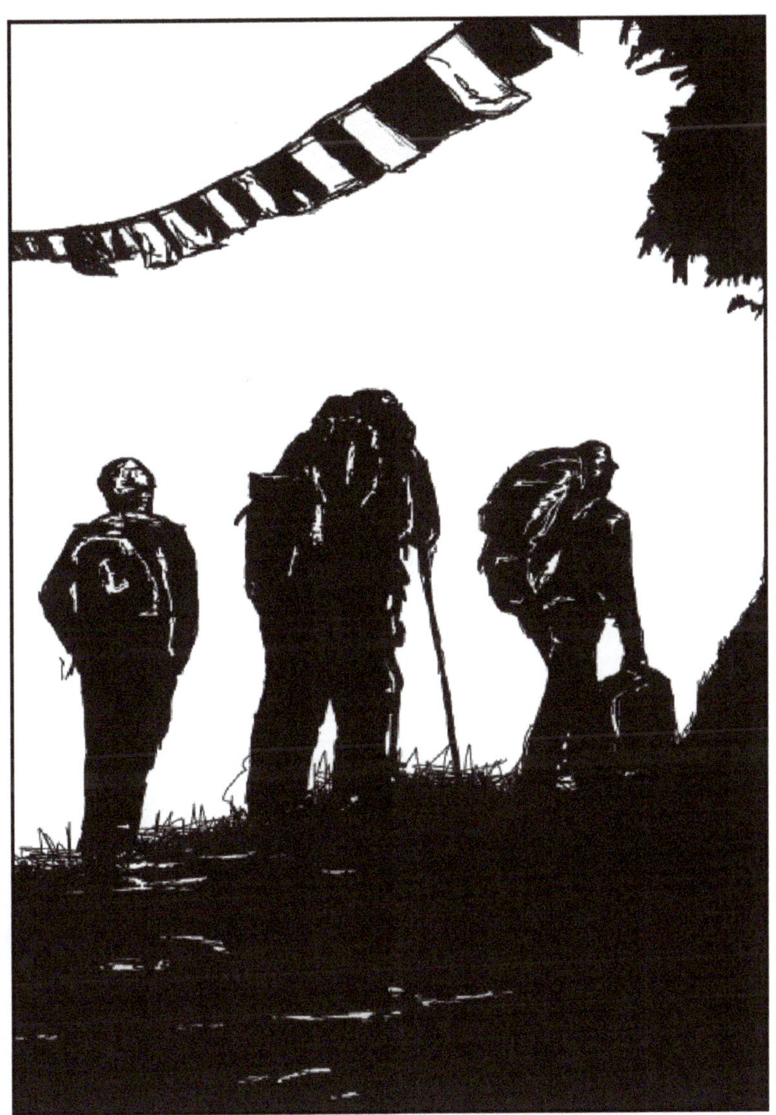

As we trek all you see are backpacks and the ground
As you climb those damn steps, sometimes up sometimes down
You are focused and tired, climbing steady climbing slow
As the scenery passes by all covered in snow
As I raise my head slow to scan what's there to see
3 trekkers with their packs head down just like me
So slow and so steep the mountains large they do rise
I finally reach the top, yerahhh now where is my prize?
In a line we all wander up the hills with our guides
Until we reach the very top to the vistas oh so wide.

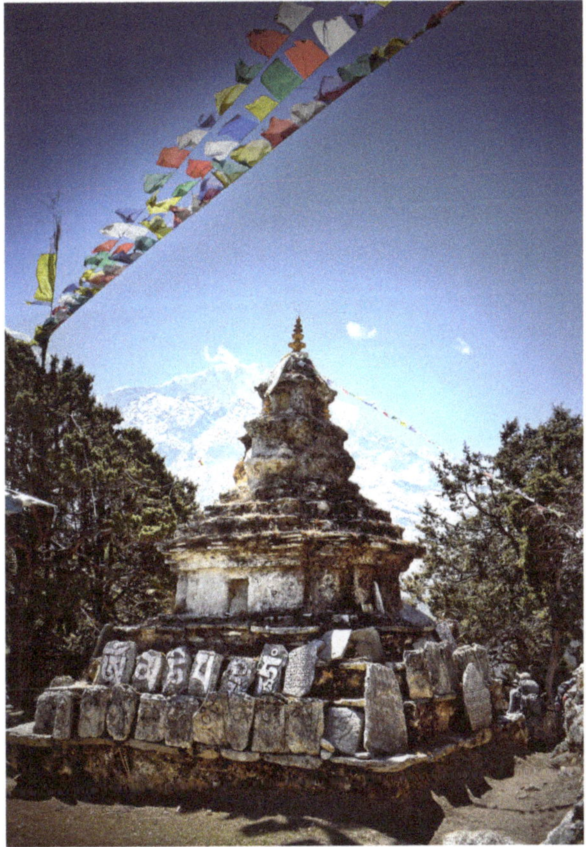

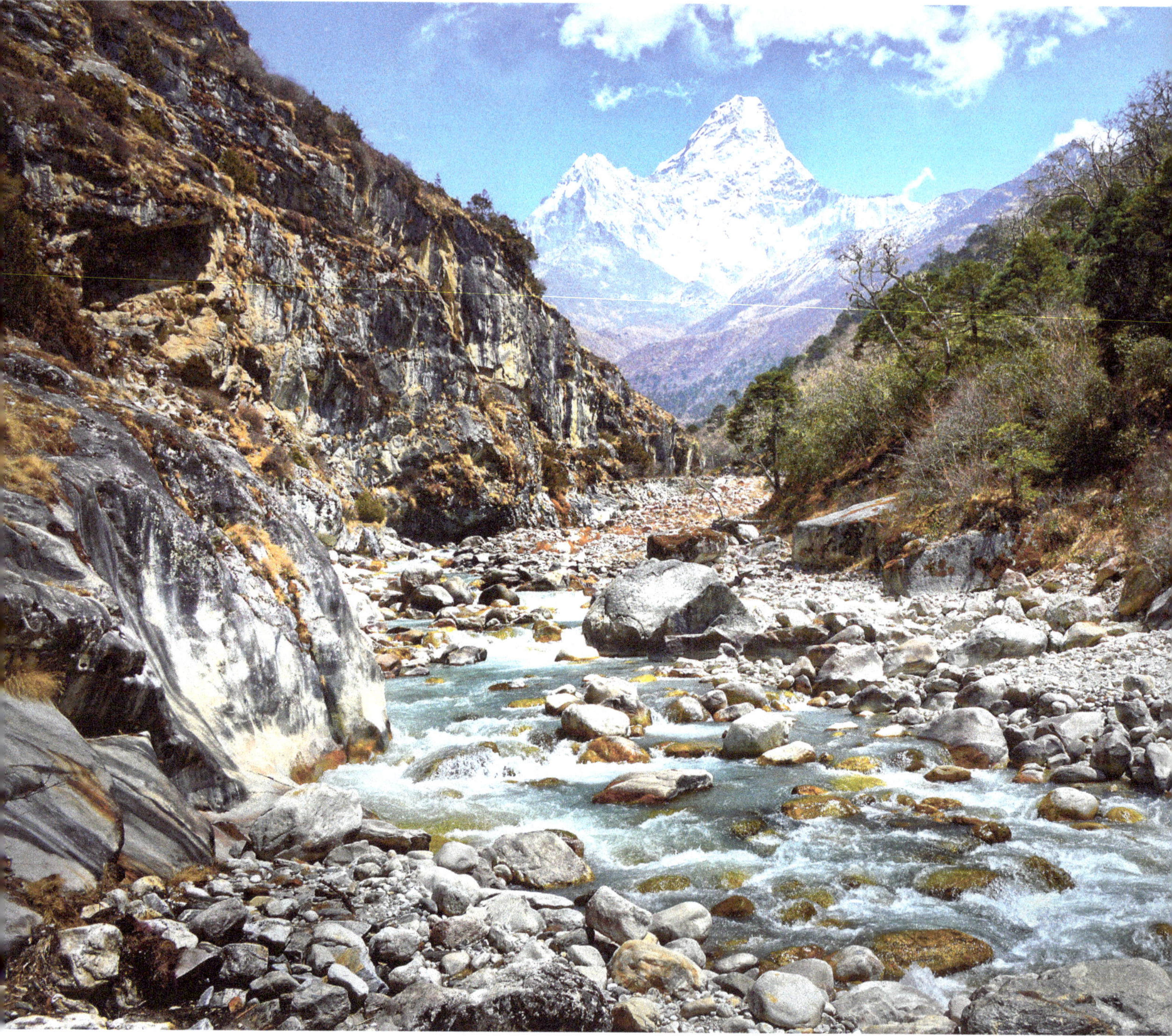

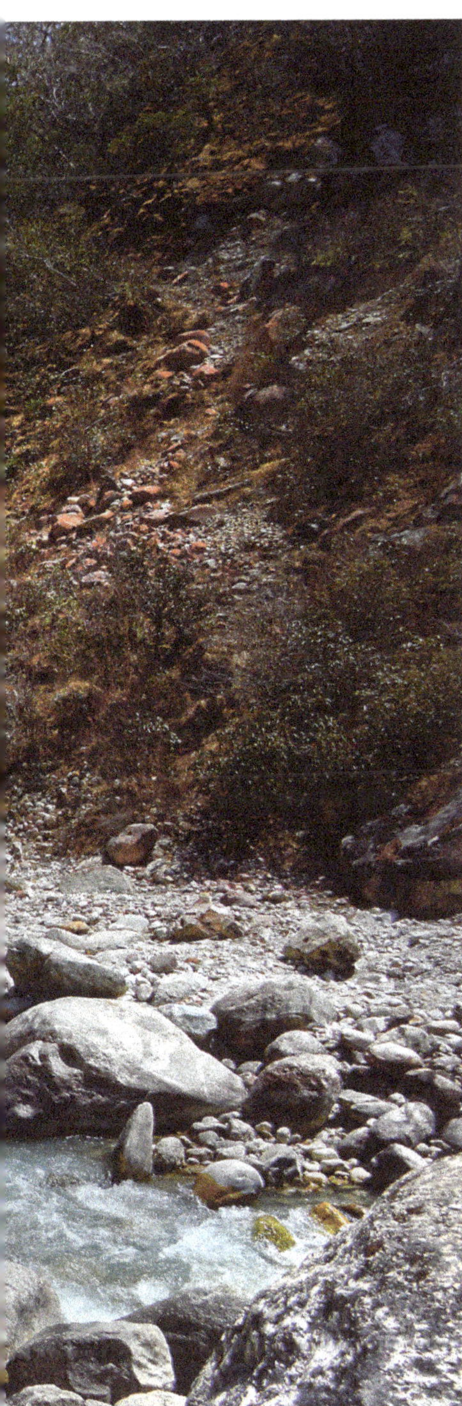

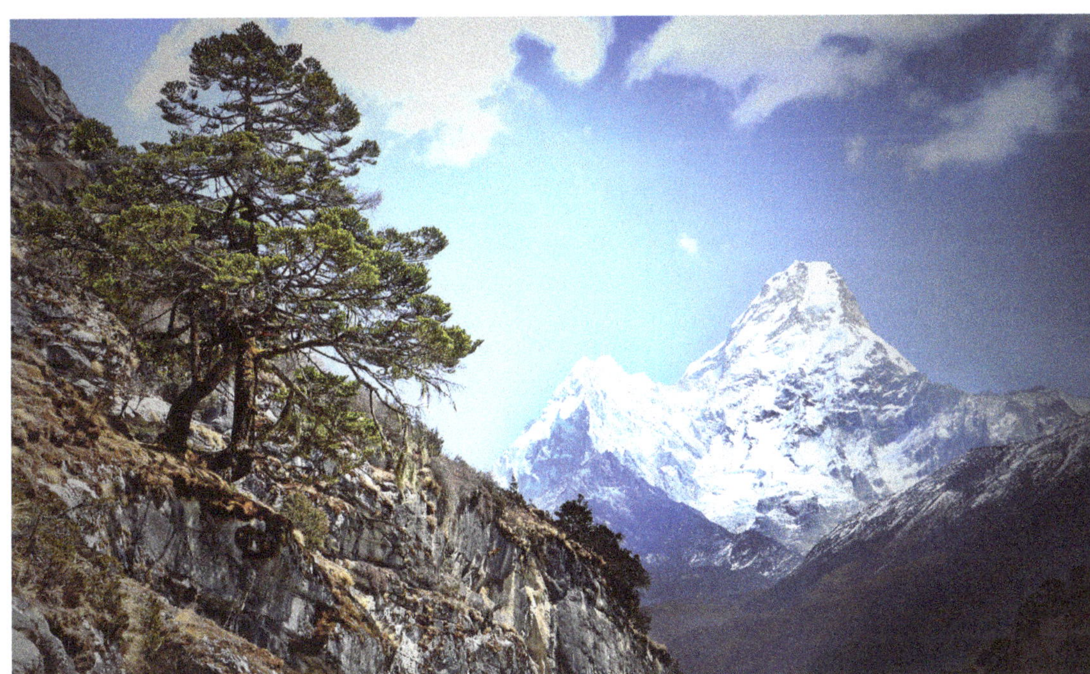

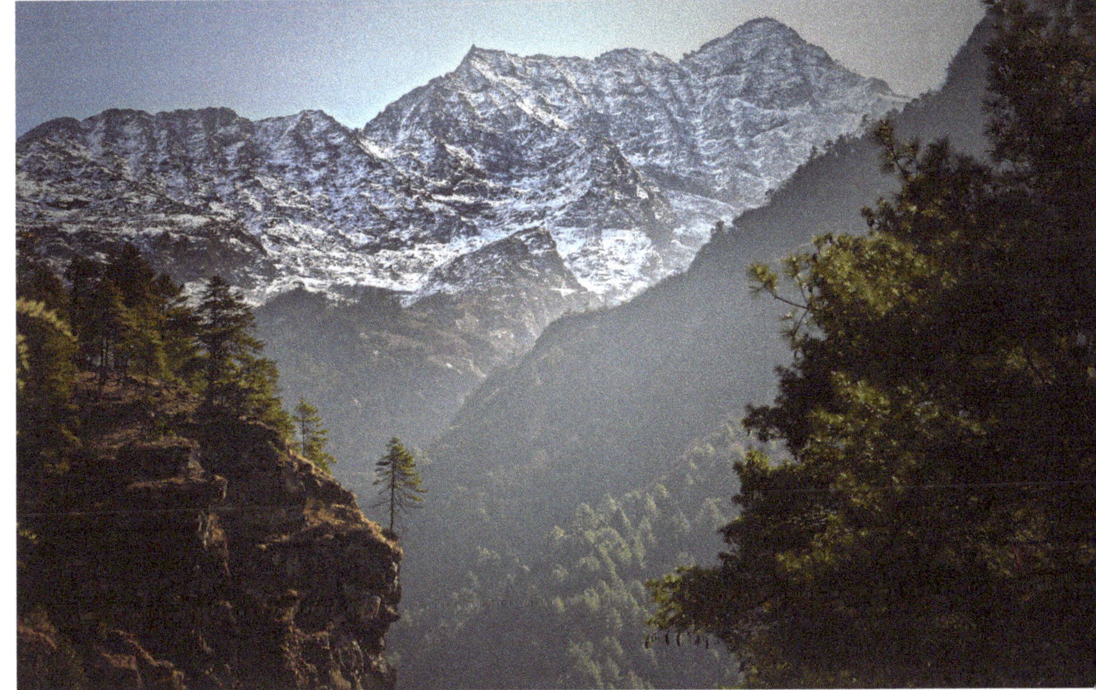

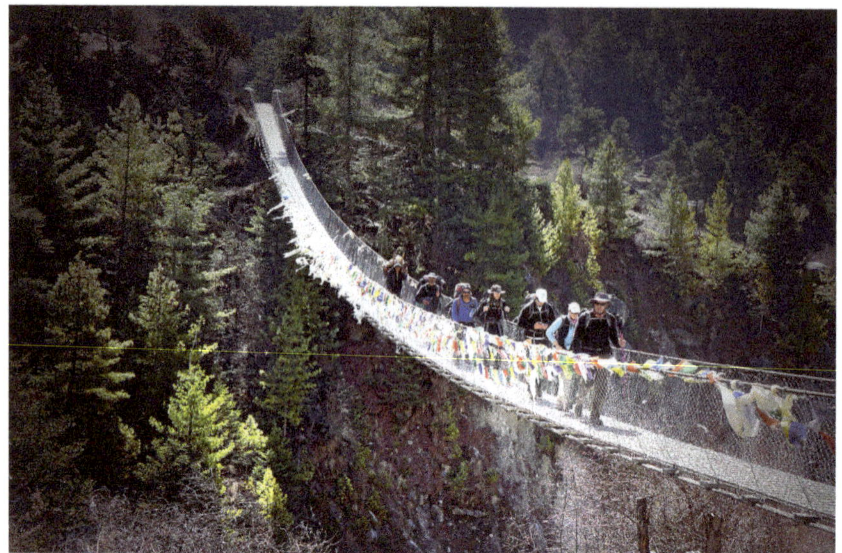

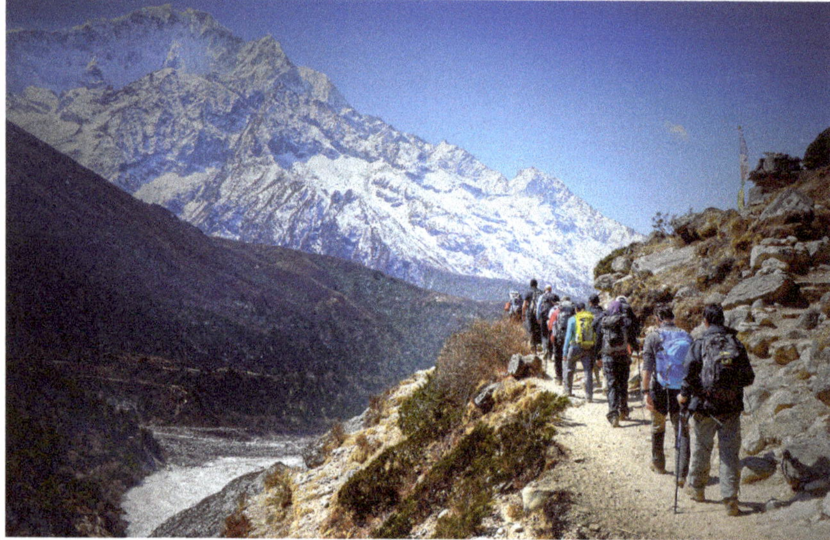

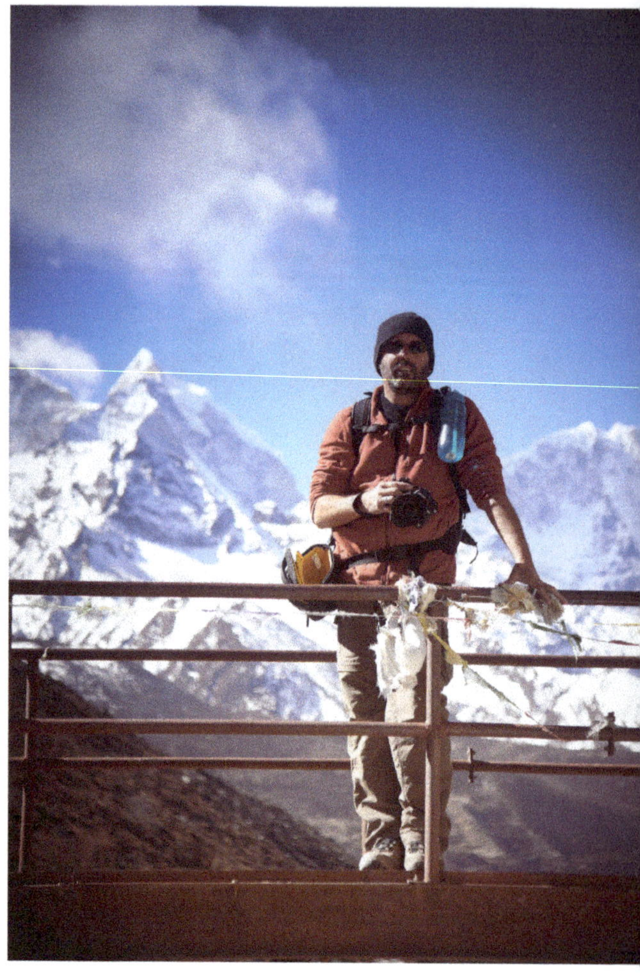

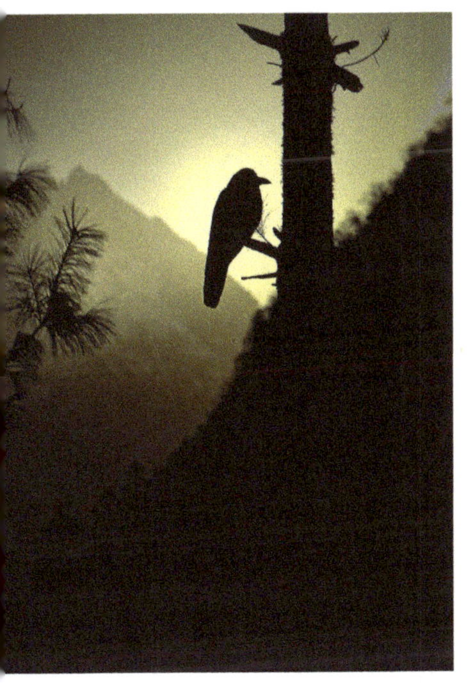
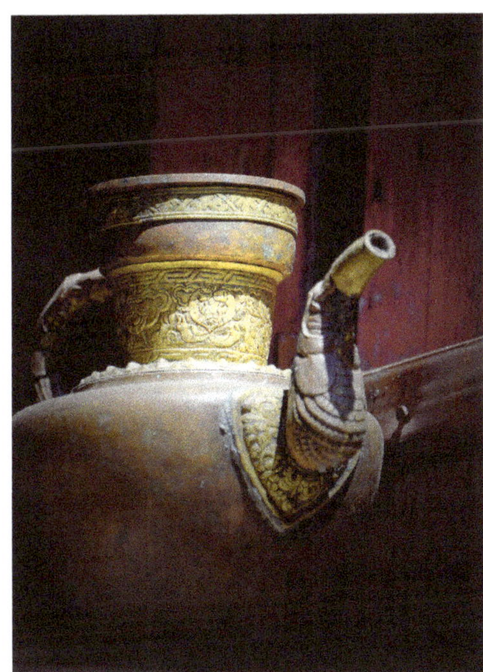
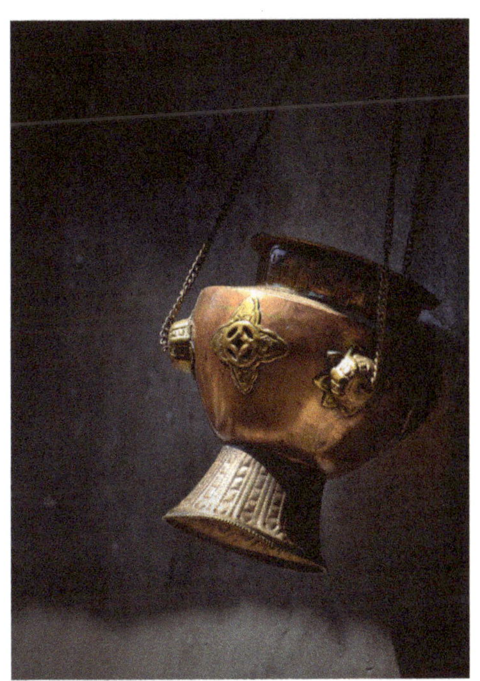
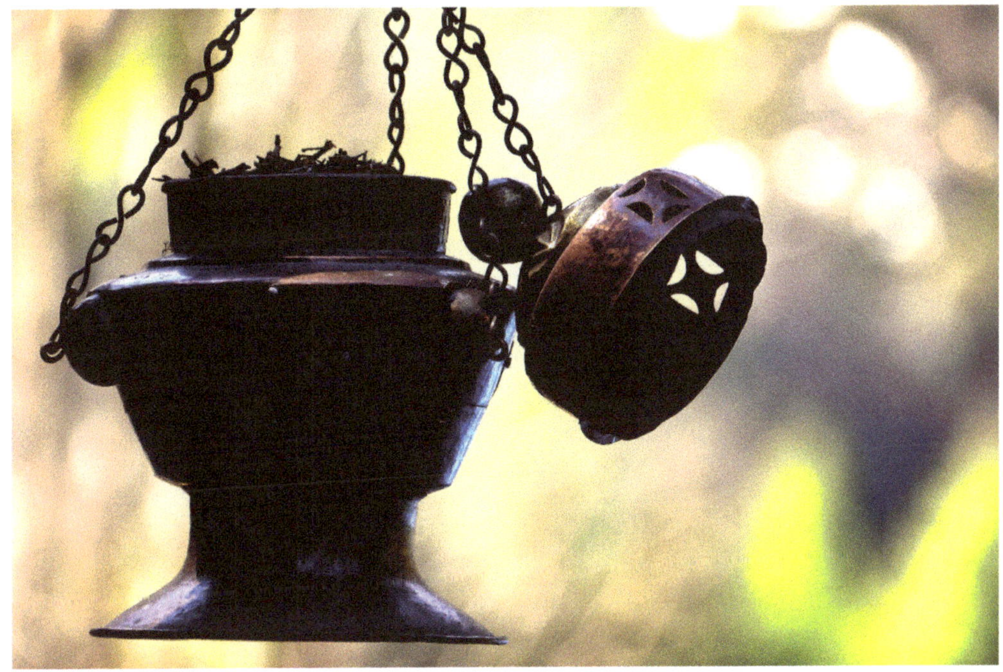

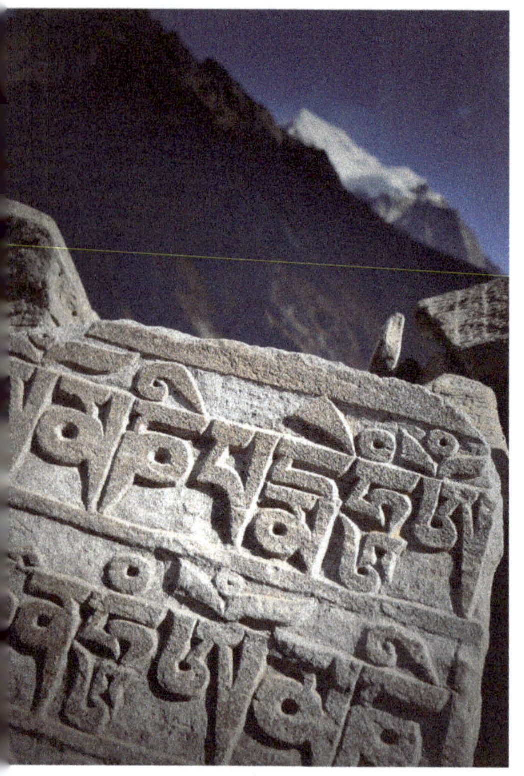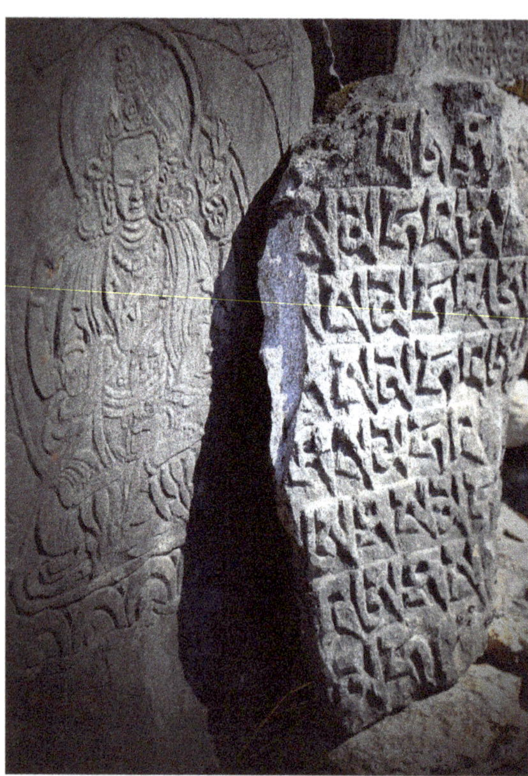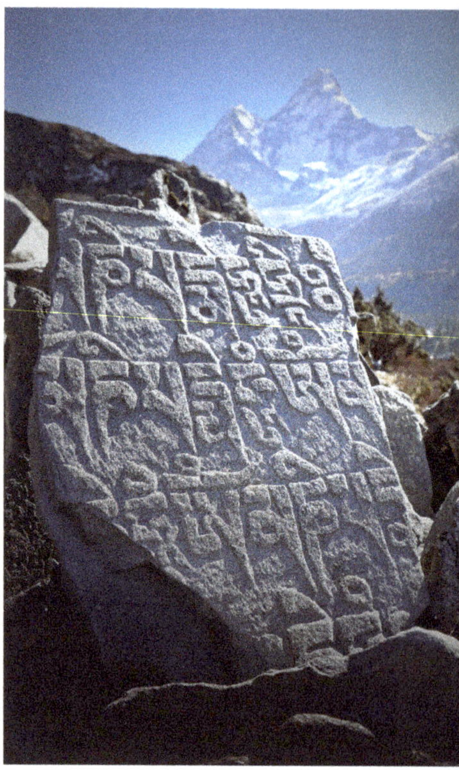

Mani Stones

All along the trail are the Mani Stones and tablets. These all have Buddhist prayers carved into the stone and they are to do with making the path protected by the good spirits. I loved seeing them placed as walls or as monument structures along the trail as they seemed to guide you along. I took heaps of photos, trying to show the lettering and placements of them and trying to convey their importance to trekkers in the region. Seeing them day in day out really enforced the spiritual journey we were on.

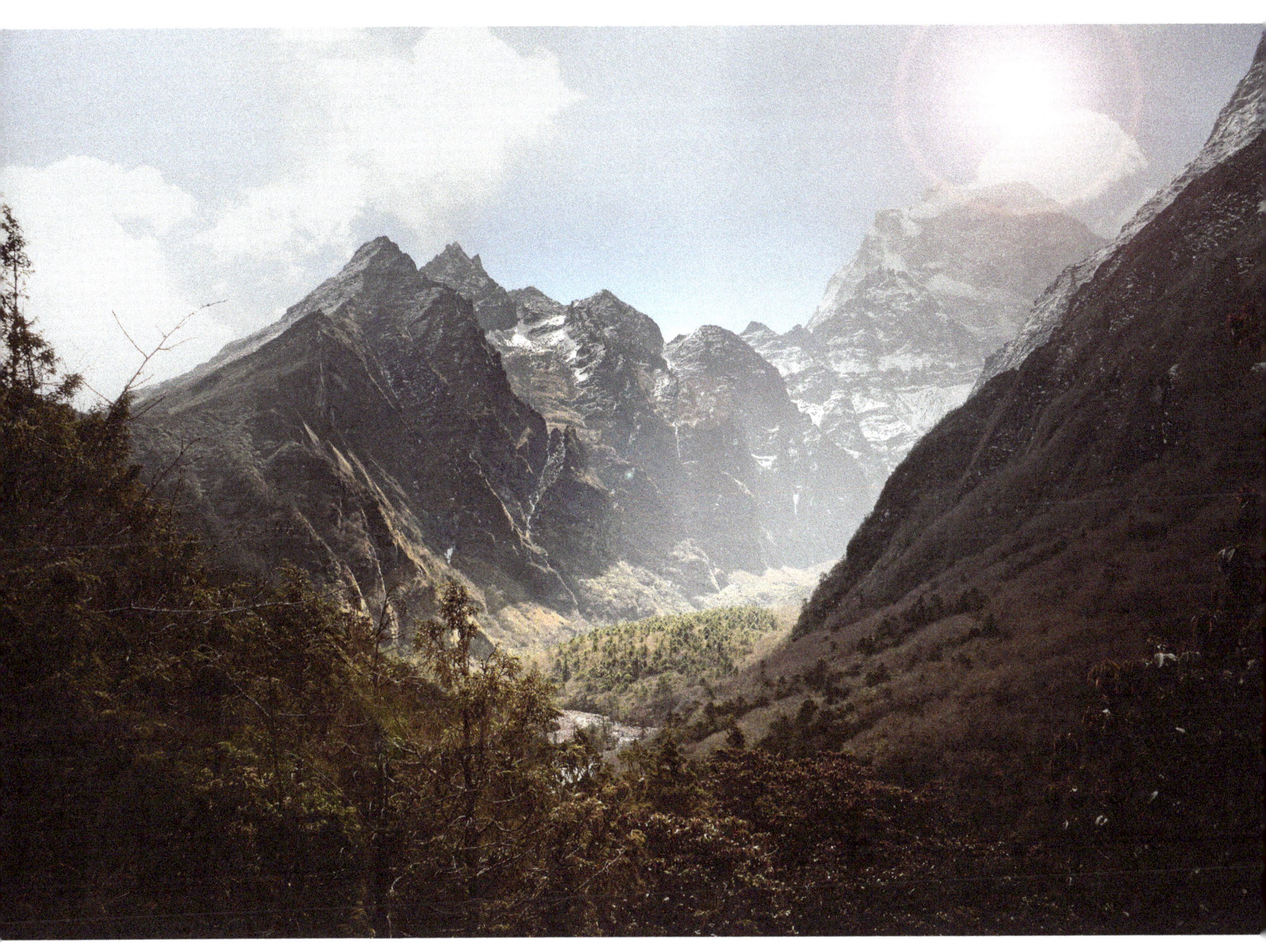

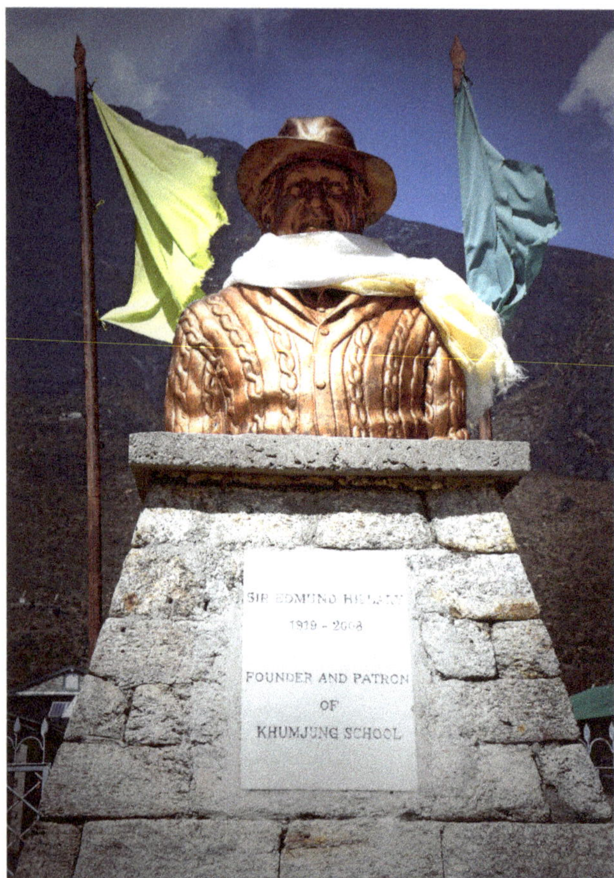

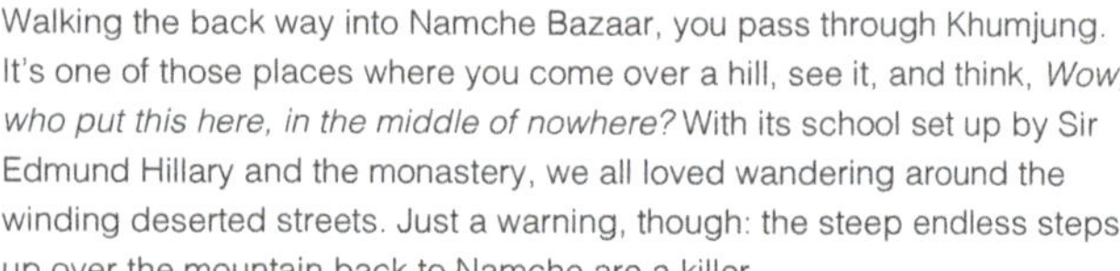

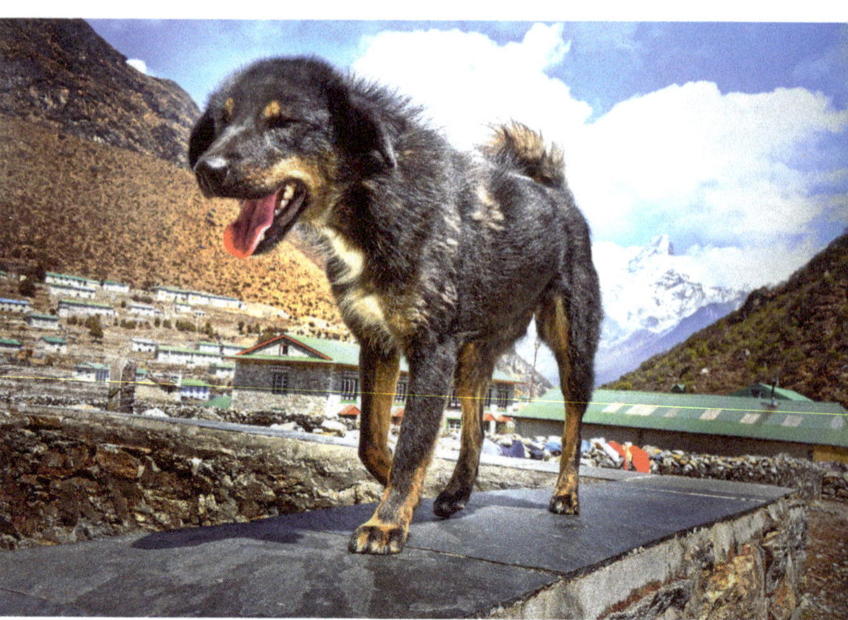

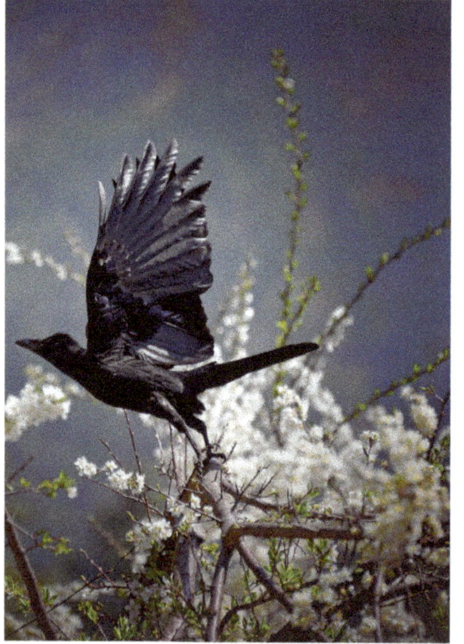

Walking the back way into Namche Bazaar, you pass through Khumjung.
It's one of those places where you come over a hill, see it, and think, *Wow,
who put this here, in the middle of nowhere?* With its school set up by Sir
Edmund Hillary and the monastery, we all loved wandering around the
winding deserted streets. Just a warning, though: the steep endless steps
up over the mountain back to Namche are a killer.

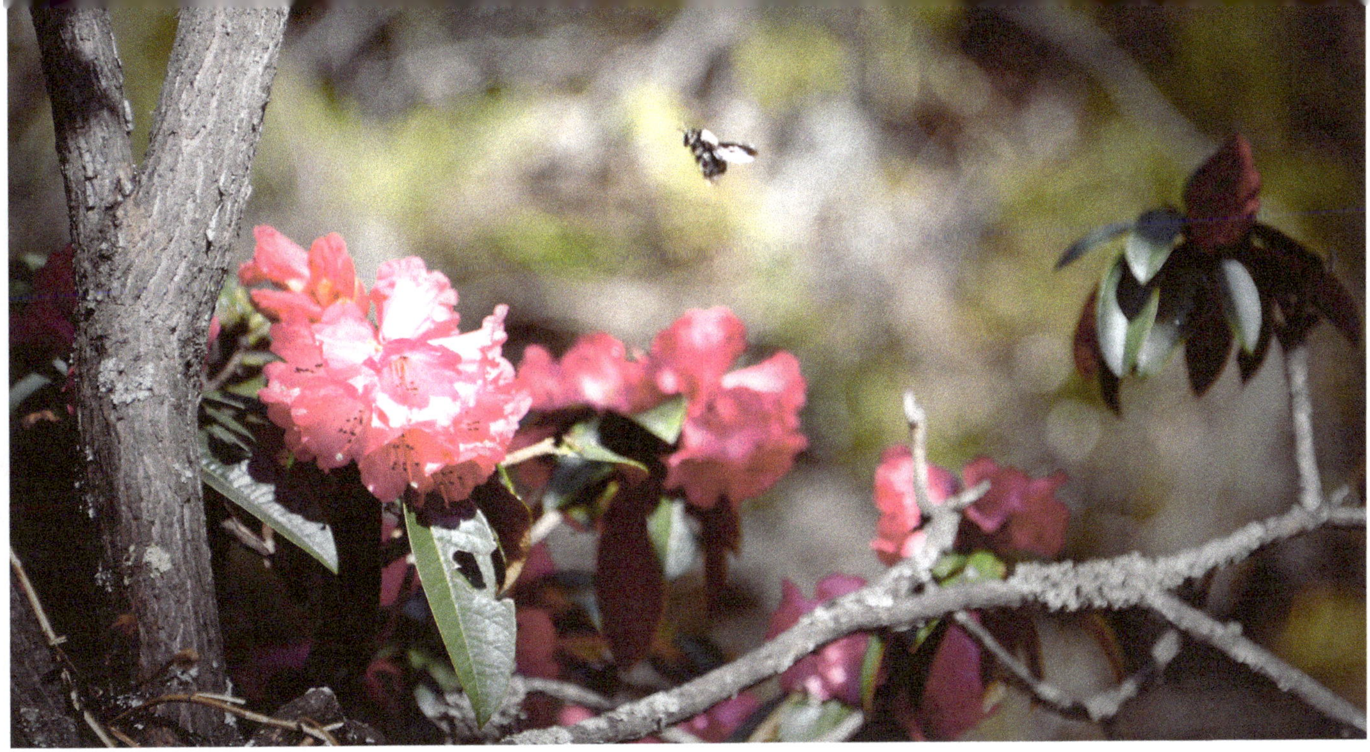

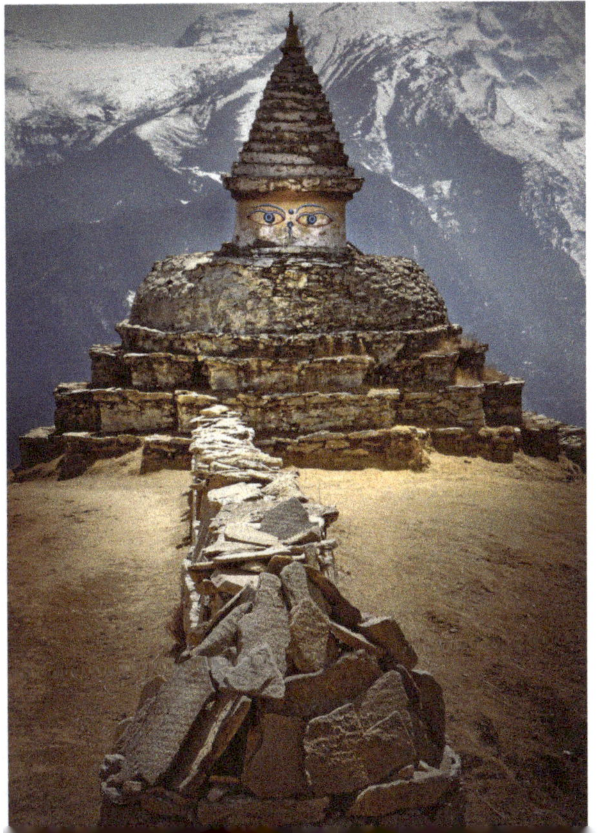

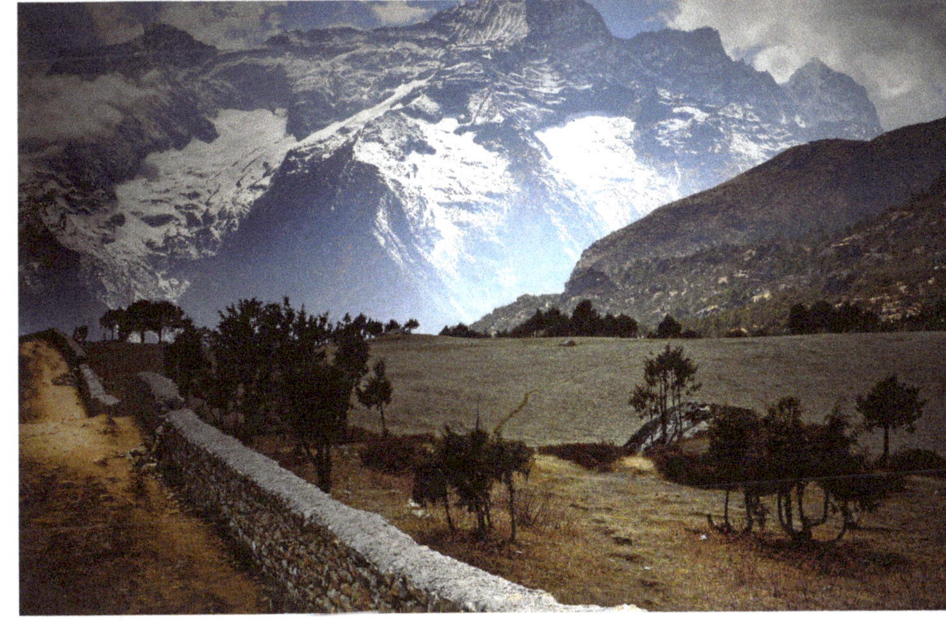

Khumjung Monastery

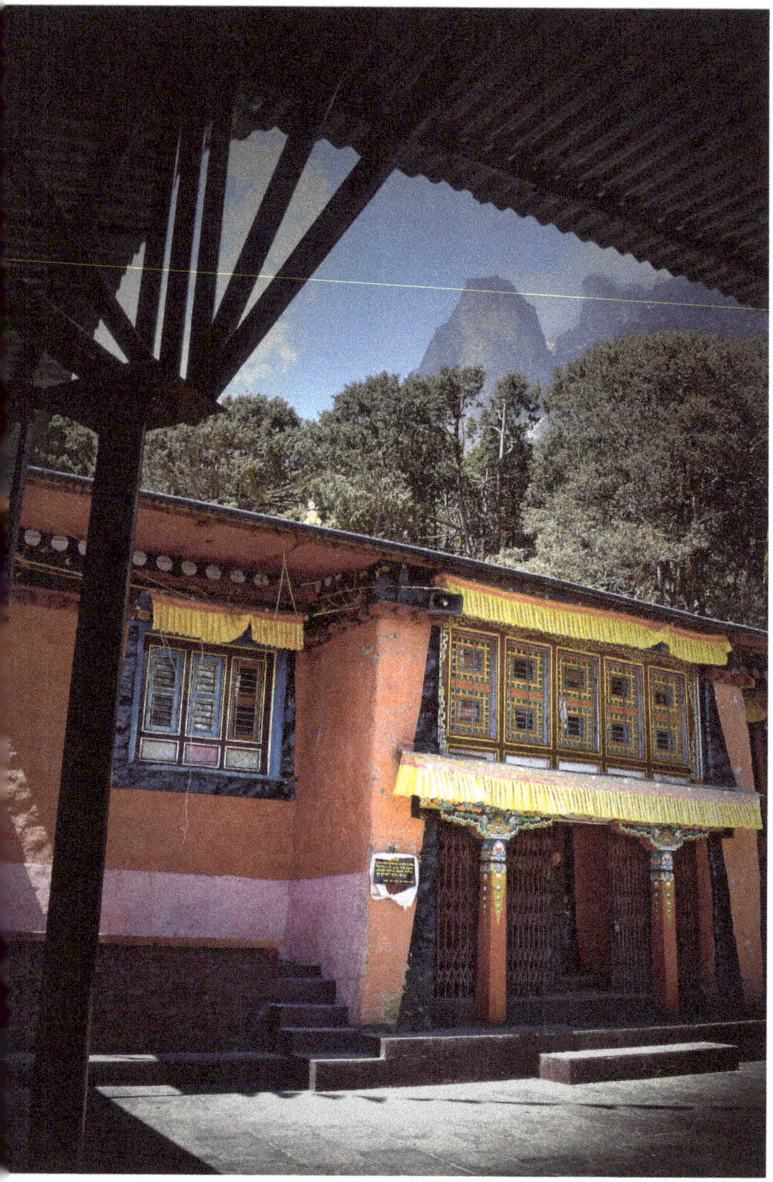

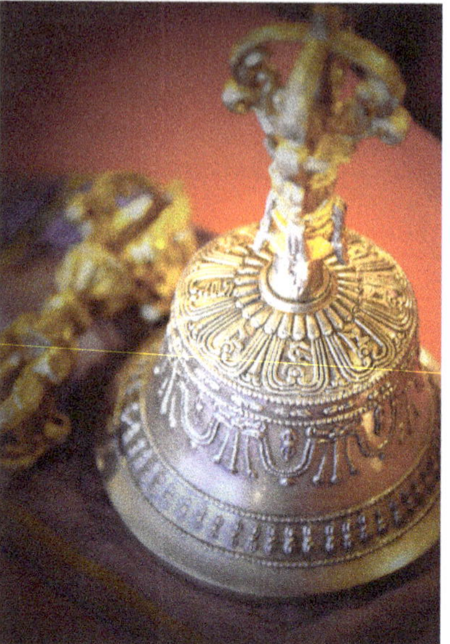

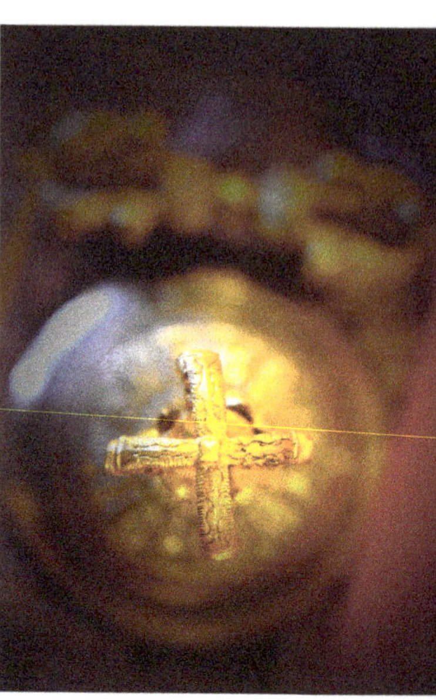

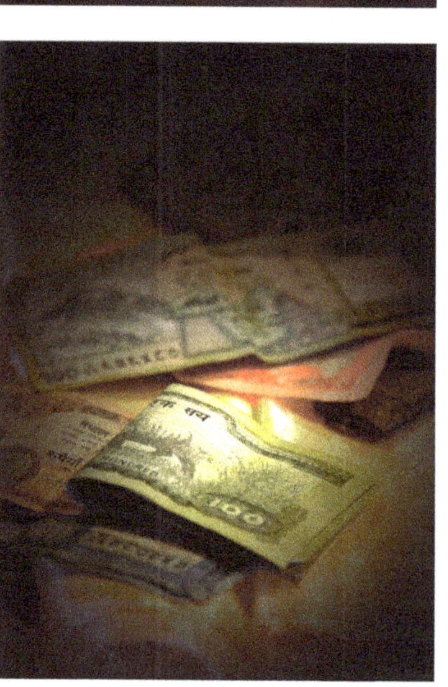

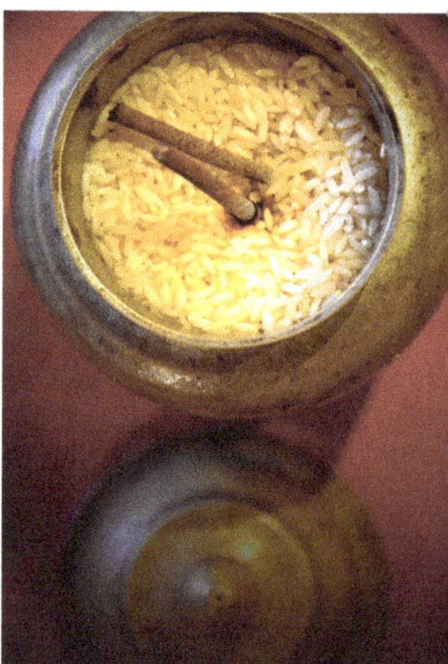

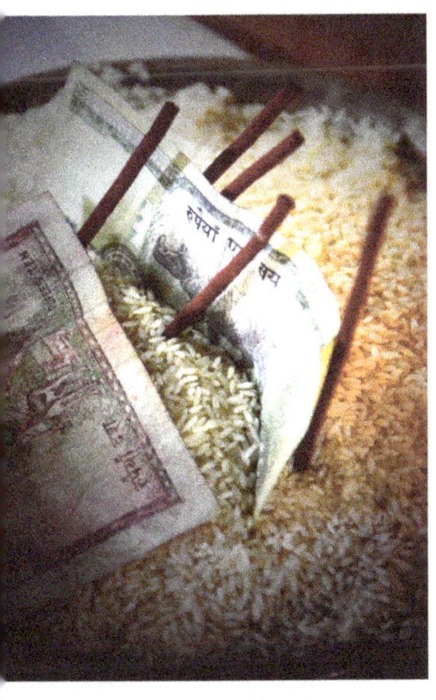
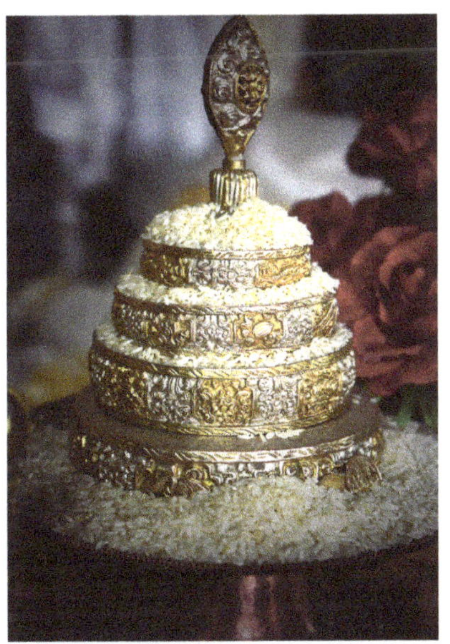
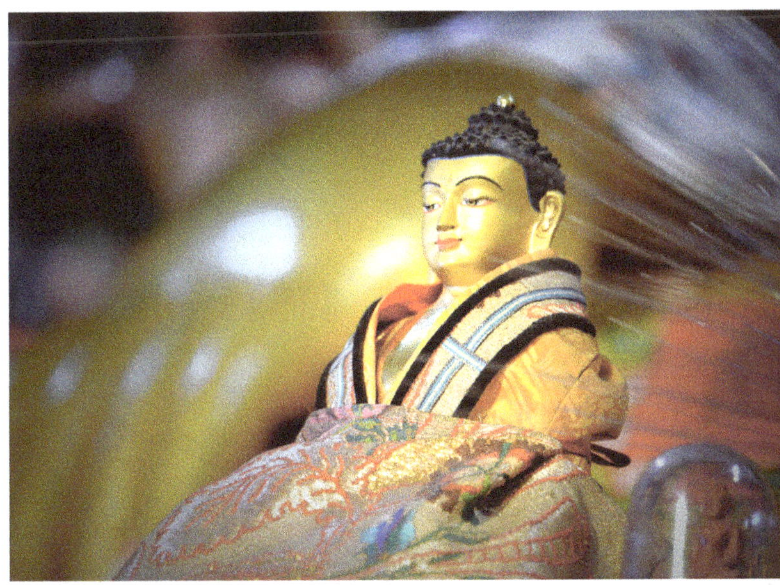
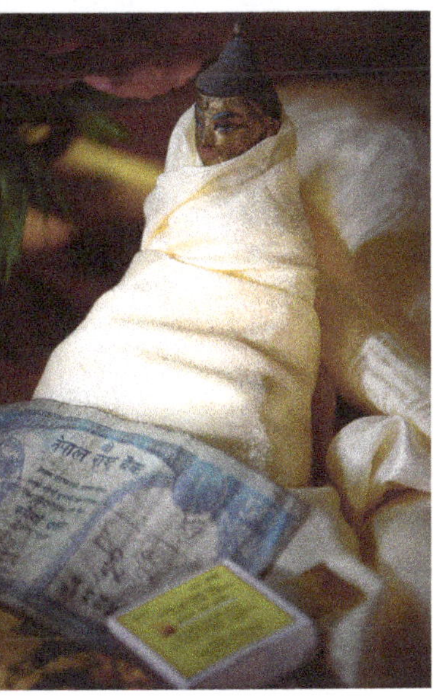
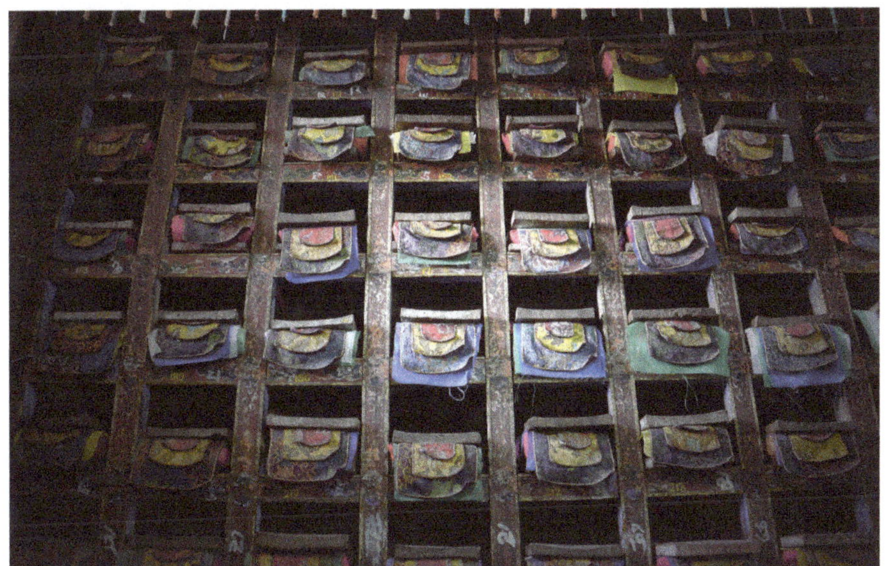

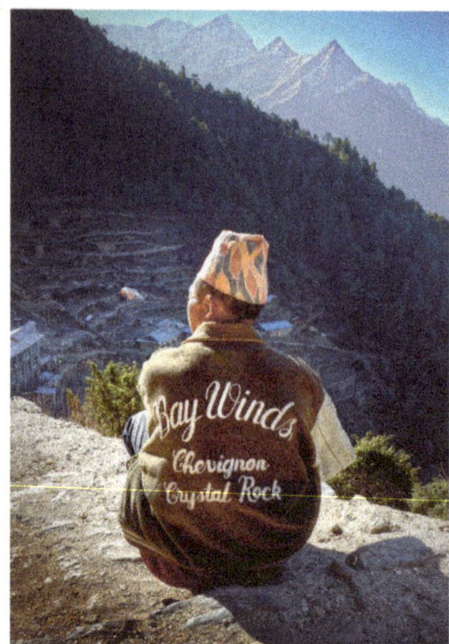

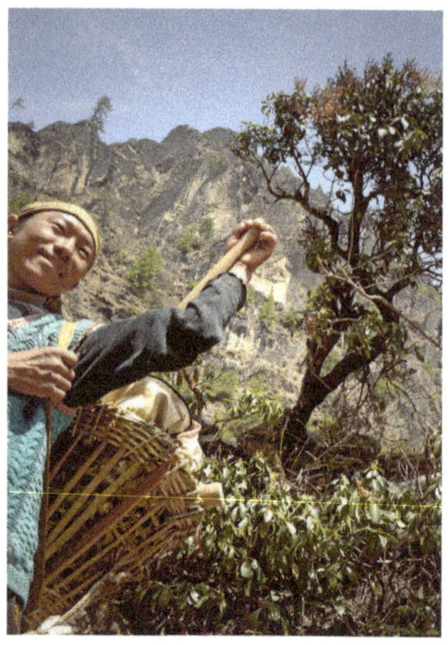

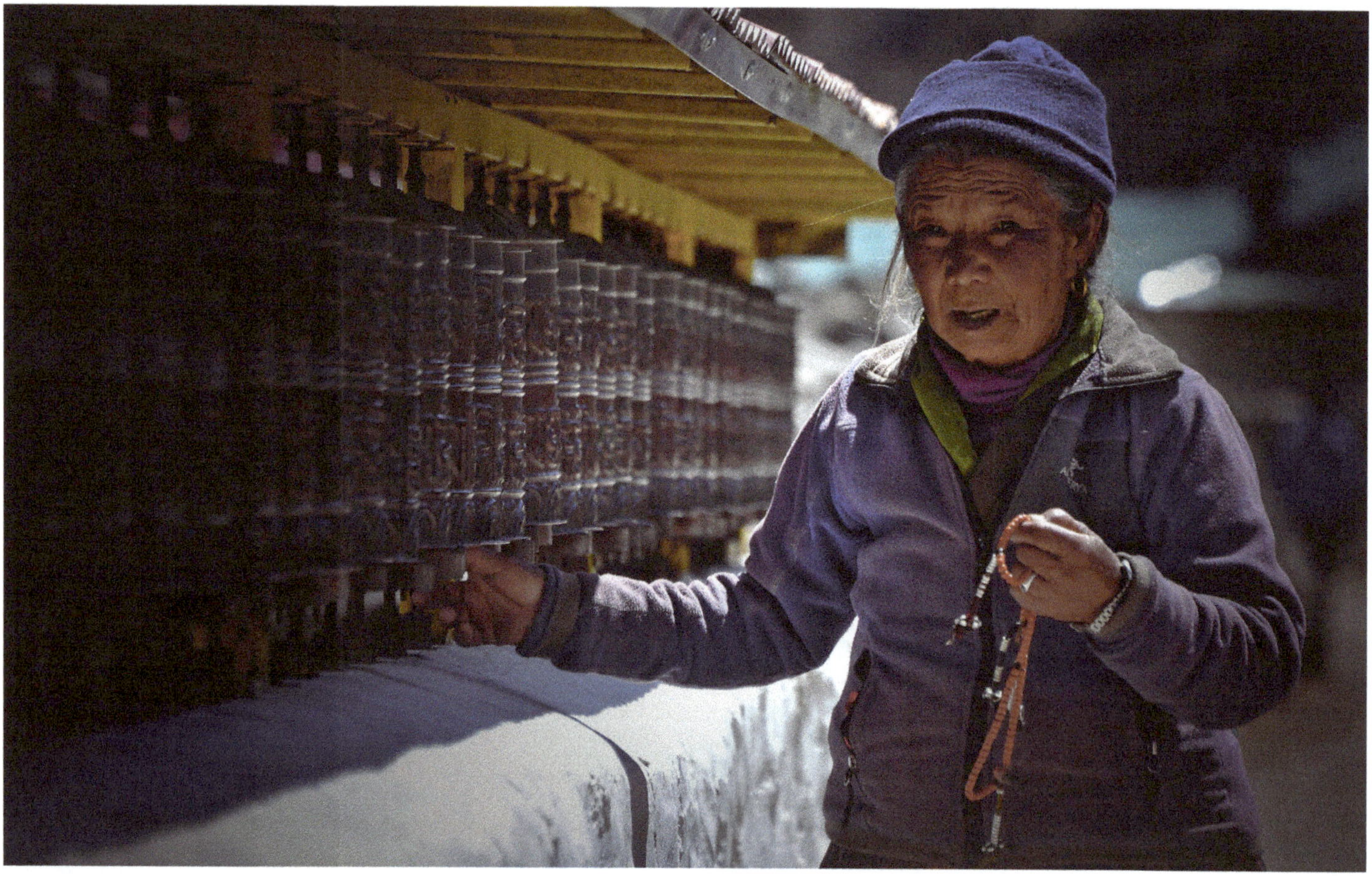

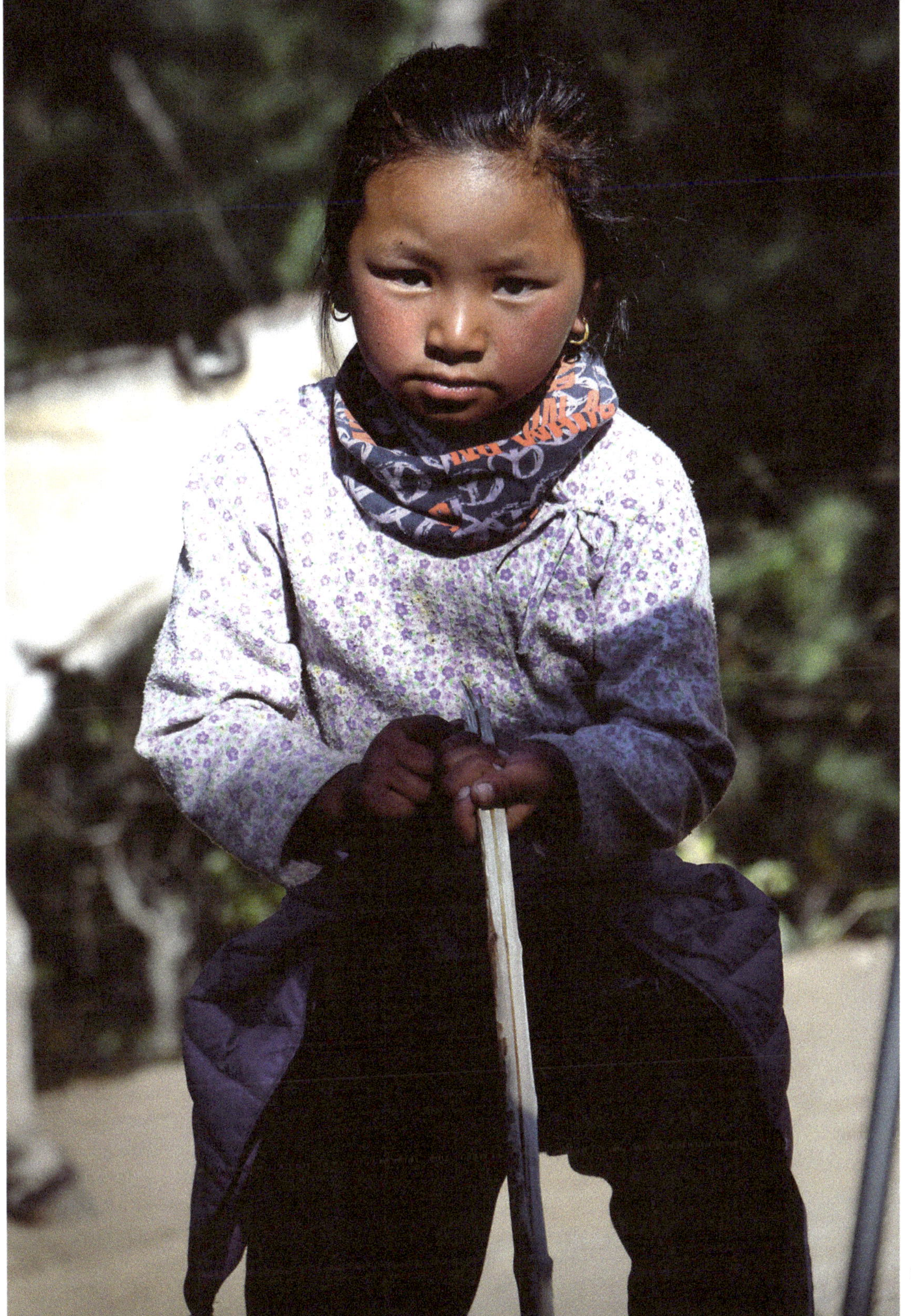

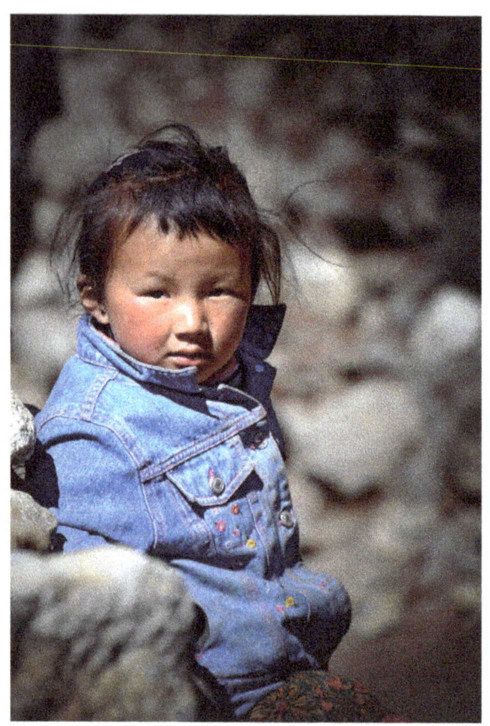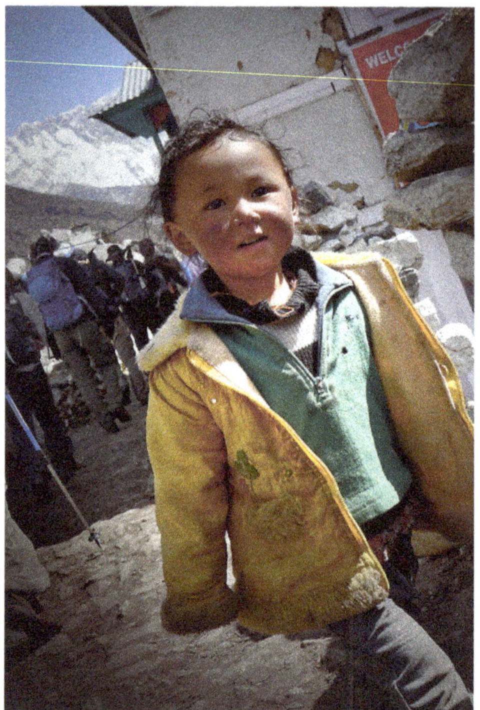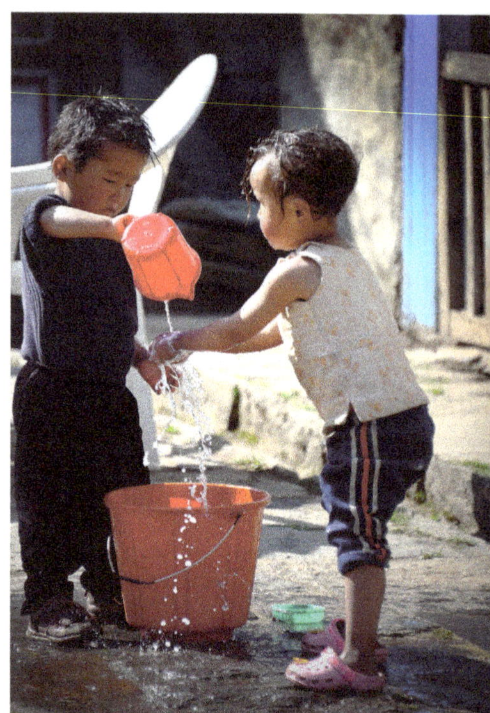

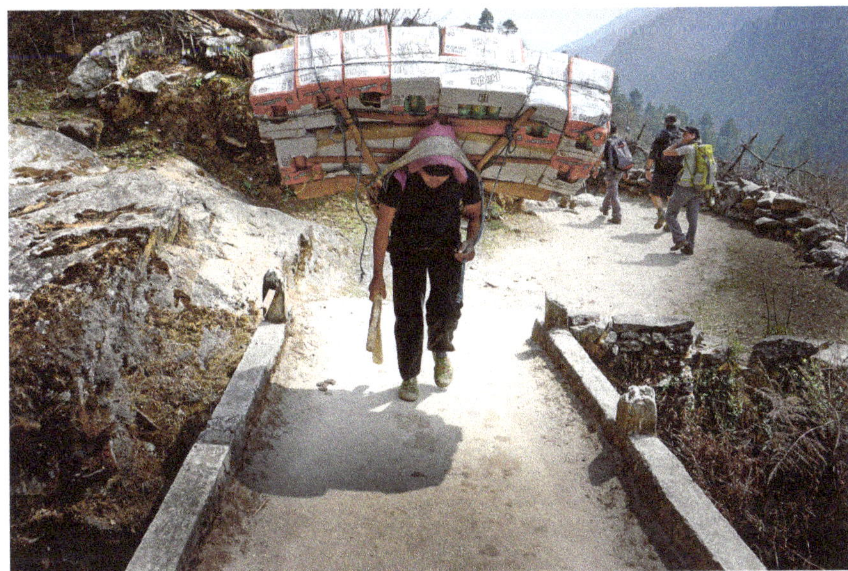

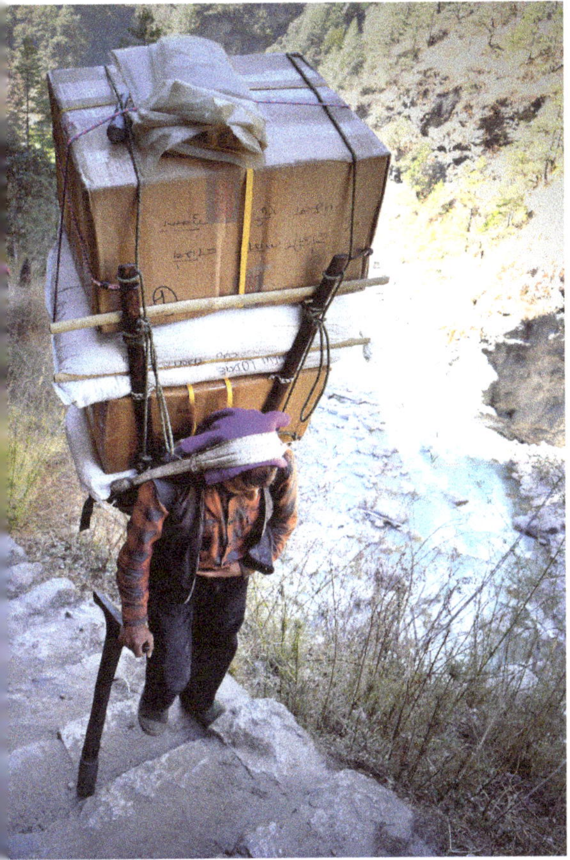

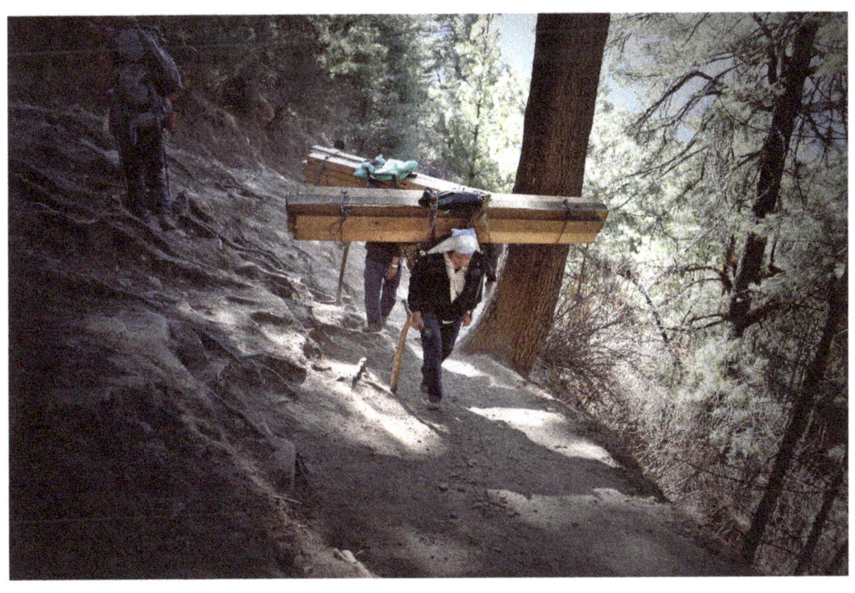

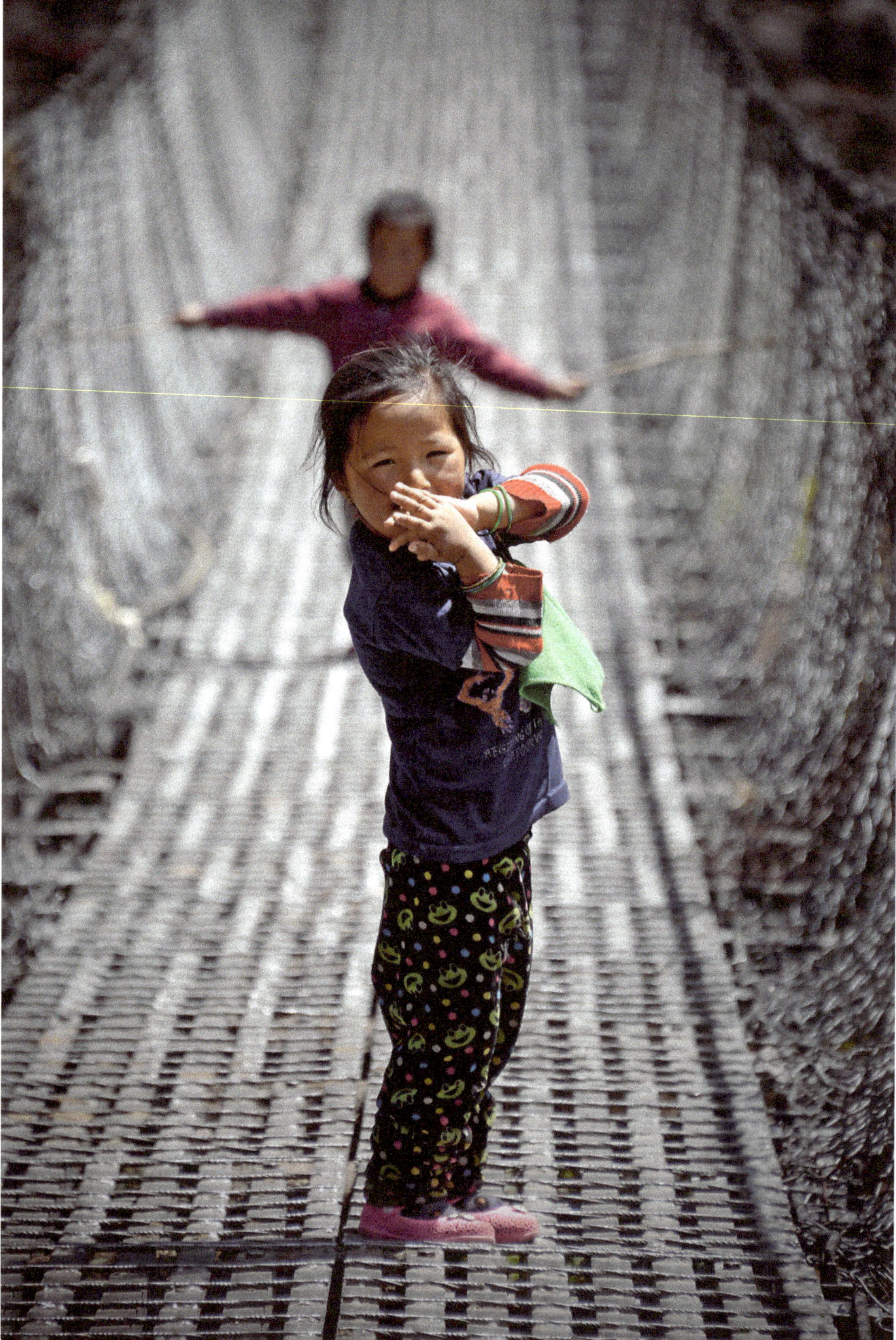

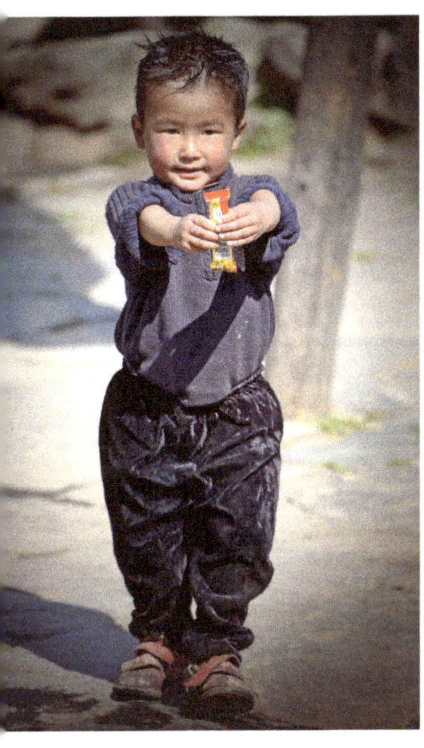
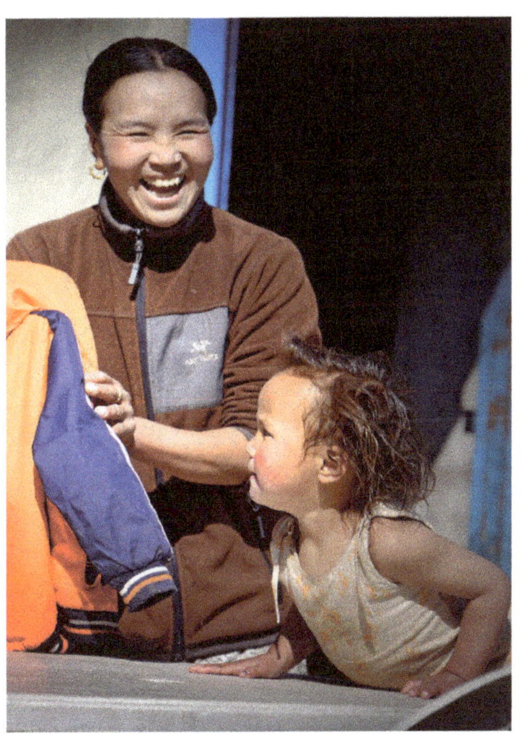
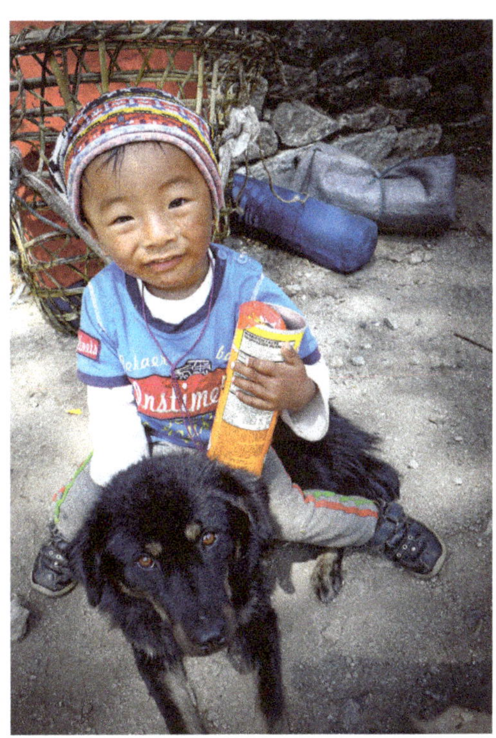

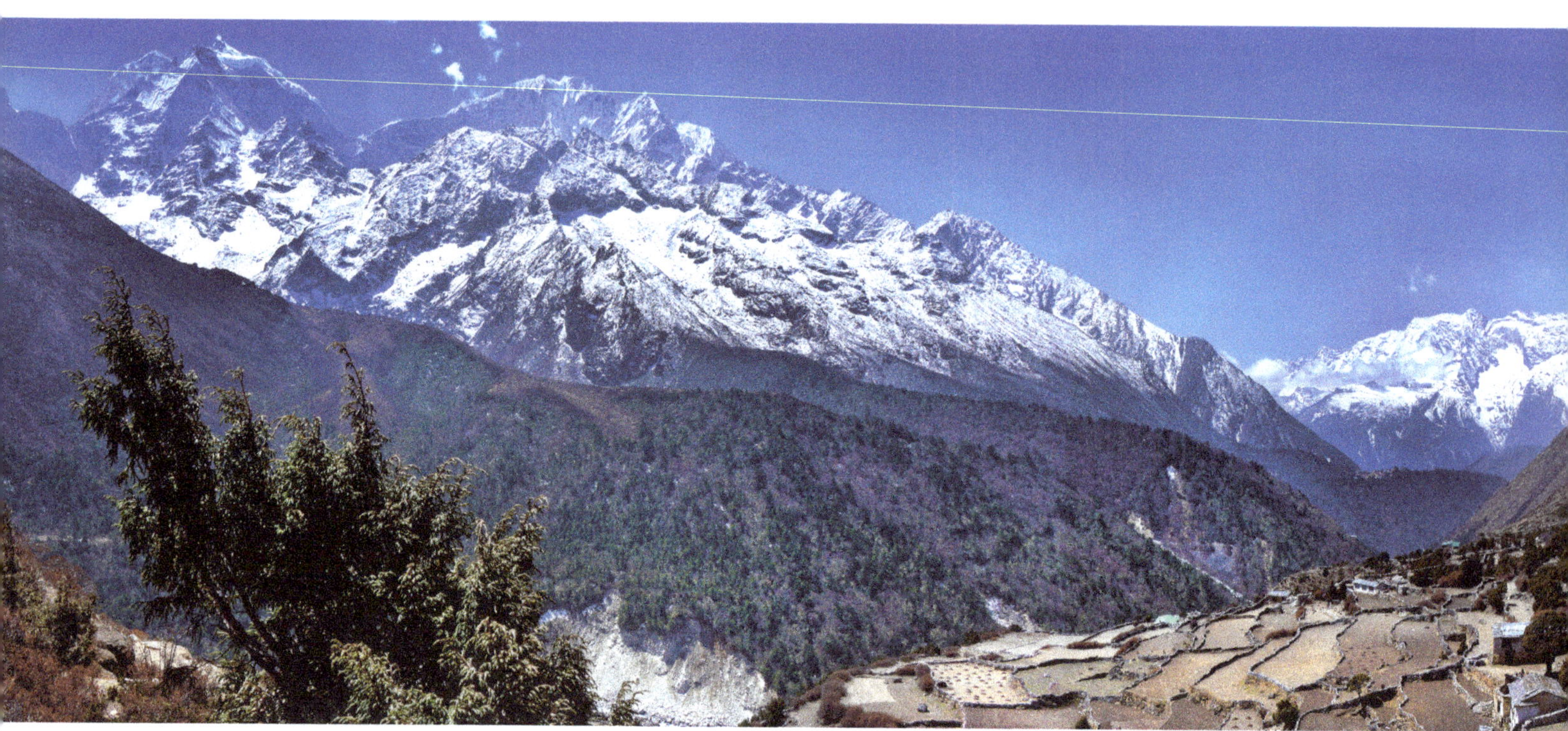

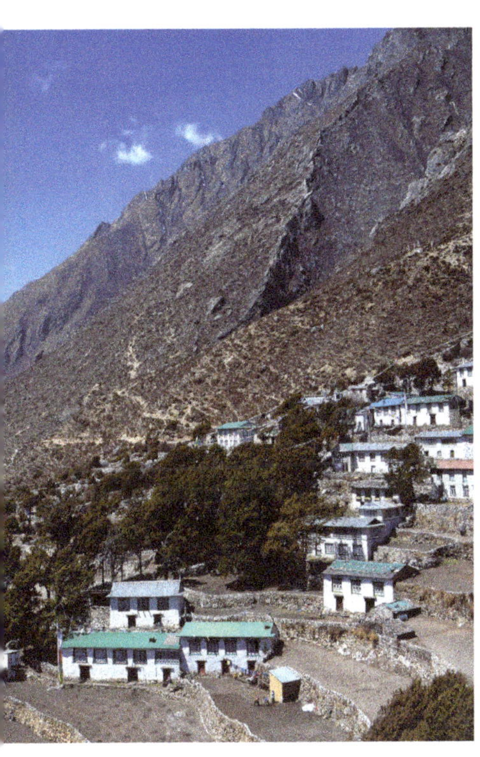

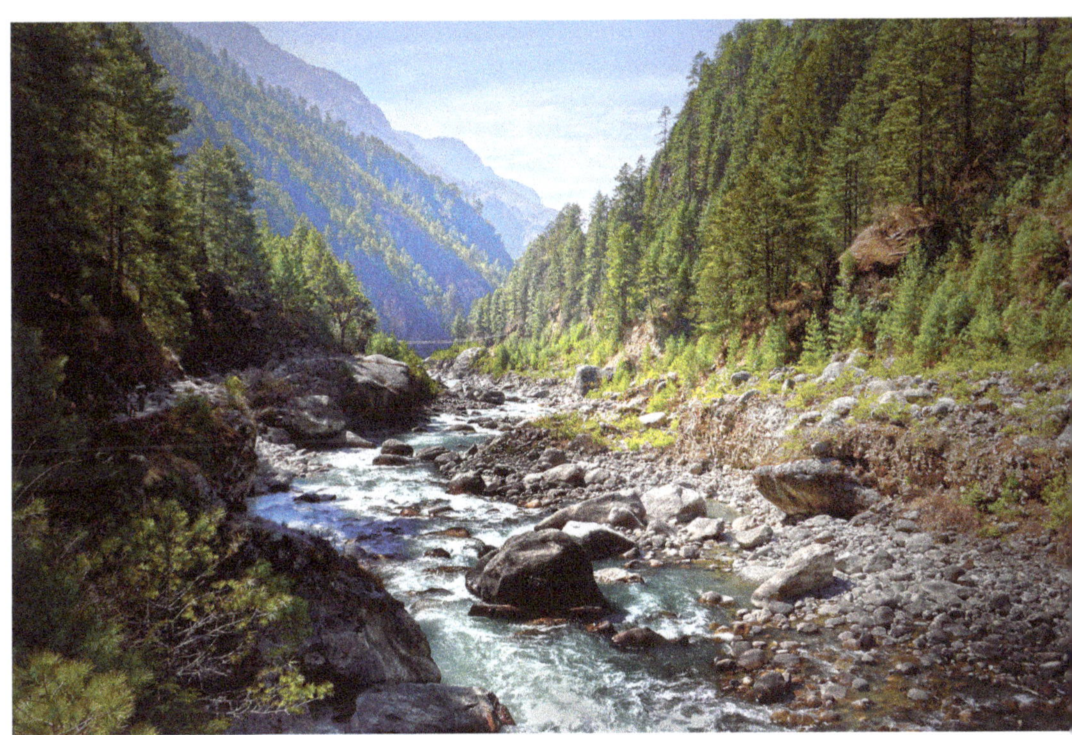

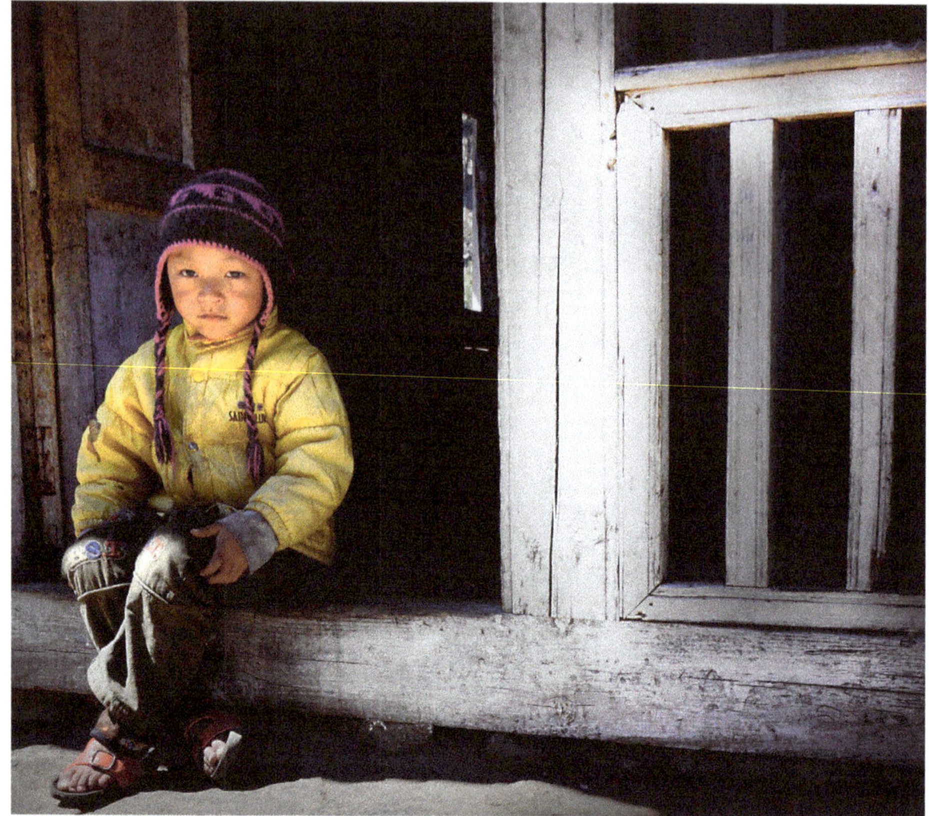

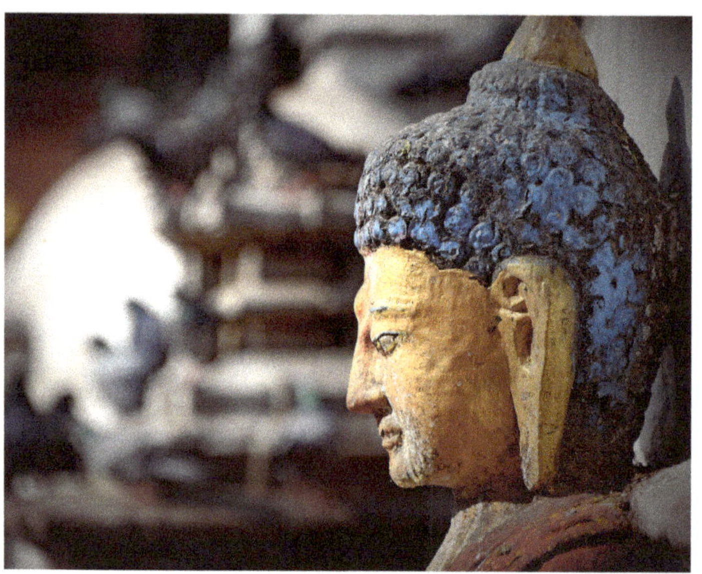

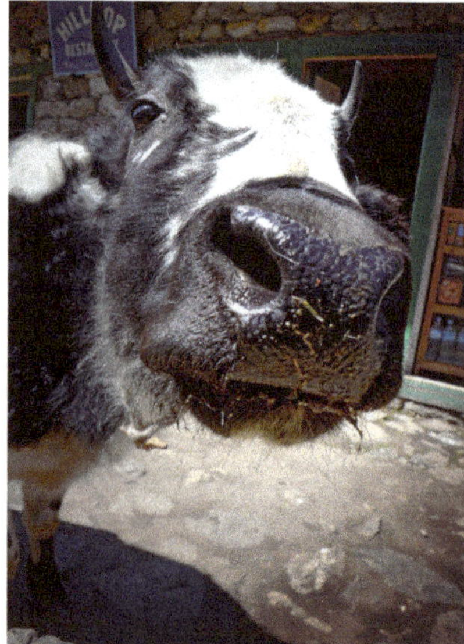

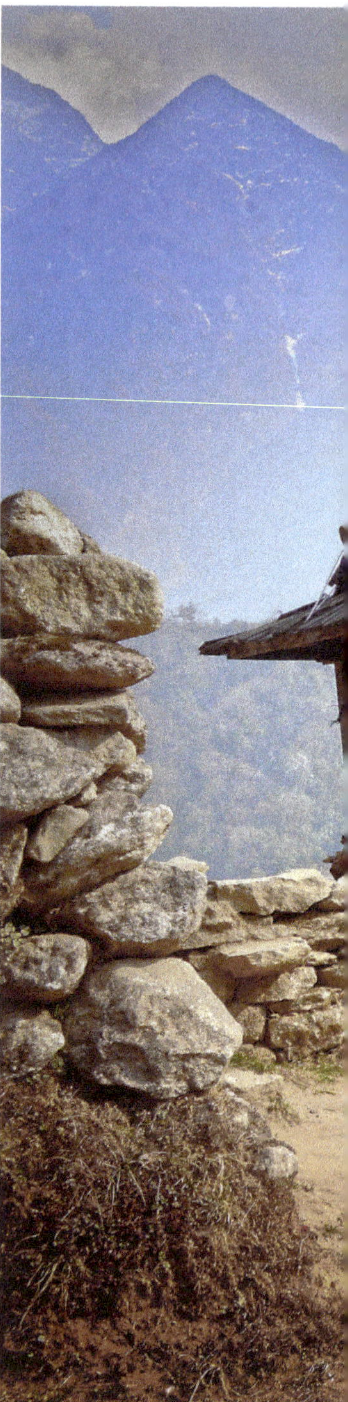

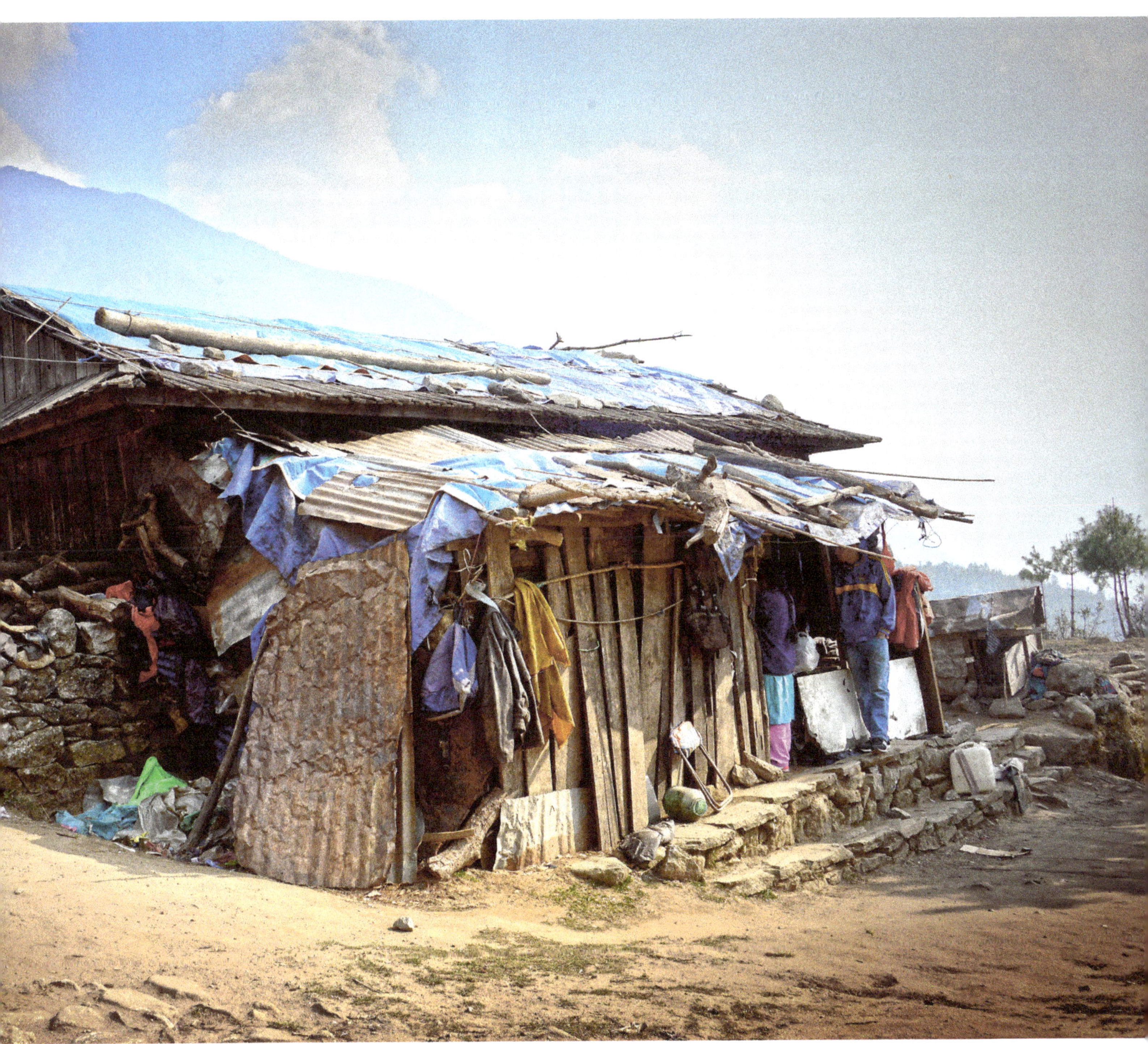

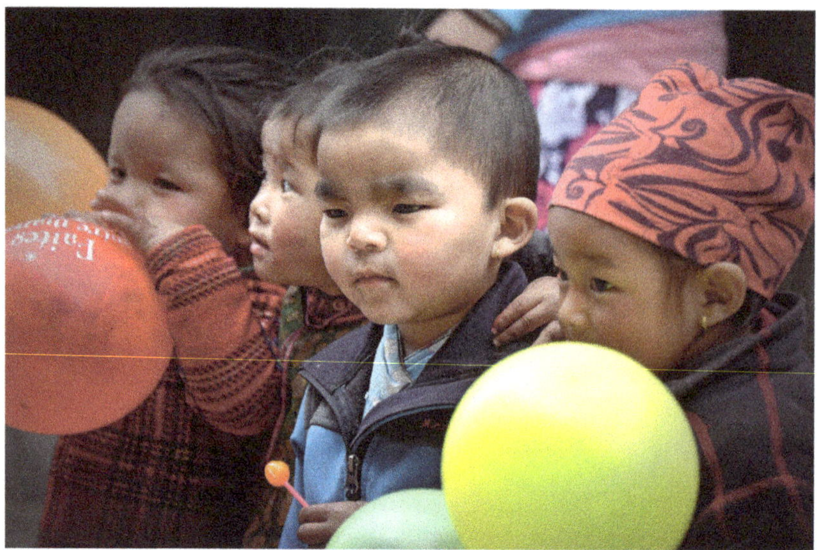

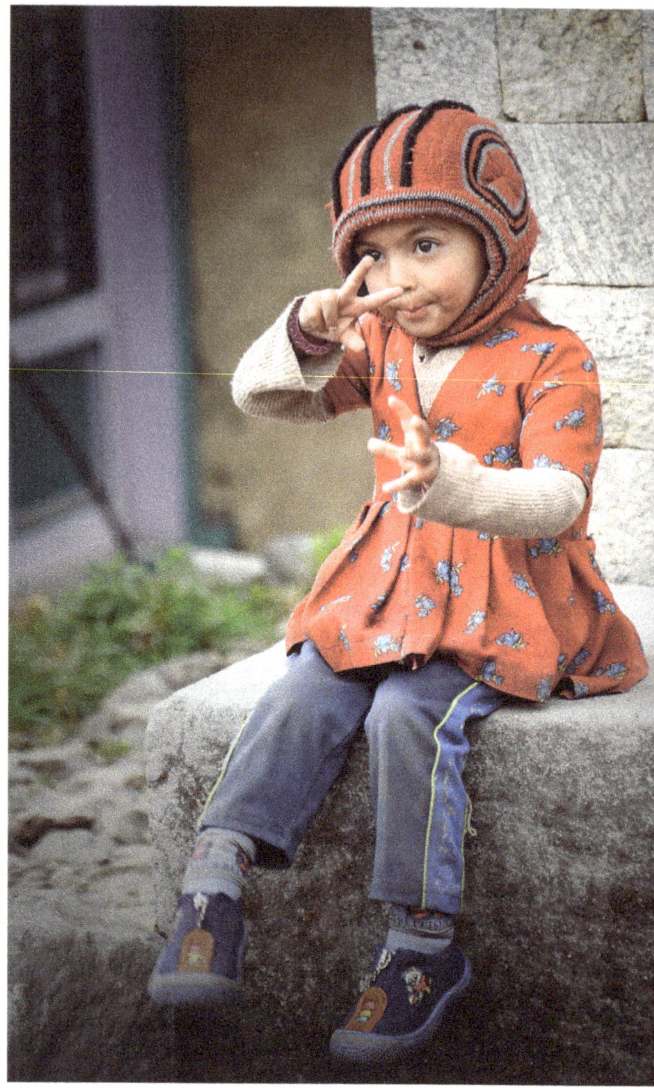

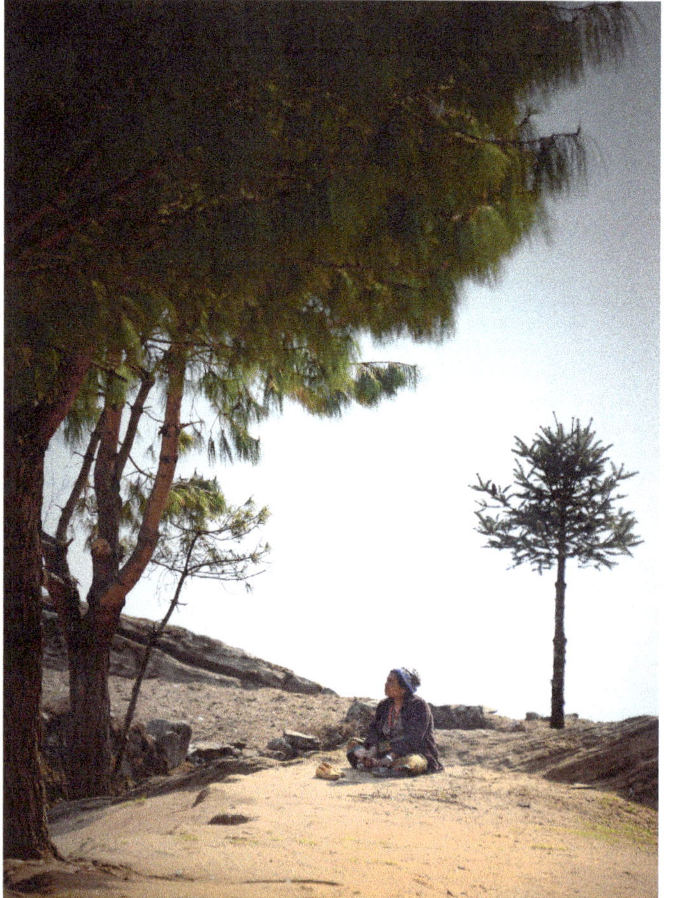

Lukla the town is an interesting mix of traditional life and flogging all the stuff trekkers need on their way out to climb the mountain. As you can see from my photos, it's the people, the children, and the dogs, who welcome you to your trek. Wandering around, mixing with them and watching their lives was a pure highlight.

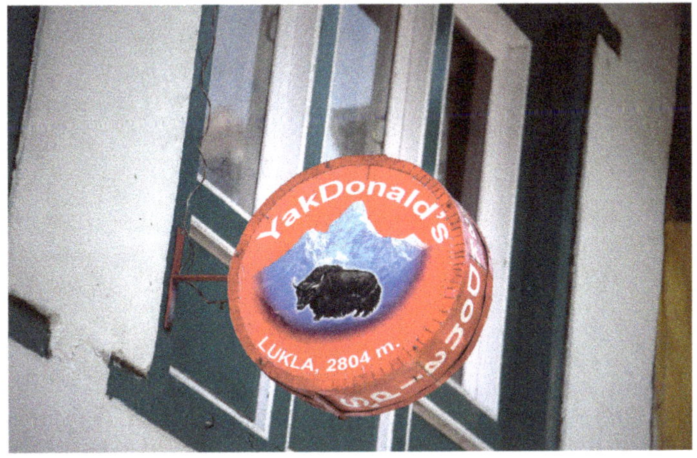

YakDonald's
LUKLA, 2804 m.

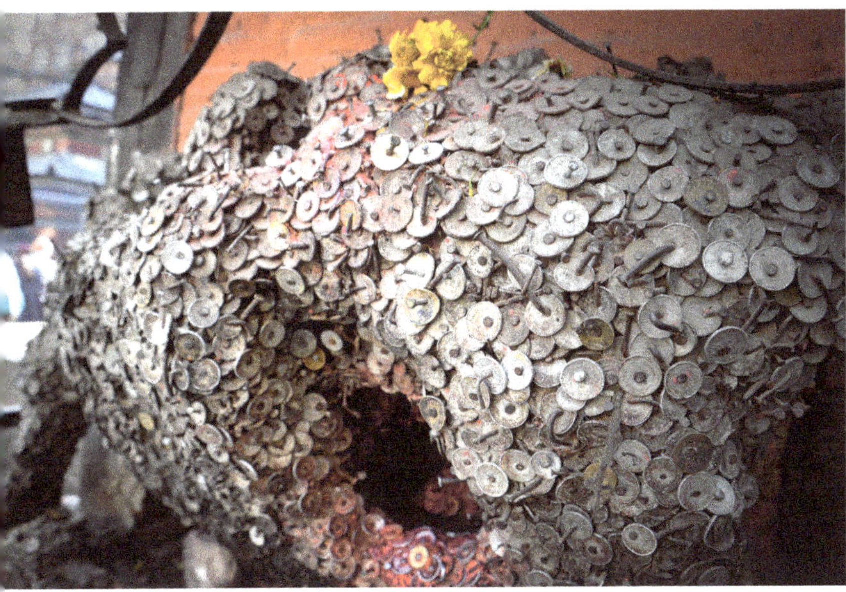

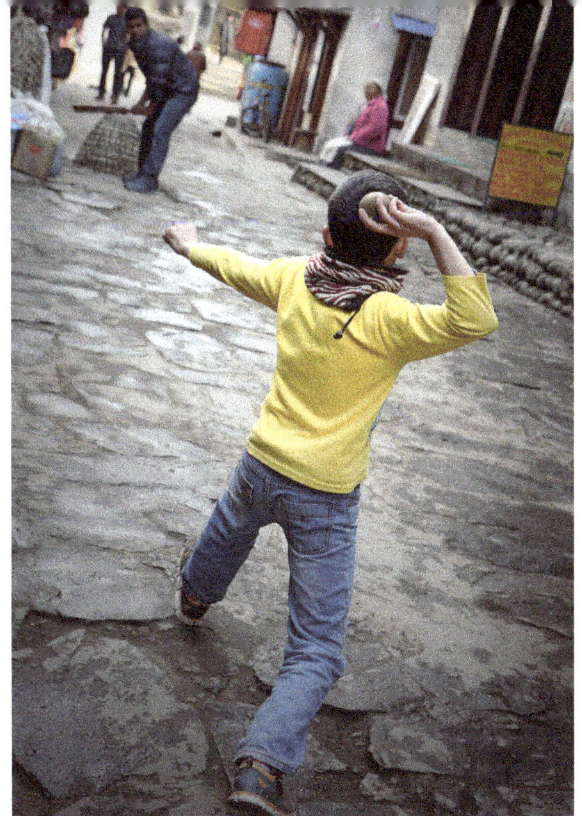

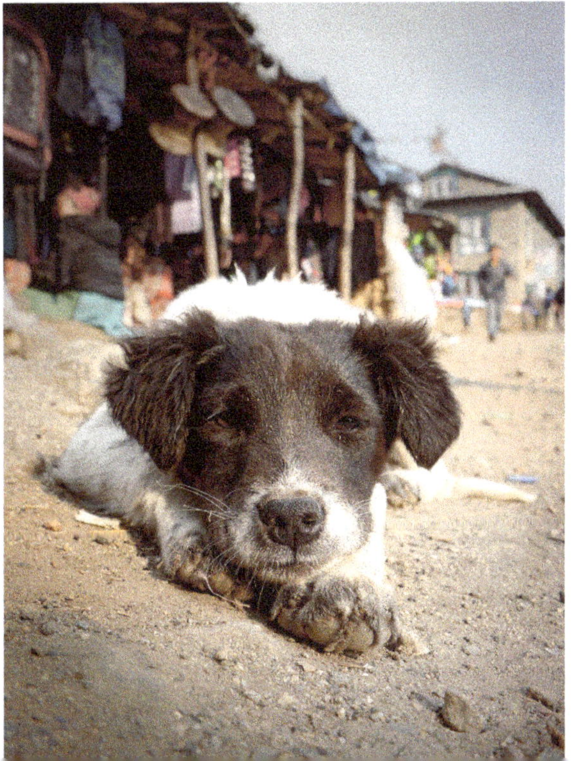

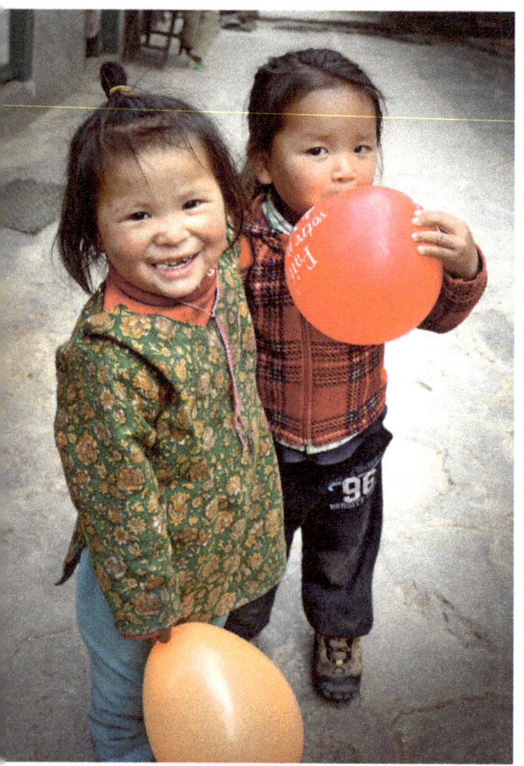 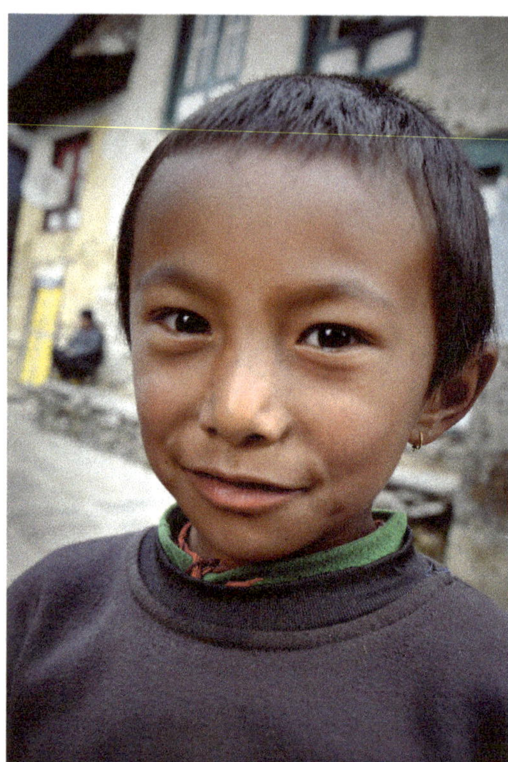 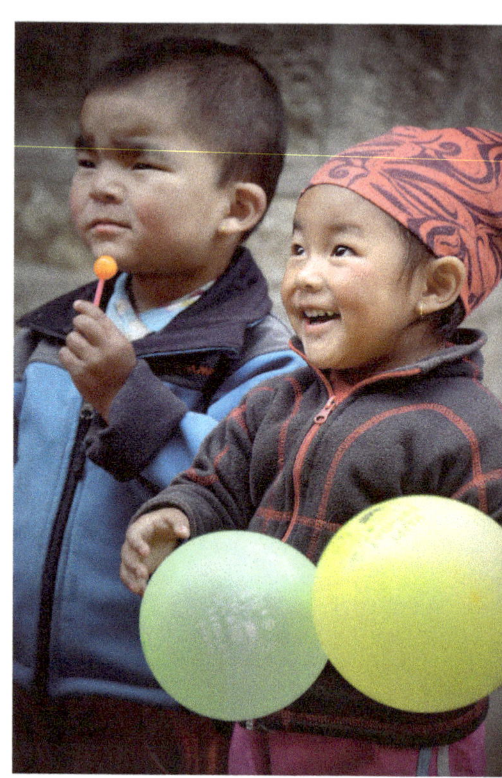

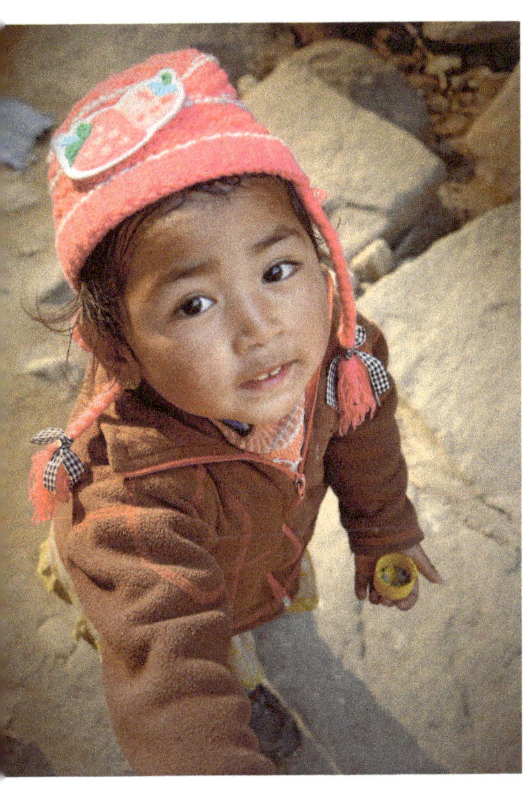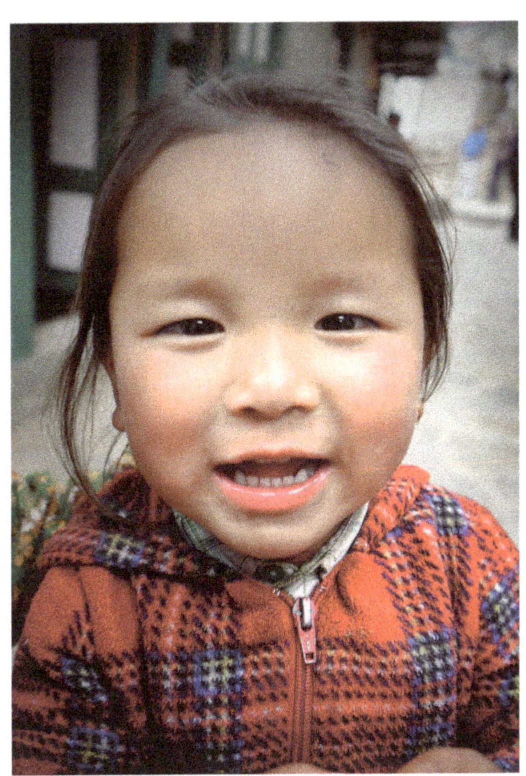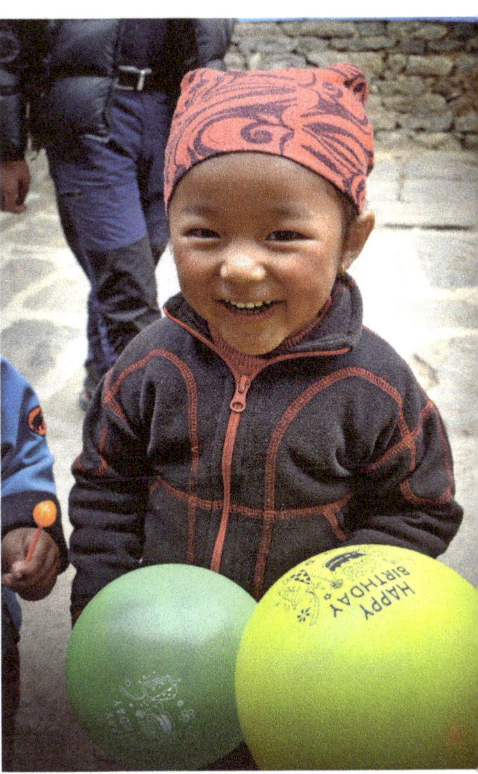

Local social games

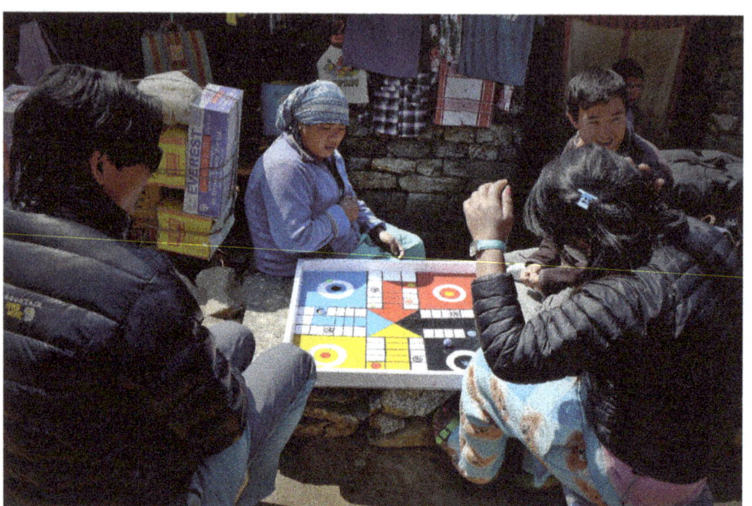

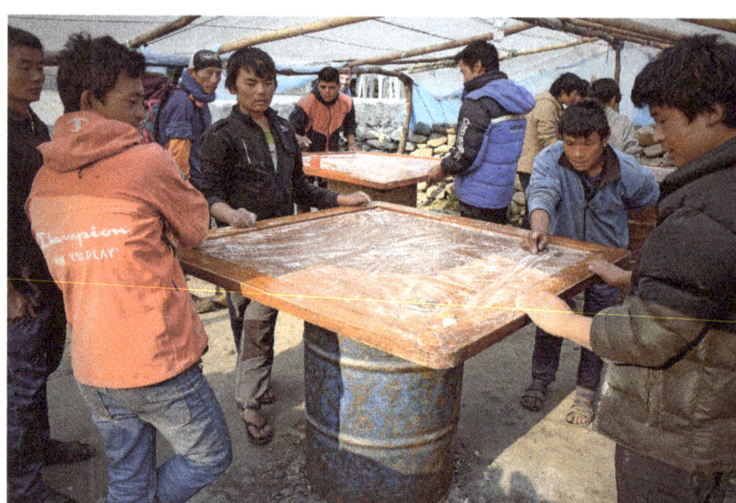

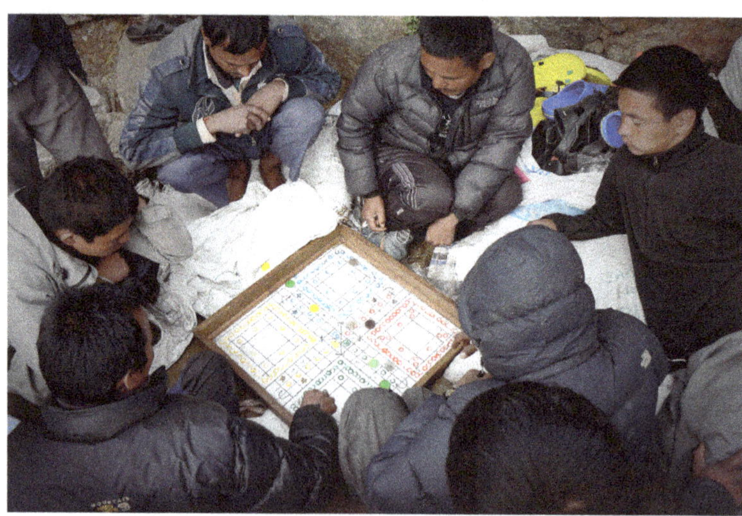

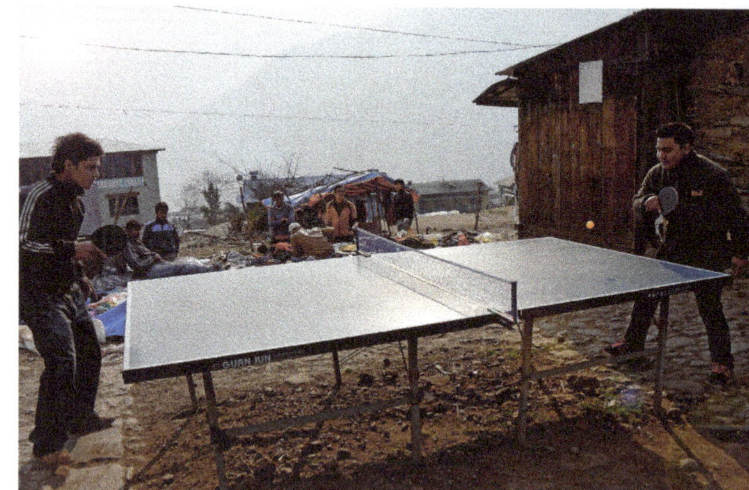

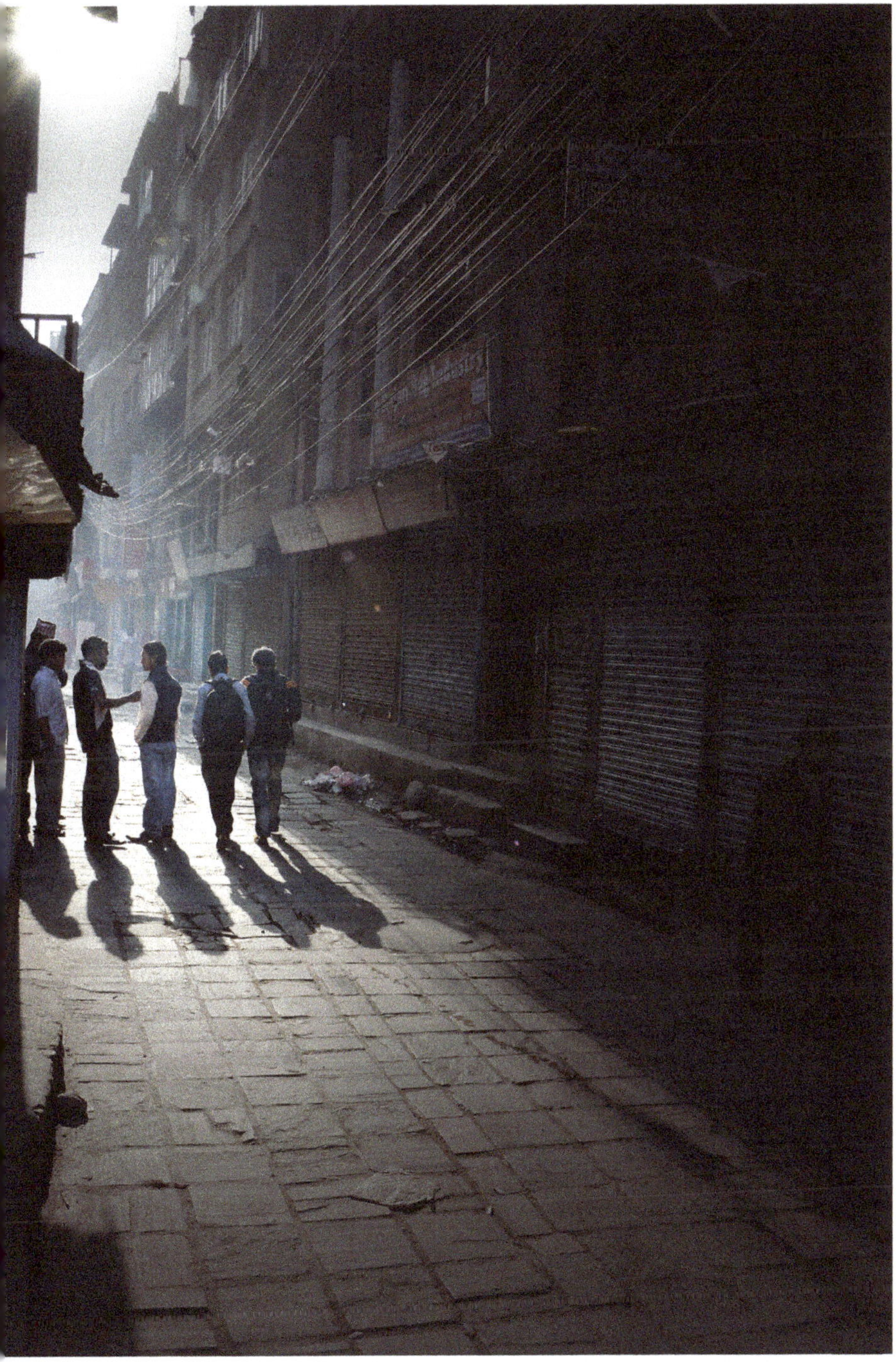

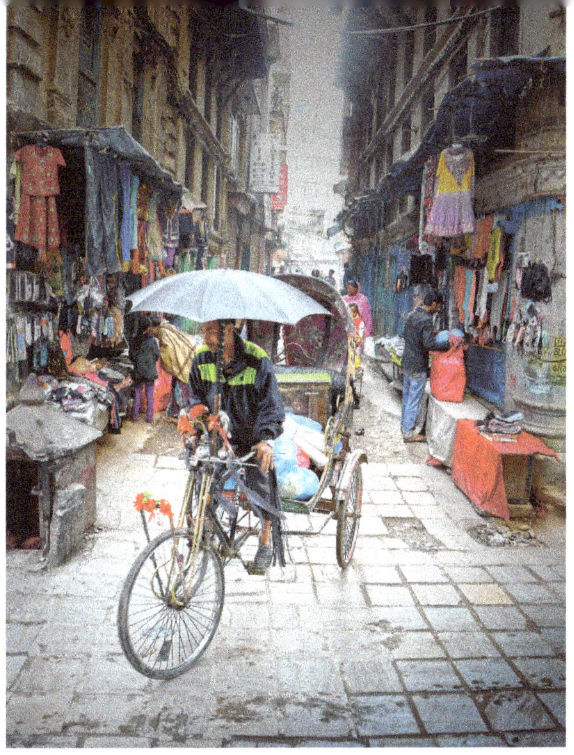

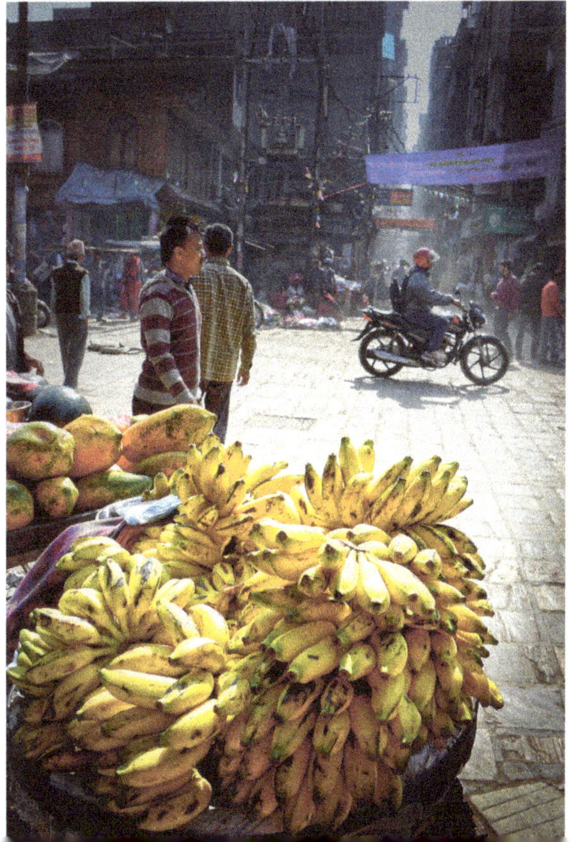

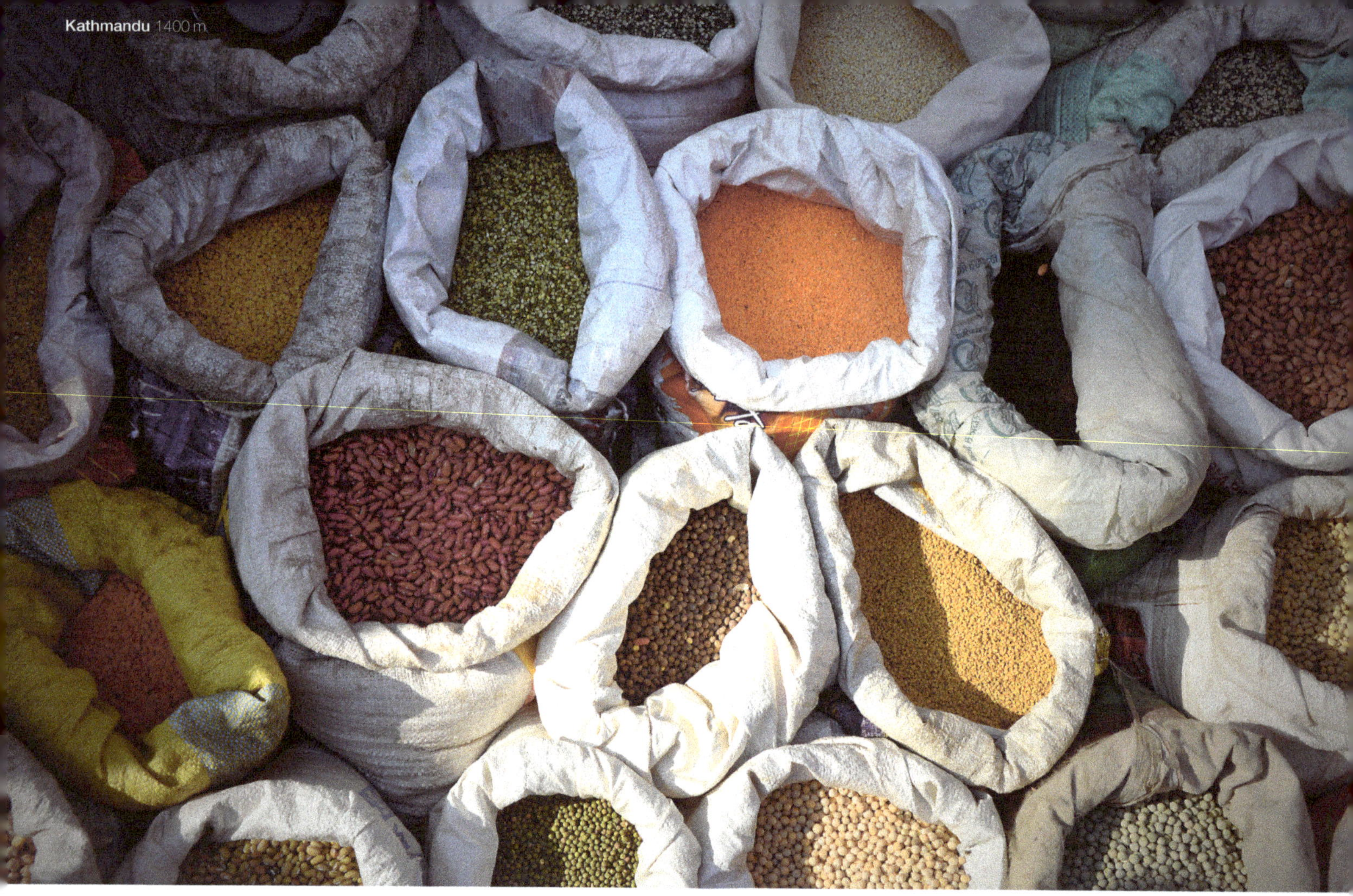

Morning street market

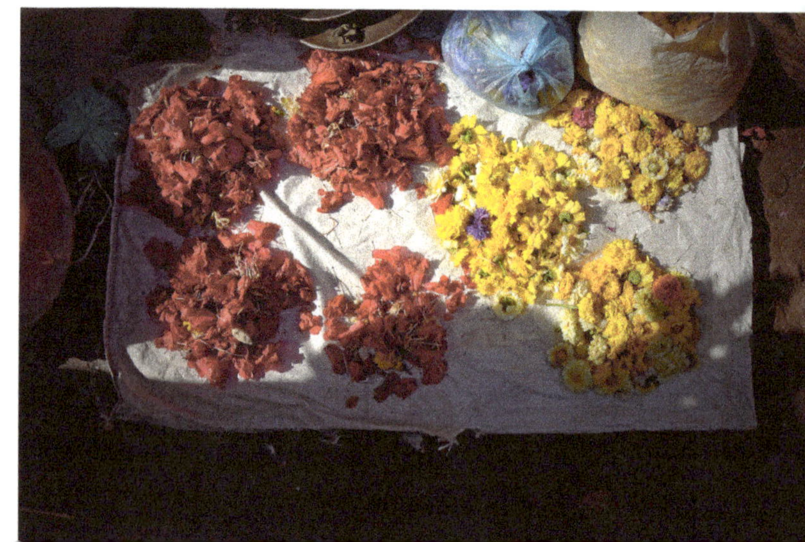

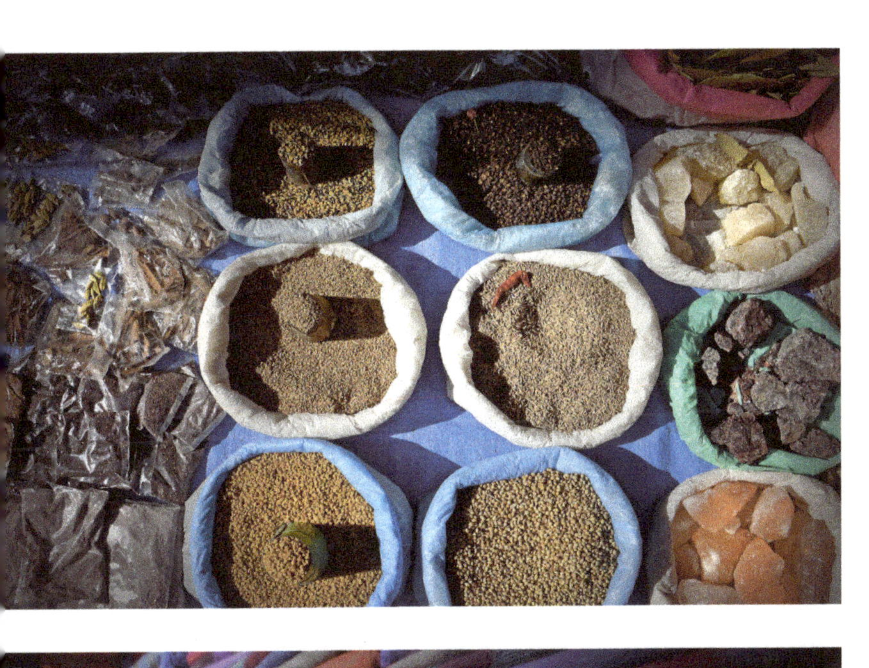

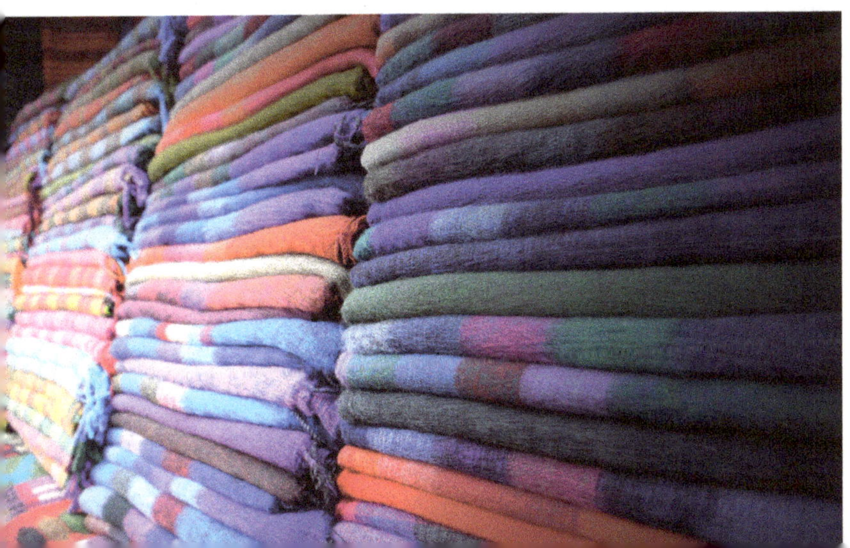

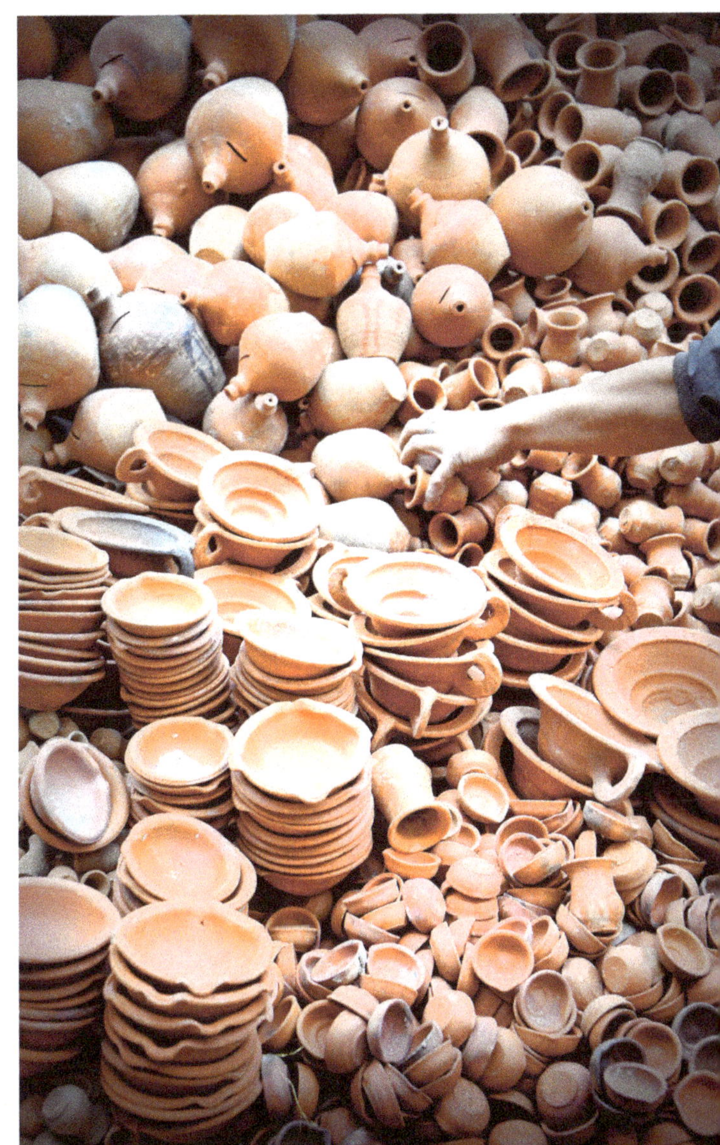

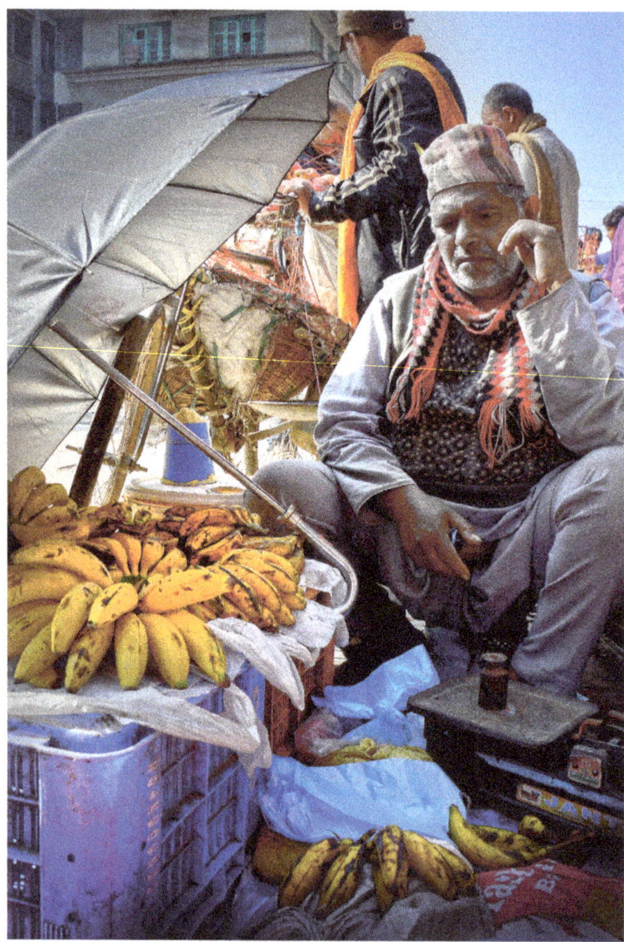

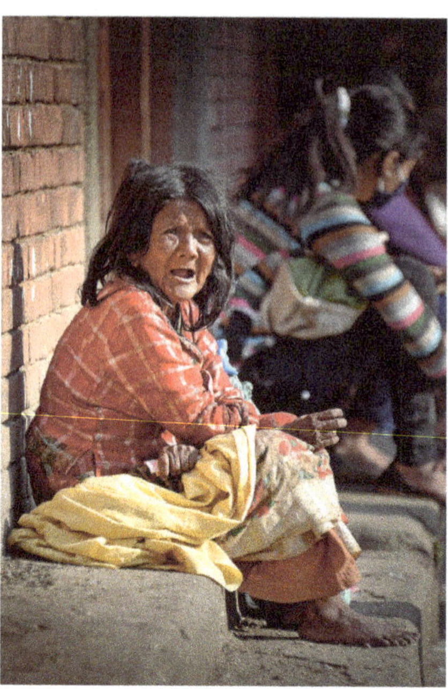

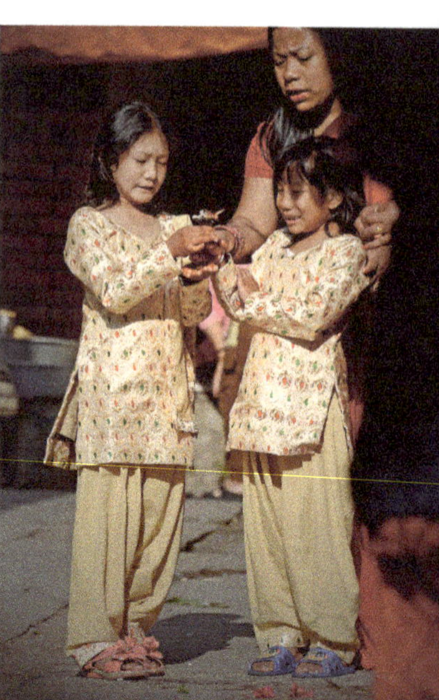

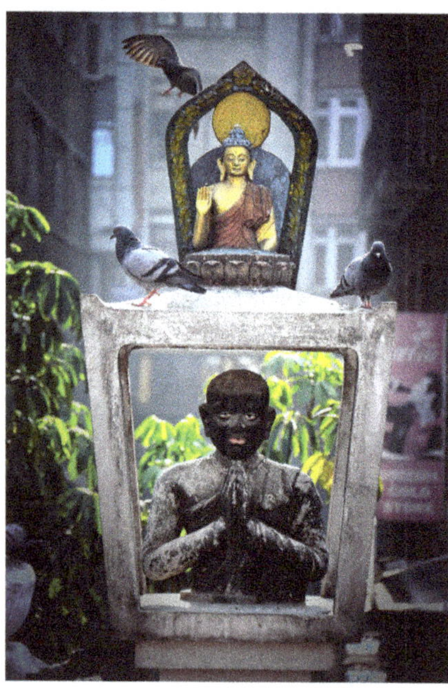

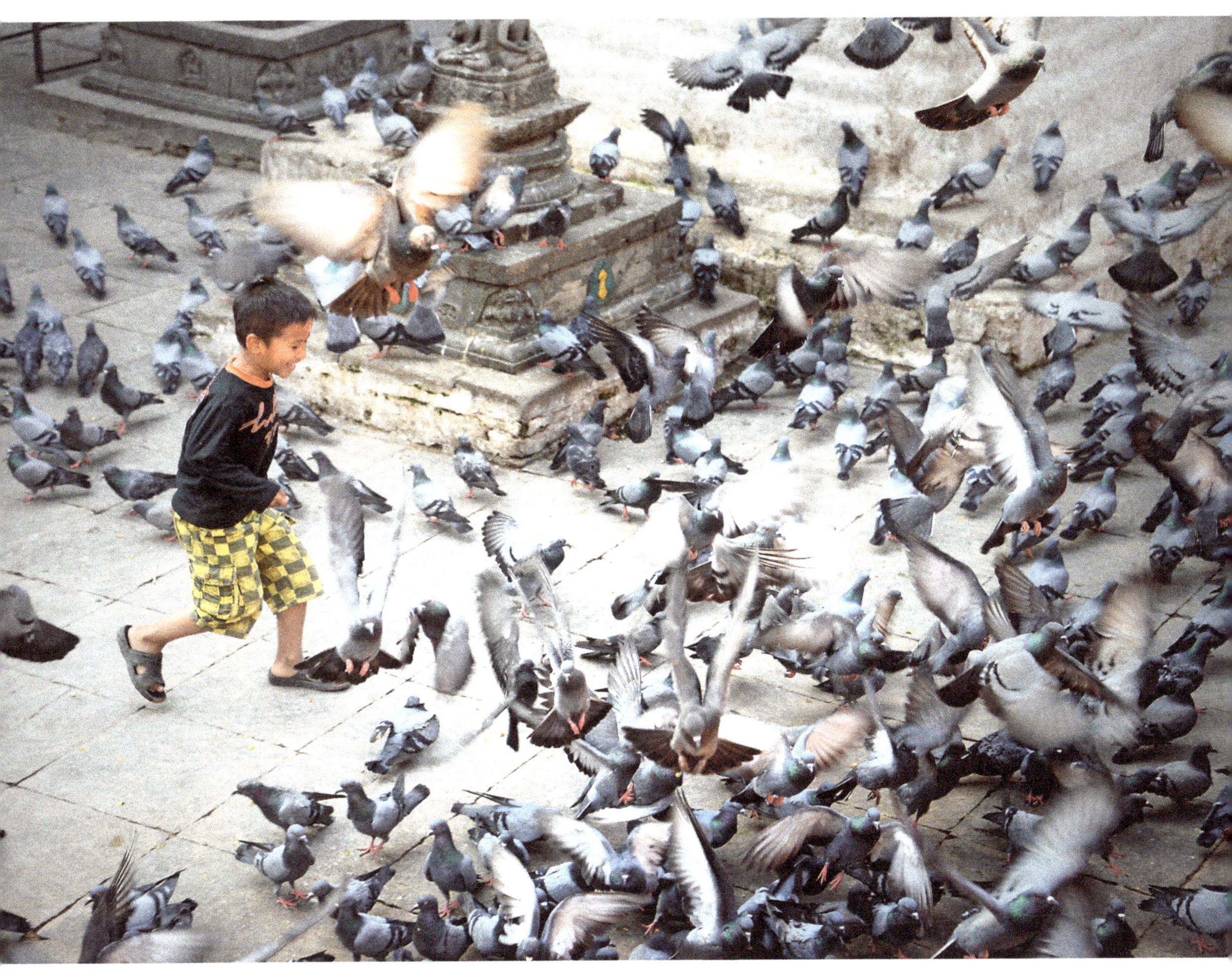

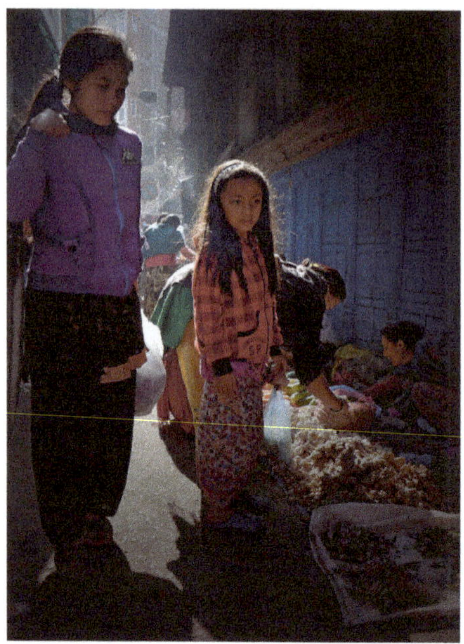

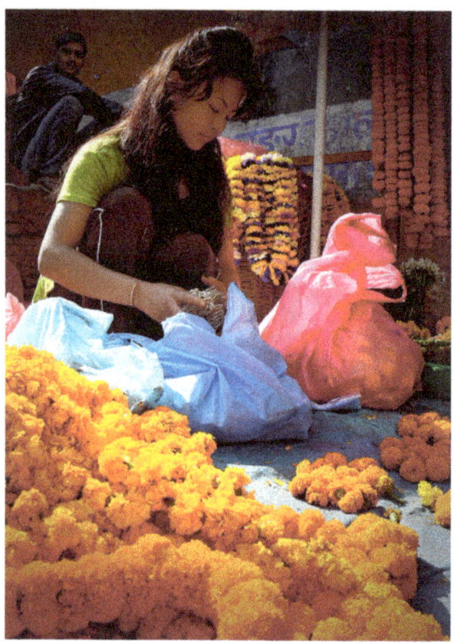

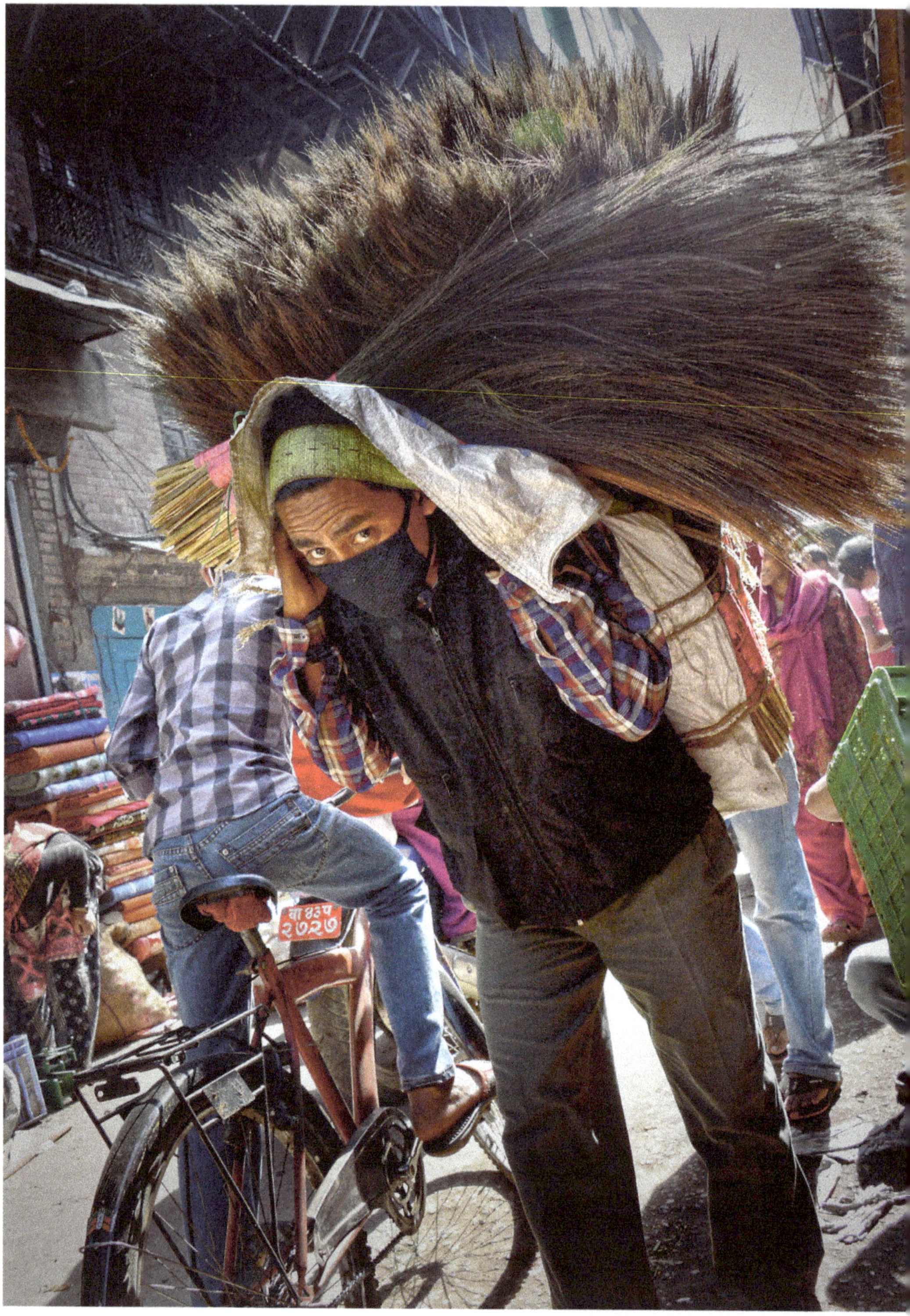

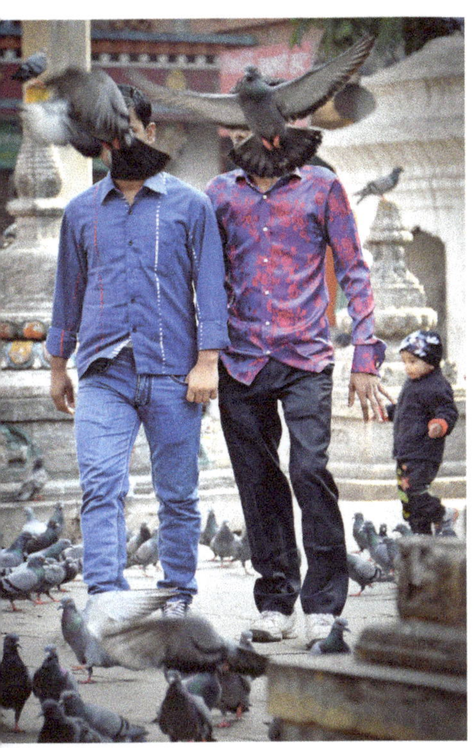
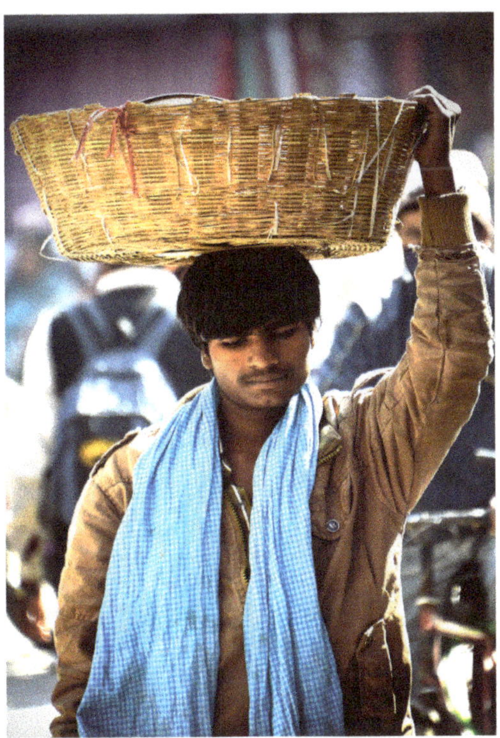
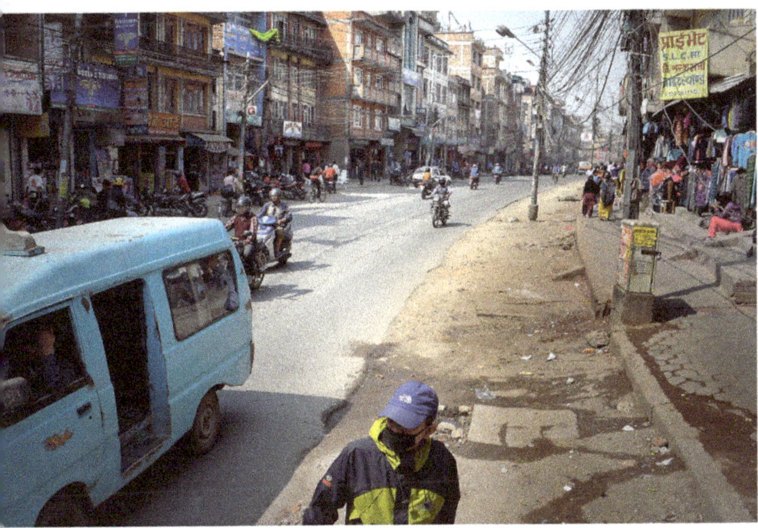
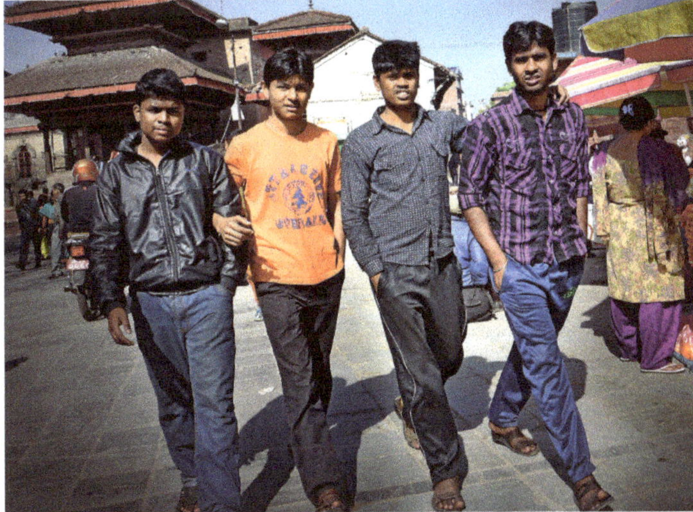

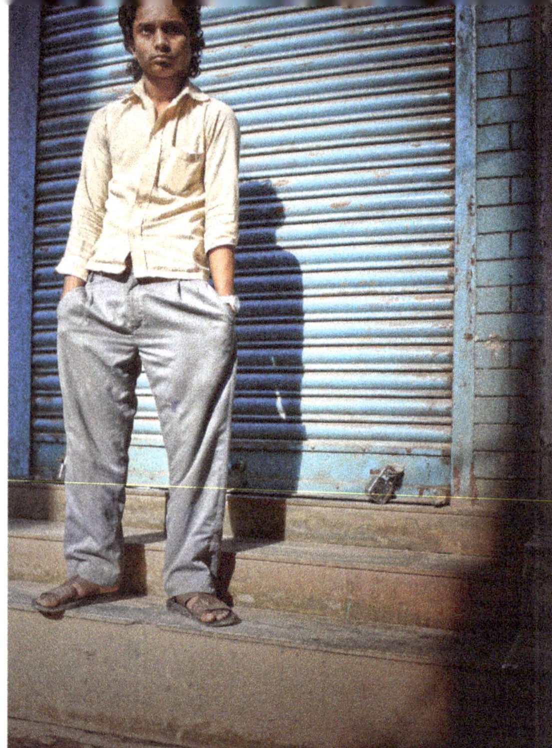

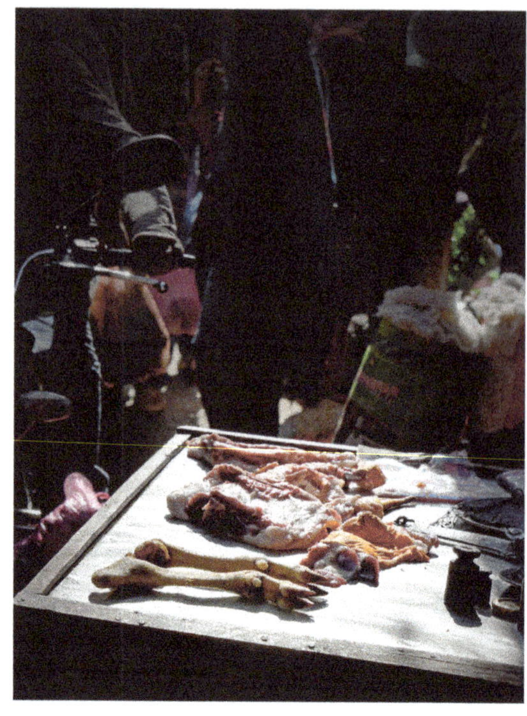

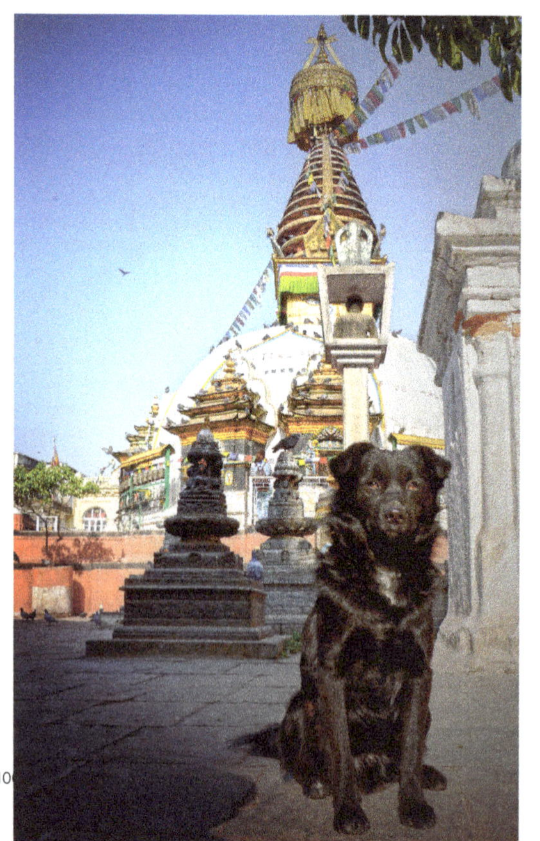

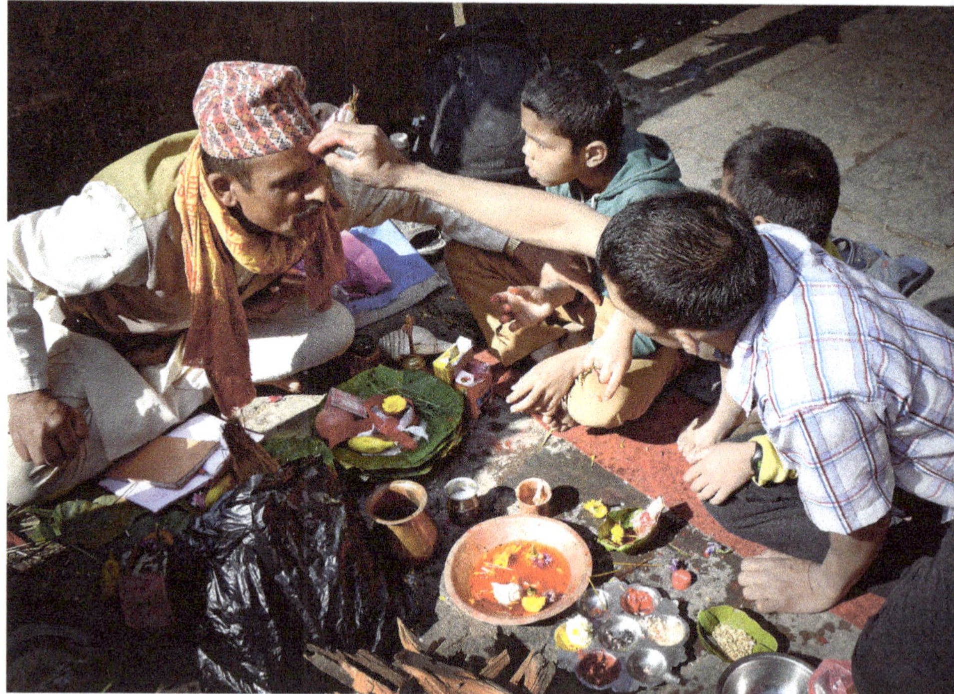

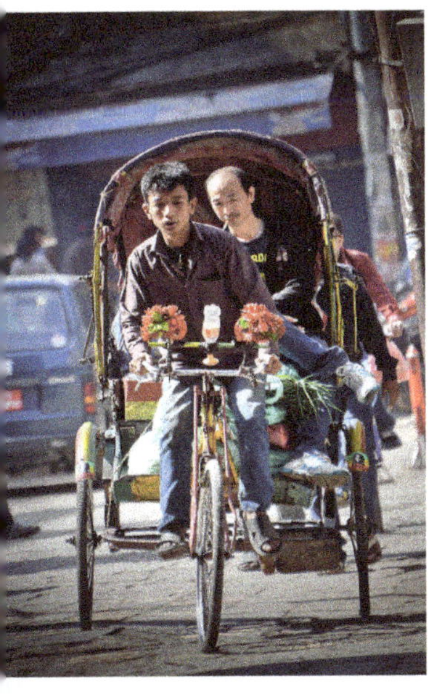
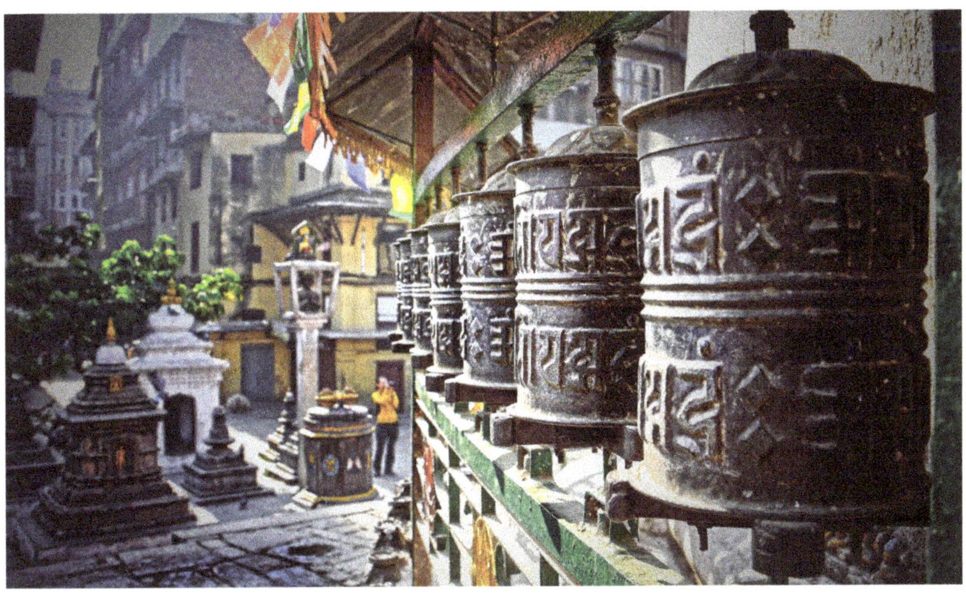
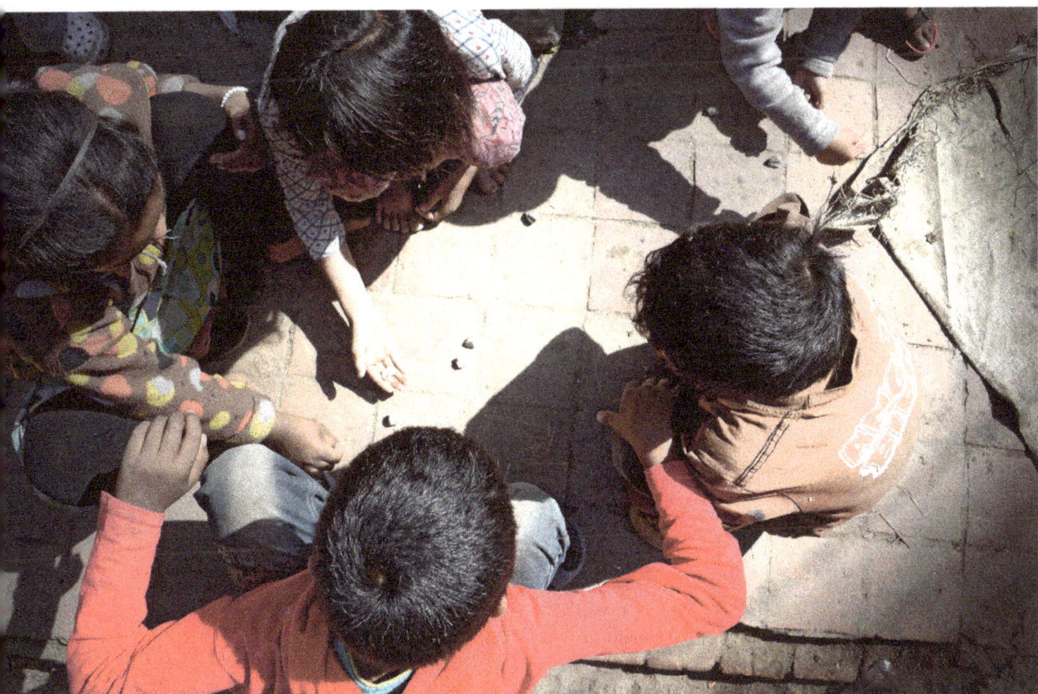
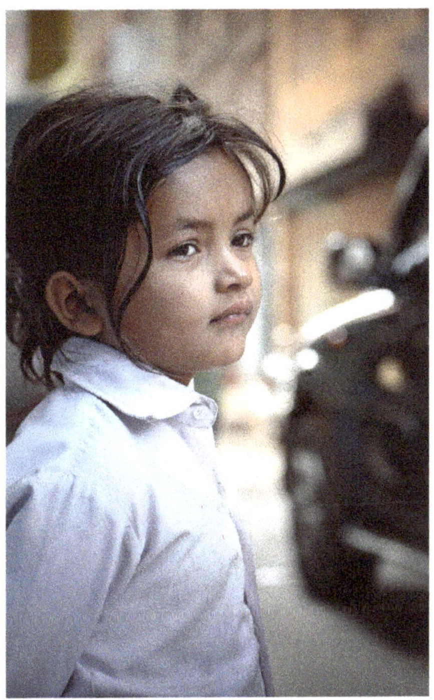

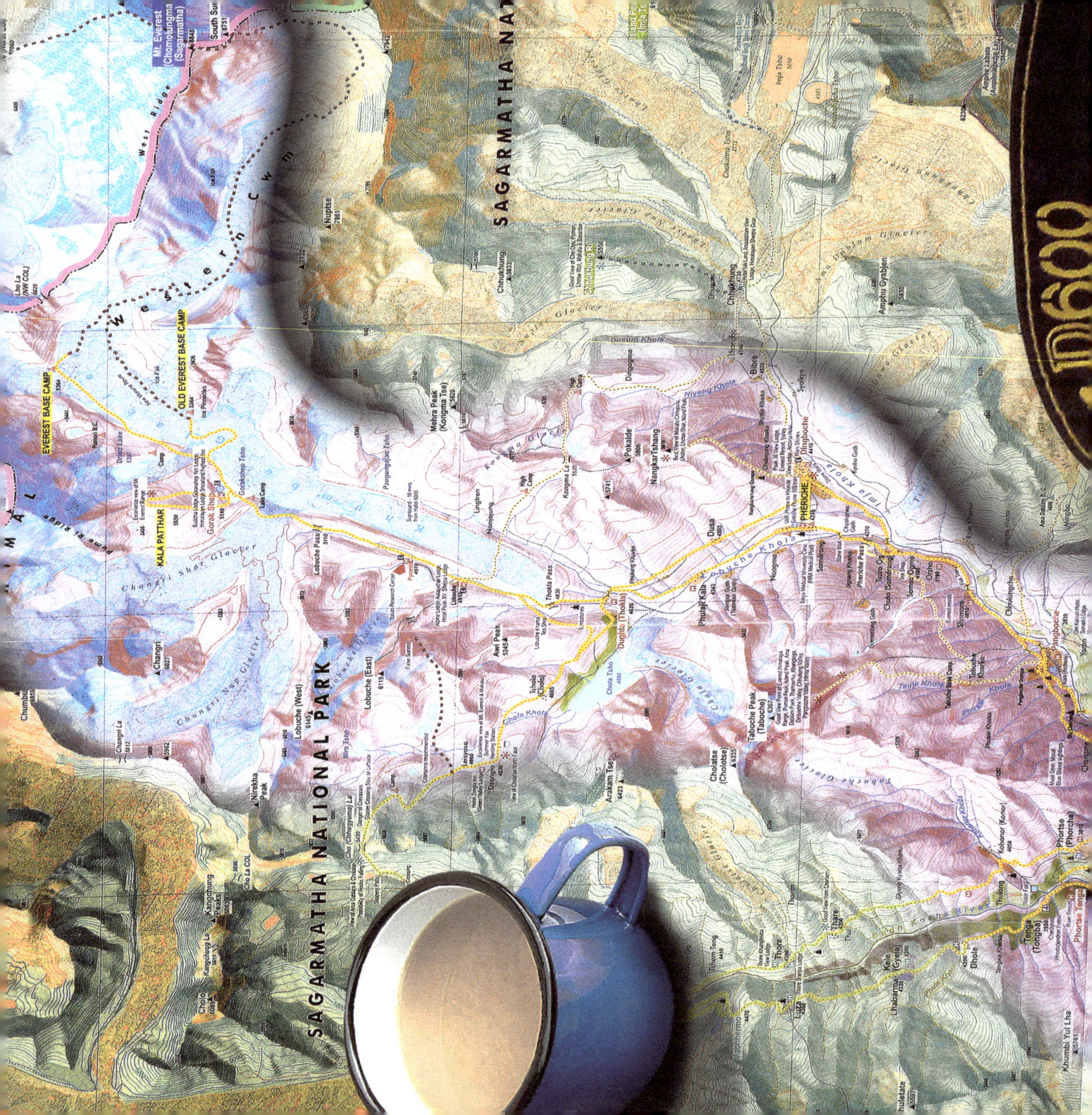

Mt. Everest (Chomolungma) (Sagarmatha)
South Summit
Lho La (NW COL)
West Ridge
Western Cwm
SAGARMATHA NATIONAL PARK
EVEREST BASE CAMP
OLD EVEREST BASE CAMP
KALA PATTHAR
Gorak Shep
Nuptse
Chhukhung
Mehra Peak (Kongma Tse)
Nangkartshang
Pokalde
Dingboche
Bibre
Dusa
PHERICHE
Lobuche Pass
Tshola Pass
Thukla Pass
Pheriche Pass
Phulji Gaun
Dughla (Thokla)
Lobuche (West)
Lobuche (East)
Awi Peak
Tshola (Chola)
Taboche Peak (Taboche)
Cholatse (Cholatse)
Arakam Tse
Changri
Nirekha Peak
Kangchung Peaks
Changri La
Cho La COL
Chola
SAGARMATHA NATIONAL PARK
Pangboche
Shomare
Orsho
Pangboche
Phortse (Phorche)
Kolonar (Konar)
Phortse Tenga
Tengi (Tongba)
Bhole
Kele (Gyele)
Thore
Tsare
Khumbi Yul Lha
Imja Khola
Imja Tse
Island Peak
Changri Shar Glacier
Changri Nup Glacier
Khumbu Glacier
Nuptse Glacier
Lhotse Glacier
Cho La Glacier
Taboche Glacier
Ama Dablam Glacier

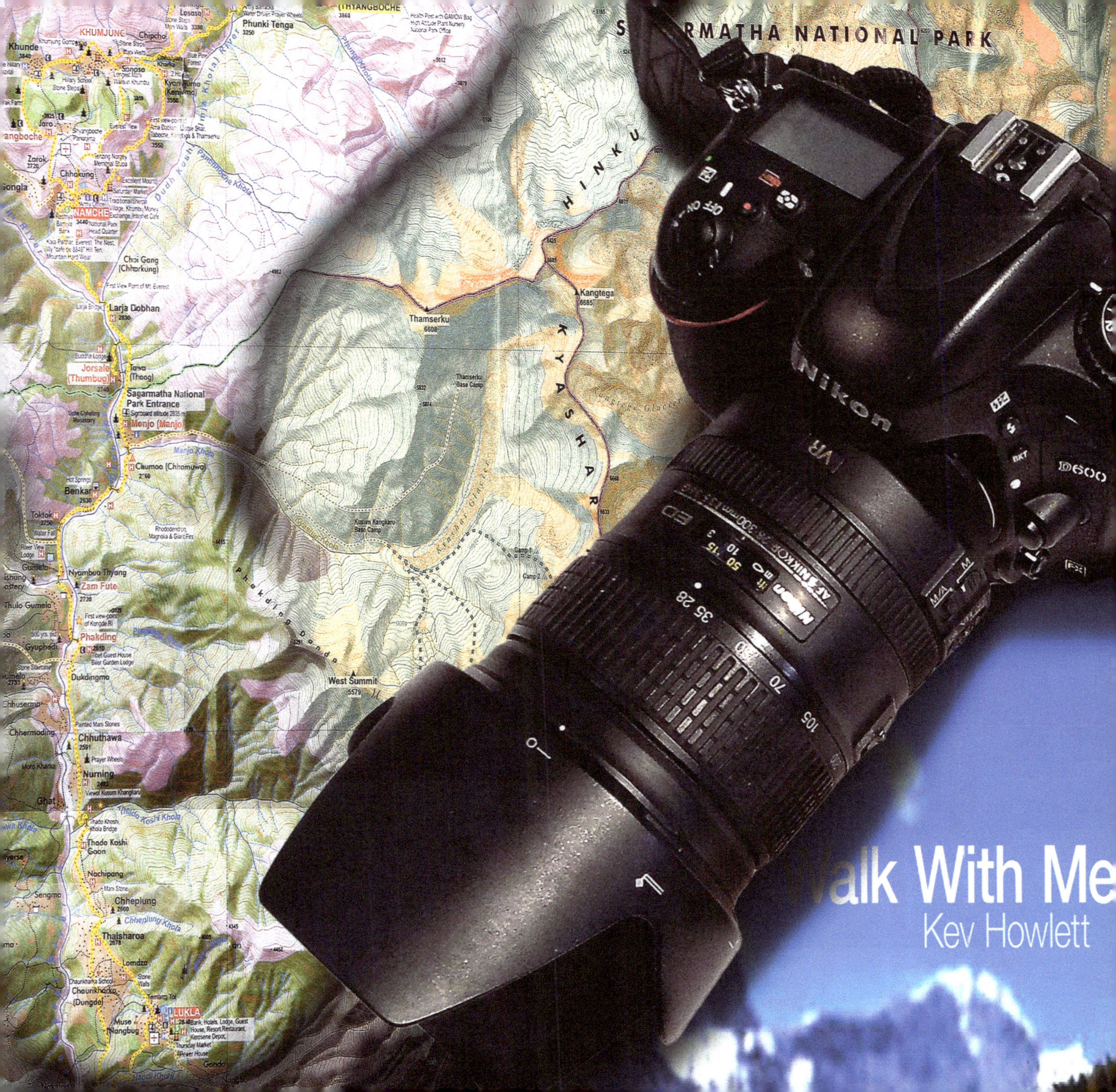

Walk With Me
Kev Howlett

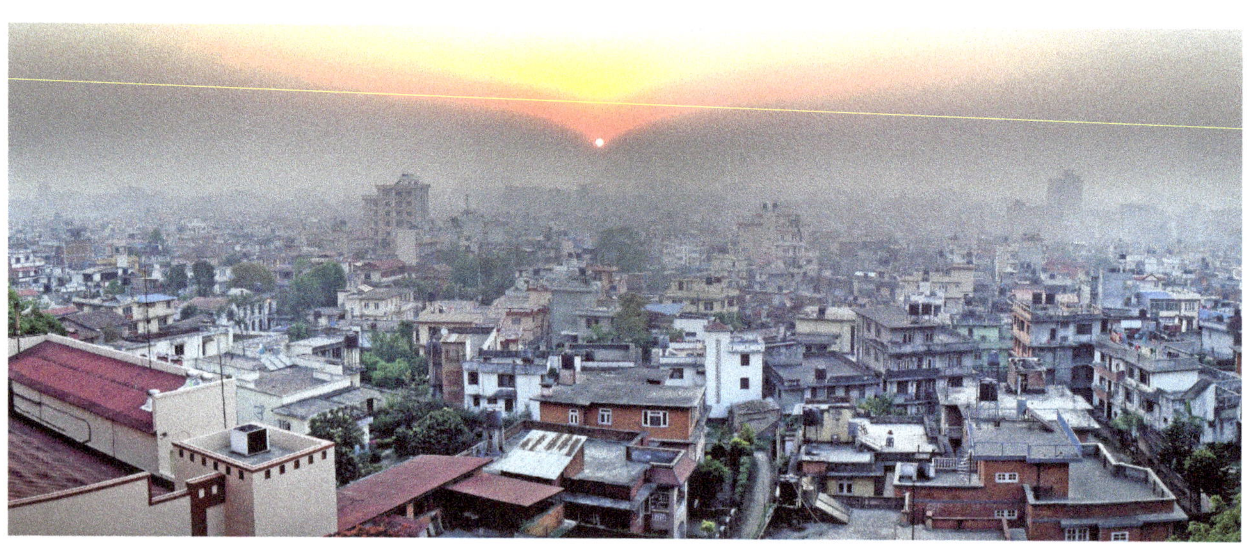

Walk With Me would not have been possible without the generous support of the following:

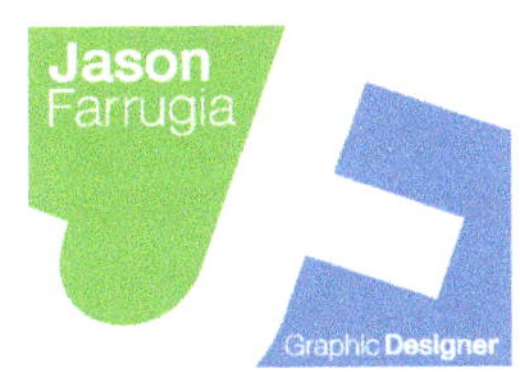

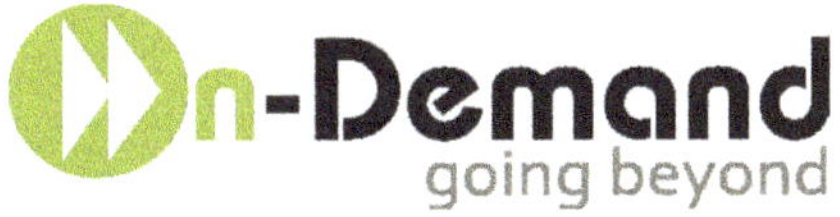

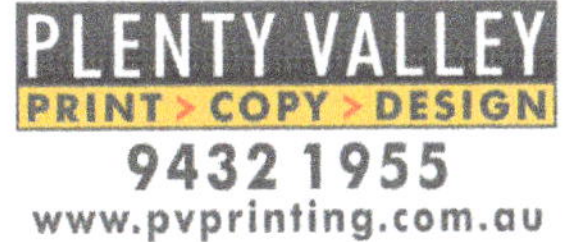

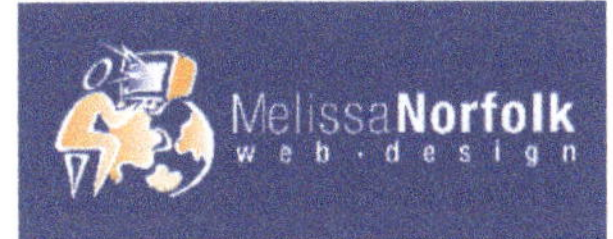

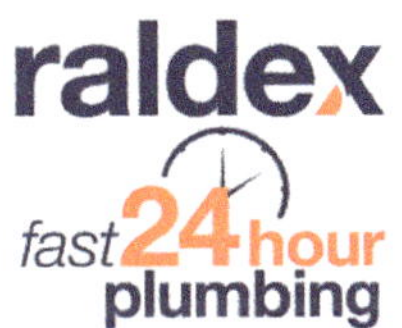

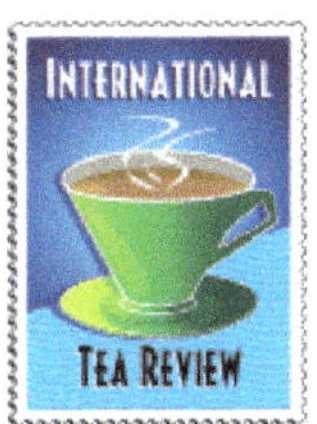

Adrienne Liebmann
Anthony Kilner
Ariel Skippen
Barbara Geary
Billy Tisdall
Carol Challis
Carole Howlett
Choice Legal, Lawyer and Business Consultants
Christine Fenwick
Christine Lewis
Dale Eldridge
Daniel Mcshane
Dave Saunders
Dawn MacKenzie
Debra Schuckar
Eltham Motors
Gary Haspell
Gene Deubel

Jan & George Leighfield
Gina Boothroyd
Heather Davis
Helen Krionas
Ian Crockett
International Coffee Preview
Jackie Mutimer
Jamie Thomas
Jane McGrath
Jane Saunders
Janet Geary
Jocelyn Harewood
Jodie Grayson
Joe Dolce
Judith Chivers
Julie Jackson
Julie Thorn
Justin Fankhauser

Kate, James & Dean (Landers)
Kavisha Mazzella
Kaye & Jaye White
Krystle Herdy
Les Zigomanis
Lin van Hek
Lisa Roberts
Lynden Boehm
Mandy Burton
Marcello D'Amico
Maria Vavala
Melissa Baker
Michelle Endersby
Mike Nicholls
Natalie Coish
Natalie & Dave Geary
Nigel Laxton
Niki Grosios
Pam Fallon

Patrick Psaila
Paul Robinson
Robin & Gay Miller
Sara Van Hecke
Scott Hearse
Sher Hazeldine
Srinivas Gorantala
Steve & Tracey Gibbs
Steven Trajkovski
Stewart & Lynda Maddison
Sue Kent
Surajo Frith
Tanya Matheson
Tess Evans
Theo & Louise Milligan
Tracey & Felix Rzezniczak
Tracy Connellan
Woodridge Insurance Services

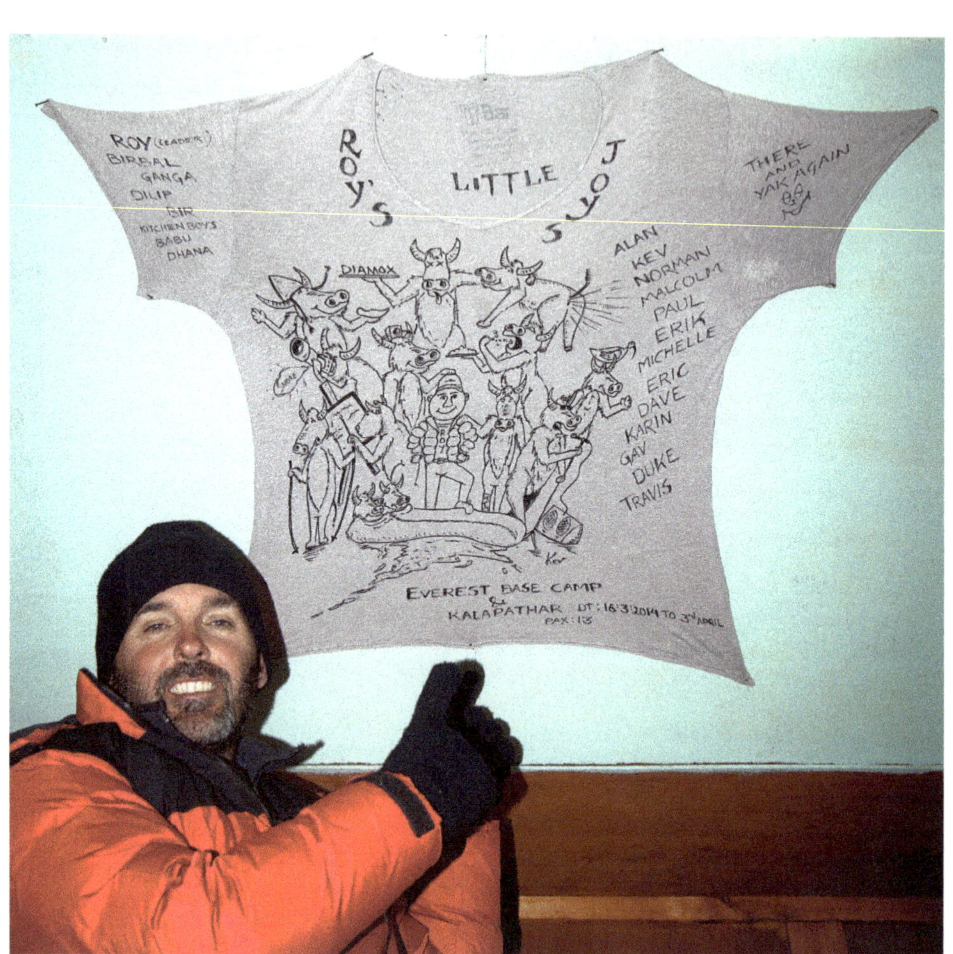
ROY (LEADER)
BIRBAL
GANGA
DILIP
BIR
KITCHEN BOYS
BABU
DHANA
ROY'S LITTLE JOY'S
THERE AND YAK AGAIN
DIAMOX
ALAN
KEV
NORMAN
MALCOLM
PAUL
ERIK
MICHELLE
ERIC
DAVE
KARIN
GAV
DUKE
TRAVIS
Kev
EVEREST BASE CAMP
&
KALAPATHAR DT: 16'3'2014 TO 3RD APRIL
PAX: 13